India's Industrial Policy and Performance

This book assesses the performance of Indian industries from the perspectives of trade, investment, policy, and development incentives. It evaluates the relevance and the macro- and microeconomic impact of industrial policy on growth in different sectors of industry.

The book examines India's key policy initiatives and economic and institutional plans through many decades and examines their short and long-term effects on industrial environment and performance. It measures India's strategic policies and efforts to promote industrialization against similar initiatives in countries like Germany, Japan, South Korea, and Taiwan. The volume also contextualizes the performance of different sectors of industry such as automobiles, electronics and information technology, and pharmaceuticals, among others, within the larger framework of global economic scenario and competition.

This book will be of great interest to researchers and students of economics, political economy, industrial development and policy, and South Asia studies.

Nitya Nanda is Director of the Council for Social Development, a social science think tank based in New Delhi. His areas of interest include international trade, industrialization, development and environment issues. He has been a consultant for several UN organizations, including UNCTAD, UNESCAP, and UNDP, and the European Commission. He has also been a consultant for different government ministries and agencies in India and contributed to formulating policies. He has published many articles in journals and edited books, as well as pieces in magazines and newspapers. He has also authored and edited several volumes, including *Expanding Frontiers of Global Trade Rules* (2009), *Hydro-Politics in GBM Basin* (2015), and *India's Resource Security* (2018).

Advance Praise

This most valuable book analyzes the industrialization experience of India since independence, situated in its wider global context. It traces the evolution of industrial policy in India, shaped by economic and political factors, to assess its impact on performance. In doing so, it highlights the critical importance of industrial policy as a determinant of both successes and failures. The author argues that the absence of industrial policy after economic liberalization in 1991 is the reason for the premature deindustrialization since then, to stress that rethinking industrial policy is essential to revive the manufacturing sector as a source of economic growth and employment creation. The book makes an important contribution to our understanding of complex issues and contentious debates on industrialization. It should interest students, researchers and policy practitioners in India and elsewhere in the developing world.

> Deepak Nayyar, Emeritus Professor of Economics, Jawaharlal Nehru University, New Delhi; Honorary Fellow of Balliol College, Oxford; and former Vice Chancellor, University of Delhi

This volume provides a balanced and well-researched discussion of the evolution of industrial policy in India, and of its likely impact on economic performance, since the 1950s. It debunks the commonly held view that the best industrial policy is no policy. Such research is very timely given the premature de-industrialization of India, despite the recent rapid growth acceleration. It is a "must read" for those engaged in public policy design and the study of alternative development theories and for graduate students in economics.

> Giovanni Andrea Cornia, Honorary Professor of Economics, University of Florence and former Director, UNU-WIDER, Helsinki

This is a comprehensive work on industrial policy by Nitya Nanda as he covers multiple facets of industrial policy for developing countries and with specific focus on India. Given the renewed focus on industrial policy and the role of state in India, this will be an extremely relevant book for students, academicians, and policymakers.

Parthapratim Pal, Professor, Indian Institute of Management Calcutta, Kolkata

I am happy that such a study has been conducted. The volume should be of immense use to policy makers in their effort to re-orient the industrial policy to bring a competitive manufacturing sector in the country quickly. It should also encourage other researchers to explore new interpretations and to boldly experiment with different measures. It is an essential reading for students and researchers interested in industrialisation in India.

K S Chalapati Rao, Professor, Institute for Studies in Industrial Development, New Delhi

India's Industrial Policy and Performance

Growth, Competition and Competitiveness

Nitya Nanda

LONDON AND NEW YORK

First published 2022
by Routledge
2 Park Square, Milton Park, Abingdon, Oxon OX14 4RN

and by Routledge
605 Third Avenue, New York, NY 10158

Routledge is an imprint of the Taylor & Francis Group, an informa business

© 2022 Nitya Nanda

The right of Nitya Nanda to be identified as author of this work has been asserted by him in accordance with sections 77 and 78 of the Copyright, Designs and Patents Act 1988.

All rights reserved. No part of this book may be reprinted or reproduced or utilised in any form or by any electronic, mechanical, or other means, now known or hereafter invented, including photocopying and recording, or in any information storage or retrieval system, without permission in writing from the publishers.

Trademark notice: Product or corporate names may be trademarks or registered trademarks, and are used only for identification and explanation without intent to infringe.

British Library Cataloguing-in-Publication Data
A catalogue record for this book is available from the British Library

Library of Congress Cataloging-in-Publication Data
A catalog record for this book has been requested

ISBN: 978-0-367-47813-1 (hbk)
ISBN: 978-1-032-05270-0 (pbk)
ISBN: 978-1-003-04749-0 (ebk)

DOI: 10.4324/9781003047490

Typeset in Sabon
by Apex CoVantage, LLC

Dedicated to the memory of my father, who always encouraged me to look at the world and things in an unconventional way!

Contents

List of figures	x
List of tables	xii
List of boxes	xiii
Preface	xiv
List of abbreviations	xvii

1	Introduction	1
2	Industrial policy and performance: the key issues	11
3	The Indian context of industrial policy and performance	39
4	India's industrial performance: assessments and policy linkages	75
5	Intensity of competition in Indian industry	135
6	Concluding observations	153
	References	170
	Index	187

Figures

3.1	Hodrick-Prescott Trends of Growth Rates (per cent)	51
3.2	Period-wise Hodrick-Prescott Trends of Growth Rates (per cent)	54
3.3	Period-wise Linear Trends of Growth Rates (per cent)	54
3.4	Share of Different Sectors in GDP (per cent)	55
3.5	Falling Tariffs: Income Group Wise, 1988–2012 (per cent)	58
3.6	Falling Tariffs: Region/Country Wise, 1988–2012 (per cent)	59
4.1a	GCR of Different Manufacturing Industries of India (1/4)	86
4.1b	GCR of Different Manufacturing Industries of India (2/4)	87
4.1c	GCR of Different Manufacturing Industries of India (3/4)	87
4.1d	GCR of Different Manufacturing Industries of India (4/4)	88
4.2a	CPI of Different Manufacturing Sectors of India (1/4)	88
4.2b	CPI of Different Manufacturing Sectors of India (2/4)	89
4.2c	CPI of Different Manufacturing Sectors of India (3/4)	89
4.2d	CPI of Different Manufacturing Sectors of India (4/4)	90
4.3a	Share of Different Countries in Global Industrial Production (per cent) (1/2)	91
4.3b	Share of Different Countries in Global Industrial Production (per cent) (2/2)	91
4.4	Growth of Industrial Production in Different Countries and the World (in billion 2008–09 US dollars)	92
4.5a	Value Added in Select Manufacturing Sectors in the US (in billion US 2008–09 dollars)	93
4.5b	Value Added in Select Manufacturing Sectors in Japan (in billion US 2008–09 dollars)	93
4.6	Share of Select Countries in Global Industrial Production (including Germany) (per cent)	94
4.7	Growth of Select Manufacturing Sectors in Germany (in million US 2008–09 dollars)	94
4.8a	GCR of Select Countries in Textiles	96
4.8b	GCR of Select Countries in Wearing Apparel	96
4.8c	GCR of Select Countries in Chemical Products	97
4.8d	GCR of Select Countries in Electronic Goods	97

4.8e	GCR of Select Countries in Vehicles	98
4.8f	GCR of Select Countries in Computers and Office Equipment	98
4.8g	GCR of Select Countries in Petroleum Products	99
4.8h	GCR of Select Countries in Basic Metals	99
4.9a	ACA of Select Manufacturing Sectors of India (1/3)	100
4.9b	ACA of Select Manufacturing Sectors of India (2/3)	101
4.9c	ACA of Select Manufacturing Sectors of India (3/3)	101

Tables

2.1	Payments for Use of IPRs by Country Groups (BoP, current billion US dollars)	25
3.1	Growth Rates of GDP and Different Sectors	53
3.2	Savings and Capital Formation in India (per cent)	57
3.3	Milestones in Economic Policy Reforms Since 1980	71
3.4	Growth of Central Public Sector Enterprises	71
4.1	Changing Tariff Profile of India (tariffs in per cent)	115
4.2	Structure and Growth in the Electronics Industry	129
4.3	Policy Factors Influencing Performance in Select Industries in India	133
5.1	Summary of λ_i (adjustment coefficient for short-run profit) and P_{ip} (long-term profit)	146
5.2	Distribution of Adjustment Coefficient of Short-run Profit (λ_i)	147
5.3	Distribution of Long-term Profit Rates (P_{ip})	147
5.4	Decomposition of Profit Rates by Industry	148
5.5	Test of Equality of Long-term Profit by Industry	149
5.6	Strength of Dynamic Competition in Indian Manufacturing Industries	150
5.7	Composite Index for Intensity of Competition in Indian Manufacturing	150
6.1	Competition and Measures of Performance	160

Boxes

2.1	The US trade regime: favouring developed countries!	17
2.2	History of POSCO	21
6.1	India and China: diverging industrial policy and performance	161

Preface

The spate of economic reforms that the world has seen since 1980s, in its core, had the philosophical underpinning that "no policy" is the best industrial policy that a country can have. Hence, economic reforms only meant progressive liberalization of regulatory instruments on all fronts, including domestic market, import restrictions and regulations of foreign capital. On the part of India, the objective of developing a globally competitive manufacturing sector formed the core of the economic reforms agenda in 1991. The expectation then was that foreign direct investment (FDI) with advanced technologies assisted by competitive pressure through open and free trade would improve efficiency and international competitiveness of the industrial sector. As part of the reform process, the erstwhile industrial policy framework was dismantled and progressive dilution of the FDI policy was initiated. The entire manufacturing sector was practically opened to 100 per cent FDI by 2000, defence and strategic industries being the major exception.

However, after about one and a half decades, it became clear that the manufacturing sector was in a state of stagnation. The target year for achieving the manufacturing sector's share of 25 per cent in GDP was successively pushed, the latest being 2025. However, the recent figure of the share of manufacturing sector shows how difficult it would be to reach the targeted share by 2025. This is in spite of the fact that the new government introduced the "Make in India" Initiative in 2014. It is difficult to argue if Indian industrial growth or whatever success it has achieved can be attributed to liberalized policy regime alone as India still maintains, although in bits and pieces, vestiges of an active and strategic industrial policy. The "Make in India" programme adopted by the government of India a few years back is also the proof India has not given up on industrial policy, and also a testimony to the fact that it did not have the kind of industrial policy it needed.

Meanwhile, the world has been witnessing weakening of the "Washington Consensus" and strong revival of industrial policy, both in theoretical discourse and in practice. This has been reflected in Indian policy initiative, as in August 2017, the government released a discussion paper with the objective of adopting a New Industrial Policy by October 2017. However, even after putting a lot of effort through multiple focus groups and consultations with stakeholders, a new policy could not be announced until now. This also indicates the issue of industrial policy in India is far from being settled. In any case, even announcement of the new policy need not be an end in itself. The policy needs to be dynamic and flexible, requiring adjustments, as it would move with time. It is an imperative to better understand India's long struggle to develop the manufacturing sector, and explore how India can still succeed in having a vibrant manufacturing sector.

It is also well known that India has been adopting "Industrial Policy" from time to time since Independence, and the objective has always been to promote industrialization, having higher industrial growth in particular. However, the notion of industrial policy that is being considered here is broader in scope and includes several other policies that might have a bearing on macro and micro industrial performance. Industrial policy is more about strategic efforts made to promote industrialization in a country. In this book, an attempt has been made to understand industrial performance that can combine both macro and micro performance issues and can be linked to industrial policy of the country. Characterization of the macroeconomic framework, as well as the industrial policy, is also important to understand the linkage.

The current volume makes an attempt to assess the performance of Indian industry from different perspectives, and also to evaluate the policy factors that might have been responsible for such performance. While it is more or less established that the so-called economic reforms of 1991 did not lead to substantial acceleration in overall growth rate or that of the industrial sector, and that such acceleration actually took place in the 1980s, the impacts of the reforms on performance of individual industrial sub-sectors are not yet settled. Linking policy factors to such performance is even more difficult. It is also difficult to look at economic policy regime purely in terms of a pre- and post-1991 binary. Hence, characterizing economic or industrial policy regime is also quite problematic.

Some key questions that can be raised in this context are: did India follow a planned economy model or a coordinated market economy model? If it is the latter, then how did it deviate from the variants of the model as has been followed in countries like Germany or South Korea? Did India follow an import-substituting policy or an export-led growth strategy, or a combination of both? If India followed an industrial policy regime, then what have been the key elements of such an industrial policy that might have led to whatever success India could achieve in industrial performance? The book makes an effort to address these questions by looking at macro as well as sectoral policies.

This work would not have been possible without the support of many kind souls. While it may not be possible to acknowledge all of them here, some of them deserve special mention. First of all, I would like to express my profound gratitude to Deepak Nayyar and Krishnendu Ghosh Dastidar, for their guidance, comments and suggestions. Comments and suggestions from

xvi *Preface*

K Chalapati Rao and Parthapratim Pal were also very useful. Sugato Dasgupta, Surajit Mazumdar, and Subrata Guha were also of immense help in the process. I am also grateful to Muchkund Dubey for the insights offered by him and Sheetal Bharat, who readily agreed to go through the entire document and provided some useful comments and suggestions. My thinking on this subject developed over a period of time during which I discussed these issues with several scholars, and benefitted immensely. Ha-Joon Chang, Giovani Andrea Cornia, Ajit Singh, Biswajit Dhar, Peter Drahos, Sachin Chaturvedi, Rajat Kathuria, Abhijit Das, Rajeev Kher, Pradeep S Mehta, Bipul Chatterjee, Manoj Sanyal, Pranav Kumar, Indraneel Dasgupta, Indraneel Sengupta, and Prabir Sengupta are few who deserve special mention.

I wrote the greatest part of the book during my stint at TERI. I thank Ajay Mathur for providing the enabling environment and his support. I am also grateful to my other colleagues at TERI whose support was invaluable. I worked with Saswata, Bhawna, and Souvik in different studies that helped me a lot in approaching some of the issues that I dealt with in this book. The colleagues from TERI library – Shantanu, Partho, and Maning, in particular – deserve mention for their help in accessing the relevant literature. Saroj and Bineesan were always ready to help me in data and tabulation work and formatting the manuscript and also did the proofreading. As I finished it during my stay at CSD, I also need to thank the institution and my colleagues there, Gurmeet Kaur, in particular, for her help in finding some of the references. Last, but not the least, I wish to thank three anonymous referees for their valuable comments and suggestions. Needless to say, I am solely responsible for any remaining errors and omissions, as well as the views expressed in this book.

Nitya Nanda
New Delhi
August 2020

Abbreviations

ABB	Asea Brown Boveri
ACA	absolute competitive advantage
AIDS	acquired immunodeficiency syndrome
AEPC	Apparel Export Promotion Council
AOC	Assam Oil Company
ARC	Atomic Research Centre
ASI	Annual Survey of Industries
BCPL	Bengal Chemical and Pharmaceutical Work
BHEL	Bharat Heavy Electricals Limited
BRICS	Brazil, Russia, India, China, and South Africa
CAGR	compound average growth rate
CCI	Cotton Corporation of India
C-DAC	Centre for Development of Advanced Computing
C-DoT	Centre for Development of Telematics
CKD	completely knocked down
CMC	Computer Management Corporation
CME	coordinated market economy
CPI	competitive performance index
CSD	Council for Social Development
CUTS	Consumer Unity and Trust Society
DAE	Department of Atomic Energy
DF	development finance
DFIs	development finance institutions
ECGC	Export Credit and Guarantee Corporation
ECIL	Electronics Corporation of India Limited
ELCINA	Electronic Industries Association of India
EPZ	export processing zone
ERIL	Export Risk Insurance Corporation Limited
ERP	effective rate of protection
FDI	foreign direct investment
FERA	Foreign Exchange Regulation Act
FIPB	Foreign Investment Promotion Board
FTA	free trade agreement

xviii *Abbreviations*

FYP	Five-Year Plan
GCR	global competitiveness ratio
GDP	gross domestic product
GFR	General Financial Rules
HCL	Hindustan Copper Limited
HCV	heavy commercial vehicles
HEC	Hollerith Electronic Computer
HHI	Hirschman-Herfindahl Index
IBM	International Business Machines Corporation
ICA	Indian Council of Arbitration
ICICI	Industrial Credit and Investment Corporation of India
ICV	infantry combat vehicle
IDBI	Industrial Development Bank of India
IFCI	Industrial Finance Corporation of India
IGCC	integrated gasification combined cycle
IOC	Indian Oil Corporation
IPCL	Indian Petrochemical Corporation Limited
IPR	intellectual property rights
ITA	Information Technology Agreement
KVIC	Khadi and Village Industries Commission
LCD	liquid crystal display
LCVs	light commercial vehicles
LED	light-emitting diode
LPG	liberalization, privatization and globalization
MEITY	Ministry of Electronics and Information Technology
MFA	Multi-Fibre Arrangement
MMTC	Minerals and Metals Trading Corporation
MNC	multi-national corporation
MOU	memorandum of understanding
MRTP	monopolies and restrictive trade practices
MRTPC	Monopolies and Restrictive Trade Practices Commission
MW	megawatt
NBER	National Bureau of Economic Research (of the US)
NDRC	National Development and Reforms Commission (of China)
NGO	non-governmental organization
NIC	newly industrialized countries
NIFT	National Institute of Fashion Technology
NIMZ	National Investment and Manufacturing Zone
NMP	National Manufacturing Policy
NSIC	National Small Industries Corporation
NTC	National Textile Corporation
OECD	Organization for Economic Cooperation and Development
ONGC	Oil and Natural Gas Corporation (Commission)
PCM	price-cost margin
POSCO	Pohang Iron and Steel Company

PSE	public sector enterprise
R&D	research and development
RCA	revealed comparative advantage
SAIL	Steel Authority of India Limited
SCP	structure-conduct-performance
SIA	Secretariat for Industrial Assistance
SITP	Scheme for Integrated Textile Parks
SKD	semi-knocked down
SSI	small-scale industry
STC	State Trading Corporation
TADF	Technology Acquisition and Development Fund
TERI	The Energy and Resources Institute
TEXPROCIL	The Cotton Textiles Export Promotion Council
TFP	total factor productivity
TISCO	Tata Iron and Steel Company
TNC	transnational corporation
TRATs	Textile Restructuring Assets Trusts
TRIPS	trade-related aspects of intellectual property rights
TUFS	Technology Upgradation Fund Scheme
UAE	United Arab Emirates
UK	United Kingdom
UNIDO	United Nations Industrial Development Organization
US	United States (of America)
WTO	World Trade Organization

1 Introduction

In a developing country context, industrialization is often considered to be synonymous with economic development. Immediately after Independence, India adopted the Industrial Policy Resolution, 1948, which created a mixed economy, reserving spheres for the private and public sectors. About four decades later, when India embarked on an economic reforms programme in 1991, the major instrument was the Industrial Policy Statement of July 24, 1991. The orientation of this policy was diametrically opposite to the 1948 one, though both of them intended to speed up the process of industrialization in India.

Industrial policy is the strategic effort made by a country's government to promote industrialization, particularly the development of the manufacturing sector. Unlike the broader economy-wide macroeconomic policies, industrial policies are often sector specific. Often, they are partly both – macroeconomic or horizontal, and sector-specific or selective (also called vertical). For example, a country might broadly follow an import-substituting industrialization policy whereby almost every sector enjoys some amount of protection from imports, yet some sectors might enjoy a higher or lower degree of protection, depending on the priorities and emphasis of the government. Industrial policies are normally considered interventionist and hence are opposed by mainstream economists advocating market-oriented policies.

While even mainstream economists accept the need for interventions that are intended to regulate networks and public infrastructure, or for correcting information asymmetries and promoting R&D, the debate is about whether government interventions should go beyond them. Historically, however, it is difficult to find an example where industrialization has taken place in a perfectly *laissez-faire* environment and without any state intervention beyond a level that the mainstream economists are willing to concede, be it the case of US industrialization or more recent examples of industrialization of East Asian countries or some success stories in some Latin American countries (Chang 2002; Rodrik 2004).

Even in a developed economy, it is rare to find an economic policy that does not embrace an industrial policy aspect to maintain its industrial dynamism, except for a brief period during the 1980s and 1990s when having no

DOI: 10.4324/9781003047490-1

2 Introduction

policy was accepted as the default industrial policy. Even during this period, governments in such countries continued with several initiatives that can broadly fall under industrial policy. But now, especially after the financial crisis of 2007, developed countries like the US, Germany, and Japan all have accepted the need for an industrial policy (Andreoni 2017).

While the American Recovery and Reinvestment Act (ARRA) of 2009, and the 2010 National Export Initiative, form the latest industrial policy cycle in the US, an industrial policy was active even during the administration of George W. Bush (2000–2008) in the form of the American Competitiveness Initiative. It tried to improve competitiveness by providing skills, finance, and a tax-friendly business environment, ensuring greater access to international markets through bilateral trade agreements and several technology initiatives and policies. There have been several other sectoral polices and initiatives to improve industrial performance.

Similar is the story of other countries. To give a few prominent examples of recent industrial policy measures in the developed world: the 2009 New Growth Strategy and the Industrial Structure Vision 2010, and initiatives through the Industrial Competitiveness Committee in Japan; and in Germany, the 2008 ZIM (Zentrales Innovations program Mittelstand), the Konjunkturpakete I e II (economic stimulus) in 2008, the Protection of Jobs and Modernization of Federal Republic 2008, Special Program for Large Enterprises 2008, Boosting internal demand for new cars 2008 and the 2010 High-Tech Strategy 2020.

In any case, industrial policy is a tool for effective coordination of the activities of various sectors of the economy, and so, quite important for successful industrialization. Despite criticism from many quarters, there is growing consensus in the recent development literature that state intervention is often necessary. While the current debate has shifted away from dismissing industrial policy to recognizing its relevance, the best ways of promoting industrialization are still widely debated, particularly in the context of the global trade regime whereby some of the industrial policies used earlier have now been restricted or outlawed (Rodrik 2009; Dubey 2020).

1.1 The Indian Context

As indicated before, while the 1948 industrial policy of India put emphasis on the role of the public sector, the 1991 industrial policy put emphasis on the role of foreign capital and technology to drive the industrialization process. The real industrial policy in the post-Independence era, however, came with the 1956 Industrial Policy Resolution, which, along with the role of the public sector, put emphasis on heavy industry to create the industrial base in the country.

The shift between 1948 and 1956 was guided by the adoption of the Constitution of India and the initial experience with the industrialization process, the success of the First Five Year Plan in particular. This policy remained in

Introduction 3

force until 1977, when another Industrial Policy was adopted, though the changes were not so drastic. There was an added emphasis on the small-scale sector to promote industrialization in backward areas, and it created District Industries Centres.

The next Industrial Policy was to come in 1980, emphasizing capacity utilization and productivity, and export-oriented and import-substituting units. Interestingly, this was the first time when consumer interest and prices and quality issues were mentioned in the industrial policy document. The 1990 Industrial Policy could not create any impact, as the 1991 Industrial Policy soon came along. It enhanced the role of foreign investment and foreign technology, reduced the role of the public sector, instituted a series of liberalization measures including removal of licensing requirements, and removed some provisions of the Monopolies and Restrictive Trade Practices Act 1969. The 1991 Industrial Policy is the longest lasting policy so far. Broadly speaking, however, one can argue that pre-1991 policies were essentially similar. On the other hand, it can also be argued whether India has any industrial policy as such in the post-1991 economic policy framework.

It is quite obvious that when we talk about industrial policy or industrialization strategy, it is not just what has been discussed in the government policy document that has been named industrial policy, but that it is a much broader concept which includes several other policy domains including trade policy, investment policy, state involvement, banking and financial policy, and so on. In all these areas, the country went for more liberalized environment which was in line with the philosophy that having no policy is the default policy. Accordingly, characterizing the overall development or industrialization strategy of the country is quite difficult.

The dominant narrative is that prior to 1991, India followed an import-substituting industrialization policy. While this might have been partly true, it is questionable also if this has indeed been the industrialization strategy of India. Import substitution may not have been the only reason that India might have imposed high import barriers. Dealing with a shortage of foreign exchange and the felt need to discourage conspicuous consumption could have been other reasons. Moreover, India also adopted several policies and programmes to encourage exports, as well.

On the other hand, it is also difficult to argue that India simply dumped import-substituting industrialization in the post-1991 period. The experience of the automobile industry is a clear example. Foreign investors who entered India in this sector were given targets for indigenization of their production in India in terms of sourcing of the components they used. The sector also enjoyed the protection of relatively high tariff rates. These are obviously important components of an import-substituting industrialization strategy.

Similarly, it has also been often argued that India followed a Soviet-type central planning model since the 1950s. While it is true that India used to have five-year plans, such plans were used by many other countries that have never been termed planned economies. South Korea and Taiwan had

4 *Introduction*

five-year and four-year plans, respectively. While these countries have been termed coordinated market economies like Germany, India has been compared with the former Soviet Union! Maybe Nehru's fascination for Fabian socialism was partially responsible for this, but this could also be due to India's perceived political alignment with the Soviet bloc rather than NATO (the North Atlantic Treaty Organization). Hence, along with characterizing the industrialization strategy, characterizing the overall economic policy framework is also an issue of debate.

1.2 The Problematique

Now the question is how these different industrial policies were successful (or otherwise) in creating the desired outcomes. This is indeed a difficult question, as industrial growth performance is not determined by industrial policies only. Not only macroeconomic policies, but also other socio-economic factors and political situations, as well as global economic and geo-political issues, play an important role in this regard. For example, the famous 1991 reforms were triggered by the economic crisis that was in turn triggered by higher oil prices and decline in exports due to the Gulf War of 1990–91 waged by the US-led coalition forces in response to the Iraqi invasion of Kuwait.

However, as explained previously, overall industrial growth rates may not truly reflect the performance of industrial policies. Industrial policies are not macroeconomic policies. Even though overall industrial policies were adopted from time to time, they put varying emphasis on different sectors of the economy. Moreover, strategic industrial policy would also require deep understanding of how different sub-sectors in the manufacturing sector have been performing, and how these different levels of performance are linked to different policy variables.

When it comes to industrialization and industrial performance in India, it is now well accepted that India had only limited success. It could not match the performance of the East Asian countries, and at the same time, it did not go the African way (Nayyar 2006). While India maintained its growth momentum for a long time, even after its policy shift in 1991, an inconvenient truth is that its success in getting ahead in terms of growth in manufacturing remains elusive. India's share of manufacturing increased steadily during 1950–1980, and it continued to rise slowly until the mid-1990s, but it became stagnant thereafter and even experienced a decline since 2008 (Raihan 2020). GDP data for the period after 2013–14 are not truly comparable; nevertheless, the share of manufacturing in GDP continued to decline even after 2013–14, and Nayyar (2019) observed that between 1990 and 2016, the share of manufacturing has declined from 19.7 per cent to 16.5 per cent. According to Basole and Narayan (2020), the share of manufacturing further declined to 14.9 per cent in 2017.

Compared to other Asian countries, India's manufacturing output (as a share of GDP) peaked too early, and at a much lower level (Nayyar 2019).

This has raised the concern of premature deindustrialization in India. While traditionally deindustrialization has been defined as a decline in the share of manufacturing in total employment, in recent literature, it has also been defined in terms of decline in the share of manufacturing output in GDP. Tregenna (2009), however, suggested that deindustrialization should be defined in terms of a sustained decline in both the share of manufacturing in total employment as well its share in GDP. Basole and Narayan (2020) estimated that between 2011 and 2017, the share of manufacturing in total employment has witnessed a marginal decline from 12.6 per cent to 12.1 per cent. A premature deindustrialization in India, therefore, seems to be real.

The question arises whether this limited success was due to any conscious strategies and policies adopted in India, or if it was just due to market forces. This, of course, would require understanding first if India had an industrial policy and how it changed over time. Some key questions that can be raised in this context are: did India follow a planned economy model or a coordinated market economy model? If it is the latter, then how did it deviate from the variants of the model as followed in countries like Germany and South Korea? Did India follow an import-substituting policy or an export-led growth strategy, or a combination of both? If India followed an industrial policy regime, then it would be pertinent to look at the elements of such an industrial policy that might have led to whatever success India could achieve in industrial performance.

Against this backdrop, it would be useful to examine if India followed an "industrial policy" and a combination of import-substituting and export-led growth strategies, as was followed in several coordinated market economies; and if the industrial policy, as well as elements of a coordinated market economy framework, played a positive role in the limited success in industrialization and industrial performance of India.

1.3 The Analytical Framework

The analytical framework used in this book is that of structuralist economics, which views an economic system as not just a system of variables determined in the market but essentially as a socio-economic process. As against the neo-classical construct of a market-guided equilibrating mechanism, the structuralist construct views the economic system as a non-equilibrating evolutionary process (Street and James 1982). Human beings are not seen as rational decision makers with the primary motive of utility maximization; their behaviour is also influenced by historical and cultural conditioning.

An important component of structuralist economics is the context, both in the sense of time and space (Baghirathan et al 2004). Hence, this framework rejects the idea of a one-size-fits-all type policy prescriptions for all types of economies at all times. In fact, the same country might have to follow different policy regimes at different points of time, not just due to socio-economic and cultural changes within the country but also due to changes in the global

6 Introduction

environment. As described by di Filippo (2009), structuralist economics has four basic characteristics: a historic structural perspective, a systemic reading of society, a global outlook, and a multidimensional approach.

In a broad sense, the origins of structuralism have been traced to the emergence of the doctrine of market failure in England during the 1930s and 1940s (Arndt 1985). In a sense, even Keynes was influenced by this line of thought, as he argued that the economy would not get out of depression simply through market forces and the government needed to act to enhance effective demand and stimulate output expansion (Baghirathan et al 2004). However, the framework emerged after the market failure doctrine was synthesized with the Latin American structuralist theory of inflation developed by the ECLAC (Economic Commission for Latin America and the Caribbean). The ECLAC termed its analysis "structuralist" in the mid-1950s as, in contrast to monetarist view of inflation, it argued that the persistent inflation in Latin America was a cost-push phenomenon, driven primarily by supply rigidities of the agricultural sector, and money was endogenous to it.

It has, however, been pointed out that, while the term "structuralism" had been in use for quite some time in other disciplines like linguistics, anthropology, and philosophy, some elements of current structuralist economics can be traced to the "structuralist" economic school in France (Blankenburg et al 2008). But it has also been argued that what is now understood by structuralist economics has no direct link with the French structuralist school of thought. While the French school was concerned with disparities in social organizations, structuralist economics emphasized the importance of what are considered non-economic factors in macroeconomic models (Taylor 1983; Missio et al 2015).

Blankenburg et al (2008), however, argued that the importance of the French structuralist school should not be ignored. Referring to François Perroux's work, they argued that he emphasized the importance of institutions and structure over time in economic analysis as against the neo-classical approach of treating resources and technology as given. Moreover, his theory of domination, which he applied to different levels of analysis, particularly in the context of international economy, which he characterized as a relationship between "dominant" and "dominated" economies, finds echo in Latin American structuralist formulation.

As a methodological or analytical framework, structuralism emphasizes system-wide analysis. It looks at the system in its totality and the inter-relationship between its different elements rather than focusing on them in isolation. Hence, an economy cannot be analyzed in isolation. It has to be seen as a part of the global economy and the dynamics of the relationship between its constituent parts, which the ECLAC described as core and periphery. It is because of this unequal relationship and its manifestation in terms of social and technological and institutional underdevelopment that developing countries cannot afford to leave everything to market and develop. Hence, economic development will come through structural change with technological and industrial upgrading, which can come only through interventionist industrial policy.

Industrial policy is essential to deal with resource scarcity, access to technology, and externality and coordination issues in industrial development. While countries have been using industrial policy in some form or other for industrial development for a long time, structuralism provided the theoretical basis for industrial policy that justifies the role of the state beyond the correction of market failures as accepted by mainstream economics. Hence, Prebisch (1959) argued in favour of industrial policy as a process in which governments deliberately try to bring about structural change in their economies. Industrial policy and its relationship with industrial performance in the context of India is the subject matter of this volume.

Structuralist economics got a new flavour when Justin Yifu Lin (2011), the then World Bank Chief Economist, argued for rethinking development strategy, broadly in line with structuralist economic policy. His suggested strategy came out of a synthesis of ideas from structuralist and neo-classical economics. While he termed it as "New Structural Economics", in essence, his framework was structuralist in nature, fortified with some ideas and tools from neo-classical economics. His work gave more acceptability to structuralist economics and more so the need for interventionist industrial policy, as his arguments were based on experience from China, which saw substantial economic transformation and industrial development in recent decades.

While it is now widely recognized that strategic industrial policy is essential for development of low-income countries, Lin (2017) argued that developing countries need to continue with industrial policy for some time. Even middle-income developing countries need to follow industrial policy, but in their case, the policy needs to be much more customized for different sub-sectors depending on their position vis-à-vis the global technology frontier. He classified industries into five broad categories, namely, catching-up industries, leading-edge industries, comparative advantage-losing industries, short innovation cycle industries, and comparative-advantage-defying strategic industries, and argued that industrial policy needs to be designed keeping the status of the industry in mind. Premature abandonment of industrial policy might lead to premature deindustrialization.

But before one tries to understand the impacts of industrial policy on industrial performance, it is necessary to understand how industrial performance can be measured. The literature in this regard has been dominated by the structure-conduct-performance paradigm whereby performance has typically been measured by price-cost margin. However, such an approach has been criticized on the grounds that price-cost margin is hardly able to capture the dynamic performance of an industry. It has also been argued that industrial policy cannot influence structure and conduct beyond a point. Moreover, the structure-conduct-performance paradigm is also quite inadequate, as competition prevailing in an industry is not the only factor that determines performance.

8 Introduction

The structure-conduct-performance model recognizes that the conduct of firms is not determined by competition with each other, where several factors, such as market structure, minimum efficient size, diversification, integration, and technology play an important role. In that sense, the structure-conduct-performance model provides an alternative approach to the equilibrating mechanism of neo-classical economics, which is also compatible with structuralist economics. Industrial structure or market structure can be considered to be determined by history as well as people's behaviour, which is not limited by rational utility maximization but also cultural conditioning.

The structure-conduct-performance based research, however, in general, used qualitative assessment of factors that determined the market structure. This was quite compatible with structuralist economics, but in the language of mainstream economics, these were essentially exogenous assumptions and were considered to be a limitation. Hence, a dynamic model was developed in which the conduct was not just determined by structure and the related factors, but it also influenced the structure in the next period. The Schumpeterian innovations play an important role here, where firms are constrained by bounded rationality and limited knowledge about structural features that determine their behaviour (Antonelli 1995). While this formulation can be attributed to neo-structuralist economics, this is also compatible with structural economics as well. While structuralist economics questions the assumption of rational decision making, it does not argue that economic agents will be irrational all the time. Hence, bounded rationality and limited knowledge about the structural features are also compatible with structuralist economics. While the literature in the structure-conduct-performance framework continued to develop, criticisms surrounding it gave rise to development of two different strands of thinking: productivity and efficiency. Each of these two measures has also undergone substantial refinements and concomitant development of econometric literature involving sophisticated techniques. However, sophistication could not overcome the basic difficulty in such measures, namely, the estimation of capital.

Measuring efficiency empirically has also been quite problematic.[1] Existing techniques measure average efficiency with respect to the best performing firm in the country, while ideally, the reference point should be the best performance that is technically possible or the best performing firm that exists anywhere in the world. While an assessment of the best performance that is technically feasible is simply impossible, measuring efficiency with all the firms that exist in the world is methodologically challenging.

As industrial policy and performance have often been looked at from the lens of trade policy, trade performance has also been used as a proxy for industrial performance. The theoretical framework behind such an approach has been the theory of comparative advantage. While terms like competitive advantage or competitiveness became popular in the management literature, they did not receive much attention in the economic literature. The idea of revealed comparative advantage (RCA) developed by Balassa (1965) caught the imagination of several researchers, and a large number of studies estimated RCAs to understand performance of industrial sectors.

Intuitively, the theory of comparative advantage runs counter to structuralist economics, or its analysis of international trade and its determinants. While comparative advantage theory itself is considered inadequate to explain international trade, even in the neo-classical framework, the RCA is also considered inappropriate to capture comparative advantage as a process, or even the outcome that could come out of true comparative advantage situations, but it can still lend itself as a candidate to assess the competitive outcome. Hence, RCA could be modified appropriately to get an indicator of competitive advantage.

As the title of the book indicates, the focus here is more on industrial performance; policy issues are discussed as they are expected to influence performance. Hence, the current volume makes an attempt to assess the performance of Indian industry from different perspectives and also to evaluate the policy factors that might have been responsible for such performance.

The next chapter looks at different aspects of industrial policy based on a review of the existing literature, in particular, how different countries have used them in their industrial development process. While this chapter is entirely based on a review of literature, the subsequent three substantive chapters also include reviews of the relevant literature. These three chapters deal with three different themes, namely macro or growth performance of India, industrial performance in India, and the intensity of competition in Indian manufacturing sector. Since these three themes have followed different streams in the manner in which the existing literature has developed, mixing all of them in a grand chapter on survey of literature might not be able to do justice to the vast literature that exists, and readers will be able to relate better if they are placed in the respective chapters. Moreover, while the literature review in Chapter 2 is largely on theoretical issues and empirical evidence across the world, the review in the other chapters is largely India specific.

Chapter 3 looks at the macro context of industrial policy and assesses industrial performance in the context of the overall growth performance and related policy issues. It analyzes how industrial policy evolved over time since Independence, more with reference to what was referred to as the industrial policy in the Indian policy landscape. It also attempts to examine if there is any scope to characterize certain periods as import-substituting, while certain others as export-led industrialization policy. Therefore, a closer look at export-import policy was also given. Industrial growth rates in the context of overall growth of the economy over different time periods are looked at, essentially to understand how they evolved and how they might have been linked to changes in industrial policies and other factors.

Chapter 4 looks at the performance of Indian industry in the context of global economic performance and developments therein. This is where different methodologies and indices are used to understand performance of

10 *Introduction*

different industrial sub-sectors over time. Three such indices have been used which are either new or a modified version of the existing ones. The sub-sectors that performed differently from the average have been picked up for a closer examination, to find possible elements of industrial policy that might have made the difference. A couple of sub-sectors that had good potentials but did not perform so well have also been analyzed in some details.

Chapter 5 looks at industrial performance in the structure-conduct-performance paradigm, although with some modification to accommodate the Schumpeterian notion of dynamic competition, and measures the intensity of competition in select manufacturing sectors through persistence of the profit indicator. Using this indicator, performance of different sub-sectors is assessed in terms of profitability and competition, both from long term and short term perspectives. Here again, an attempt has been made to understand how the differences in the degree of competition and profitability were influenced by different policies and other factors.

Even though they are interconnected, the third, fourth, and fifth chapters are more or less independent, Chapter 6 tries to connect and synthesise the findings of these three chapters and to find answers to the basic questions that are central to this book. These are whether India followed a planned economy or a coordinated market economy model, and whether it followed import-substituting and export-led industrialization models in different periods; and how the different elements of industrial policy might have influenced India's success, or lack of it, in different industrial sub-sectors. Finally, an attempt is made to understand what kind of industrial policy would be feasible and desirable in the emerging context.

Note

1 Here the focus has been on technical efficiency, which is the level of output that is produced by using a given set of inputs. A firm is considered to be technically efficient if it is producing the maximum possible output from a given set of inputs. However, sometimes, allocative efficiency is also considered. Allocative efficiency occurs when the production of output takes place at (or close to) the marginal cost. The basic principle of allocative efficiency is that it ensures proper allocation of resources in accordance with the preferences of consumers.

2 Industrial policy and performance
The key issues

2.1 Introduction

Discussion of industrial performance has generally been dominated by the structure-conduct-performance (SCP) paradigm – the basic tenet of which is that the market structure of an industry influences the performance of the industry, which has often been considered to be synonymous with efficiency most often measured as profitability or price-cost margin.[1] Each firm holds a unique position in the market at any point of time. Some have small shares of the market and are under competitive stress. Others might have large shares and are subject to fewer competitive pressures. Each firm's position influences its behaviour and performance. The performance of the whole market of particular industry is the aggregate of the individual firms' performances. At the aggregate level, a higher level of market concentration would mean higher price-cost margin and poorer performance.

However, such a paradigm may not operate in a developing country, particularly at the initial stage of industrialization. In such a situation, it is likely that there would be just a few firms, meaning that concentration will be high, yet the operating firms might be struggling to post a reasonable rate of profit.

Some economists (e.g., Stigler and Kindahl 1970) believe that a perfectly competitive condition is best suited for technical advancement, since firms are always in a vulnerable position under competitive constraints. Firms will try to consolidate their position by improving product quality or reducing cost, both of which obviously need technical advancement (assuming that there is no managerial slack). If this is to be believed, then a larger market share would make a firm complacent and thereby weaken its urge to achieve technical progress.

The alternative view is that a large market share or monopoly power is good for inventive activities. Foremost among those associated with this view is Schumpeter (1950). He visualized an economy as an organism constituted by cells that are continuously dying and being replaced with better ones. The organism grows and flourishes through a process which he called "creative destruction". An economy grows and regenerates through replacement of existing products, processes, and modes of production and organization

DOI: 10.4324/9781003047490-2

12 *Industrial policy and performance*

by their improved versions. The motivational force behind the process of "creative destruction" is the quest for earning extraordinary profits through innovations.

The very nature of the process ensures that the monopoly position achieved through innovation is not a permanent one. Because others may imitate, so another new innovation becomes necessary. Innovation, however, may require a sizeable deployment of resources and a firm would also expect a commensurate return. If other firms are able to imitate a firm's new product or process as is likely to happen in case of perfect competition, that would reduce realizable rewards – and thereby, its interest to innovate. So only a firm that can establish at least temporary monopoly power through a larger market share delaying rival imitation will find innovation attractive.

Performance in a marketplace depends not only on the costs or prices of a product, but also because of goodwill or reputation that has been built over the years. Hence, an industry based in a developing country is unlikely to do well internationally, unless it has a very distinct cost or price advantage. Its reputation is yet to be built up and the quality, even if good, is unlikely to be accepted in the global marketplace, due to absence of track record.

This has been seen particularly in the development history of Japan, Korea, Taiwan, etc. As of now, China is possibly going through the stage of competition with price advantage while it is building on its quality and reputation. This is not difficult to understand, even in the microeconomic context or corporate strategy. A new entrant will always try to offer its product or services at lower prices, often much lower than costs of production, then raising the prices when it is accepted well in the market.

While market structure has very often been linked with performance of an industry, from the policy perspective, there are several other areas that might have a bearing on performance. Countries often adopt something called an industrial policy, but this could be just a subset of what in reality industrial policy might involve. For example, trade policy has long been considered to be a part of strategic industrial policy which essentially meant infant industry protection. While some economists opposed such ideas, others emphasized the need for a dynamic trade policy. Another area is public sector participation in industrial production. While the industrial policy statement might offer a broad indication of public sector participation, the actual participation depends mostly on executive decision.

In any country, technology plays an important role in industrialization. Technology adopted can come through domestic R&D and related innovation, but it is also imported from foreign sources. Hence, technology and IPR policy can also play an important role. While foreign technology can come from outright purchase or technical collaboration, foreign direct investment (FDI) is often considered to be an important mode of technology transfer. Though often contested, FDI is also considered to be a source of financing for development.

While competition has long been considered associated with industrial performance, the nature of competition-innovation – as well as long-term industrial growth – has received special attention. For example, Schumpeter emphasized that a certain degree of monopoly power is better than perfect competition to stimulate innovation and long-term industrial development in a dynamic sense. Given this, the kind of competition or regulatory policies that the state follows, as well as the kind of overall support system the state provides, also has important bearing on industrial performance.

The literature on industrial performance has recognized several factors that can affect performance. Factors like good governance, education, and health, as well as cultural factors, are well accepted as important determinants of positive industrial performance (Lensink and Kuper 2000; Acemoglu and Robinson 2012). In particular, in most Asian countries, government-promoted primary and secondary education played an important role in industrial development (Nayyar 2019).

Accumulation of capital, labour and its quality, and technology create more direct impact, and in the language of Angus Maddison can be called the proximate causes. However, here the discussions will be more on ultimate, but among them the more active factors that influence industrial performance in a more direct manner and which taken together can be termed as industrial policy (Maddison 1991). Based on the literature, the following sections discuss these factors in further detail.

2.2 Trade policy

In the development literature, the role of trade policy in increasing growth and efficiency – as well as industrialization – has long received substantial attention. With the so-called import substitution strategy failing to foster fast industrial growth in most of the developing countries, outward orientation became the catchword, with many development theorists as well as policy makers. The advocates of the free trade doctrine have put forward several arguments: the policy of indiscriminate protection of infant industries has hindered productivity gain on a significant scale and that has led to gross misallocation of resources. Once these protective trade barriers are lifted, the economy will be put on an efficient and technologically superior path of development. The promises of a liberalized trade regime are improved efficiency – both allocative and technical, scale economies and faster technological development.

However, traditional comparative advantage and free trade theories have relied mainly on allocative efficiency to explain gains from trade. Any textbook illustration of gains from trade would tell that it arises out of a movement along the production possibility frontier. It is more or less silent on what will happen if the economy is operating at a level below the frontier.[2] But renewed hopes for a liberalized trade policy regime are not based on improved allocative efficiency only.

14 *Industrial policy and performance*

The common belief is that as protection leads to monopolization of the domestic market by a few firms, liberalization would change the market structure which would be conducive to improvements in technical efficiency as well as productivity through innovations and cost-reducing investments. This argument is, of course, false because theories of industrial organization have not been able to establish that a competitive market structure would stimulate innovation and cost-reducing investments.

A study by Chenery et al. (1986) showed that growth in total factor productivity has played a major role in the overall economic growth in developed countries. In the case of developing countries, even though factor inputs have grown at a high rate, the importance of productivity growth in overall industrial performance has been low. As a matter of fact, the importance of productivity growth has been much lower in the growth of developing economies, rather, growth has largely been driven by growth in factor inputs in these countries. Given this kind of scenario, it is natural to believe that growth in productivity is the *sine qua non* for economic growth in developing countries. So it sounds very attractive when one says that an outward-oriented trade policy can help improve efficiency and productivity. But is there any reason to believe this? To answer this question, let us consider the channels through which trade liberalization is believed to achieve these.

The first line of argument is that technical efficiency increases through a reduction in X-inefficiency. Here the presumption is that protection from foreign competition discourages entrepreneurs to work hard to improve productivity and cut costs. But there are several difficulties with this argument. It assumes that domestic competition is mild enough to keep them complacent. Moreover, with optimizing behaviour of entrepreneurs, this cannot be true. In fact, the situation may be quite the opposite – an individual firm, with a larger share of the market provided by protection, may expect larger benefits out of cost improvement and may increase technological effort.

Another line of argument is based on the advantage of scale economies. It is argued that in a liberalized trade regime, domestic firms may reap the benefit of scale by capturing a portion of foreign markets. But if there are really substantial economies of scale to be gained by expanding output, then can restriction on imports stop the firms in the exporting sector from exporting more? If the answer is that it is due to exporting firms needing to use imported capital goods and raw materials, then the problem may be solved by relaxing imports of capital goods and raw materials. There is no need for indiscriminate trade liberalization.

It is also claimed that protection increases profitability, which in turn attracts new entrants and hence producers operates far below efficient scale. This argument is not a complete one, especially because of the implicit assumption that there is no barrier to entry, which has very poor basis in developing countries. Here, one may recall that while talking about X-efficiency, it is generally argued that it increases with increased level of competition (see, for example, Leibenstein 1973). If because of protection, there are too many

Industrial policy and performance 15

firms, then there will be a higher level of competition within the domestic market. So these two arguments cannot go together, unless X-efficiency discriminates between foreign and domestic competitions, for which there is no reason.

Moreover, Bardhan and Kletzer (1984) have shown that, in fact, the net dynamic effects of protection on productivity are positive. They agree with the view that protection, by sheltering inefficient firms, delays modernization of techniques and capital stocks, and thus dampens the growth of productivity and efficiency. But by considering the learning by doing effects of protection on productivity, they have shown that even though protection might lengthen the economic life of capital, there is a dynamic trade-off between its productivity depressing effect and the learning effect, and that after a certain time, the latter effect offsets the former.

Let us now turn to the empirical evidence relating to this issue. There have been a good number of studies relating trade policy to technical efficiency and productivity growth, but none of them has found any strong evidence of a country benefitting from liberalization in the form of growth in technical efficiency and productivity.[3] In some cases (e.g., Tybout et al. 1991), of course, it has been found that there has been a very little improvement in scale and technical efficiencies after liberalization. But it should be kept in mind that these countries have implemented a package of policies (called stabilization), and liberalized trade policy is only a part of it.

So, it would be unjust to attribute this improvement in scale and technical efficiencies, albeit very little, to a liberalized trade regime only. Greater macroeconomic stability would place the managers of the firms in a better position to assess the future, which will obviously help in increasing X-efficiency. Further, the study by Caves and Barton (1990) of the US manufacturing industries has shown that the degree of technical inefficiency is, in fact, inversely related to the degree of openness to the outside world.

As regards scale economics, it may be noted that, in countries like Korea, Taiwan, Brazil, and Turkey, export boom was achieved much before any attempt to liberalize was made, while in some countries (e.g., Chile), liberalization of trade led to increase in exports of primary or primary-based products with a very little scope for achieving scale economics (Baldwin 2000).

Nishimizu and Robinson (1984) analyzed the link between trade policies and industrial productivity performance. Their analysis is based on estimates of sectoral TFPs in Korea, Turkey, and Yugoslavia, with Japan as a comparator. They came to the conclusion that import-substituting trade policies had a negative impact on total factor productivity growth in the manufacturing industries, although it varied in degree across countries and sectors.

Similarly, Weiss (1992) examined the impact of trade liberalization that was undertaken in Mexico in the mid-1980s on alternative indicators of performance over the period 1975–88. He found that liberalization had a positive but relatively weak effect on labour productivity, as well as on TFP. Das (2016) makes an effort to understand the impacts of trade liberalization

16 *Industrial policy and performance*

in the form of reduction of tariff and non-tariff barriers in India during 1990–2010 on industrial performance, measured as TFP. According to him, trade liberalization made only a small impact on increase in productivity, and much of the productivity gain in the Indian manufacturing industry occurred due to internal reforms rather than trade policy reforms.

Dollar and Kraay (2001) have been widely quoted as an evidence of trade liberalization promoting economic growth. They attempted to show that a group of developing countries, or "globalizers", that have been more open to trade than others in the period between the early 1980s and the late 1990s have grown faster than those that have been less open to trade, or "non-globalizers"; and growth of trade volumes was found to be associated with higher growth of incomes. Globalizers identified by them are the top one-third in terms of their growth in trade relative to GDP between 1975–79 and 1995–97 of a group of 72 developing countries, while non-globalizers refers to the remaining developing countries in this group. However, Nanda (2008) pointed out that the non-globalizers identified by them are actually "more globalized" both in terms of trade as a share of GDP (higher trade/GDP ratio) as well as tariff barriers (lower average tariffs). It was also pointed out that the so-called non-globalizers achieved a very high trade/GDP ratio (60 per cent) even in the 1970s, which was four times higher than the so-called globalizers and double of that of rich countries. But their trade/GDP ratio has been falling during the 1980s and 1990s, despite the fact that they continued to reduce their tariffs further.

Based on the evidence cited by Dollar and Kraay (2001) themselves, it can actually be argued that the "globalized" countries have shown poorer performance compared to the "non-globalized" countries during the 1980s and 1990s. The fact that China and India, which have shown spectacular performance during this period, have been put in the category of globalizer is also quite problematic, as they were well known to be reluctant, slow, and cautious liberalizers, particularly in the 1980s and even in the 1990s, and also remained among the most protected countries. This also raises a question on most studies that adopted an elasticity approach and found that higher growth performance is linked to higher trade liberalization.

To sum up, it may be observed that neither theoretically nor empirically has the impact of a liberalized trade policy on changes in efficiency over time been strongly established. Recent economic literature has highlighted the emergence of a global value chain, particularly in the last three decades or so, where products sold in the markets have become more complicated and a typical product is manufactured by a number of firms spread over different locations in different countries. This has given one more reason to advocate free trade policy, as it is believed that such an approach would enable a country to participate in such global value addition, which in turn will stimulate industrialization.

While this might be true to some extent, it is also noteworthy that the returns from value addition on a global scale might not be equitably distributed across firms, regions, or countries. While some components or processes in the value chain offer higher returns, others might not offer much benefit except some employment to unskilled labour.

Using a similar argument, there has also been a call for reforming tariff structures to get rid of inverted duty or a negative effective rate of protection (ERP). A negative ERP would result when duties on parts and components are higher than those on the final product. On the face of it, the argument seems convincing, but favouring the so-called final product over the components might also lead to promotion of what is often called screwdriver technology – meaning that very little is really produced in the country, but only assembled by importing almost everything, often including the packaging materials, as well. It is important to recognize the limits of effective rate of protection. It is also noteworthy that when the economic case of looking at ERP was made, global value chain was not in existence and inputs actually meant raw materials rather than components.

Historically, of course, it is difficult to find examples of countries that developed on the basis of free trade policy. Barring a few exceptions, all countries have used strategic trade policies to promote industrial development (Chang 2002). For example, US trade policy still contains some remnants of strategic trade policies that it used long years ago (Box 2.1).

Box 2.1   The US trade regime: favouring developed countries!

The US trade regime today is a chaotic evolution of government policy and business community attitudes over the last nine decades. During the early twentieth century American manufacturers were enthusiastic lobbyists for tariff protection against their European rivals. Textiles and apparel mills, as the kings of the economy, got the best deals. Meanwhile, traditional developing country products – natural resources, and consumer goods like tea and rattan-matting unavailable from American sources – have always had largely free access to the American market. In newer industries like computers, biotechnology and civil aircraft etc. US manufacturers were always ahead of their rivals and never sought much protection. As a result, today's American trade regime looks like a fat man lying on its back: Low at each end, high in the middle. Importers of sophisticated computers and jumbo jets pay no tariffs at all; neither do buyers of gourmet coffee or zinc. But in the middle, on clothes, US tariffs average nearly 18 per cent. Food items have even tougher obstacles and footwear is not far behind. So, as developing countries climb out of natural resources into manufacturing and export crops, they hit the high walls of protected markets.

18 *Industrial policy and performance*

> The results are an embarrassment to the welfare conscious. To choose an egregious case, the US now collects more tariff revenue from Cambodia than from Singapore. The US revenue tables show more such surprises. The US buys about $40bn worth of goods a year from Britain and $10bn from Indonesia, but Indonesian exporters to the US pay $200mn more in tariffs than their British counterparts. Likewise, businesses in the Philippines pay substantially more than those in France; and Bangladesh pays three times as much as Spain.
>
> Source: Nanda (2008).

2.3 Public sector participation

It has become a common belief that state-owned firms are less efficient than private firms, even when operating in similar circumstances. This has also influenced the economic and industrial policies of several countries, as many of them have privatized publicly owned firms over the last few decades. Contrary to this popular belief, there is neither any theoretical rationale nor any empirical support for the claim that private firms are inherently more efficient than their public counterparts. It is true that in most of the studies it has been found that profitability in private firms is significantly higher than that of public firms. But then, profitability cannot be taken as the only and the right criterion for judging economic efficiency. It can be a good criterion for efficiency in a business sense; but efficiency in an economic sense should not be confused with it. Particularly, in no public firm is maximization of profit the stated objective.

One may, of course, argue that when both a public and a private firm are operating in a same oligopolistic market, then lower profitability in the public firm arises from lower efficiency in input use. But this need not be the same. Lower profitability of the public firm may arise due to the fact that workers' remuneration is better and that the management of input uses is no worse.

Let us now look into the results of some theoretical approaches regarding incentives and efficiency in public and private firms.[4] In their benchmark model on ownership and efficiency, Vickers and Yarrow (1988) deal with the trade-off between allocative and productive efficiencies, which results from total privatization. The objective of the firm changes from welfare maximization to profit maximization, which also brings a tendency towards higher prices. From an allocative efficiency point of view, this makes the situation worse. On the other hand, they argue that in a privatized firm, due to profit orientation, incentives to reduce costs are strengthened, so from productive efficiency point, this could improve the situation. They found that a public firm would do far better, even if the incentive and monitoring in it is slightly better than its private counterpart. But to perform better, the private firm must be significantly superior in terms of giving incentives to the managers and monitoring. Particularly, when the price elasticity of demand and elasticity of costs with respect to cost-reducing investments are low, monitoring in the private firm must be particularly accurate and far superior compared to its public counterpart, to perform better.

Latter models have relied on principal-agent approaches, which relate owners, senior management (board), and technological management. Bos and Peters (1991), for example, compare the behaviour of a price setting firm which is initially public and then is completely privatized. They come to the following conclusions:

1 The public firm sets prices according to an inverse elasticity rule, whereby the price-cost margin depends on the particular mix of the multiple goals. Marginal-cost (MC) pricing is chosen only if the simple sum of consumer and producer surplus is maximized. Privatization leads to a move towards MC pricing.
2 The manager of a public firm generally makes less effort than is efficient, but in a privatized firm, the effort is likely to be at efficient level. But there is an exceptional case when the effort of a public firm is also efficient.

Pint (1991) presents a model which suggests that the type of ownership can have implications not only for pricing, but also for production decisions. Public firms are likely to use more labour as a factor of production, while private firms are biased towards capital-intensive technologies. Public firms are also shown to be likely to produce more output and set lower prices. Thus, even though profits are likely to be lower, consumer surplus is likely to be higher in a publicly owned firm. She comes to the conclusion that both organizational forms are inefficient.

De Fraja (1993) casts doubt on the belief that the profit motive is necessarily an effective incentive for cost reduction. He is of the opinion that as long as an appropriately designed contract is enforced, there is no theoretical basis to believe that public ownership would necessarily entail weaker incentives towards cost reduction. In fact, he shows that, under certain conditions, a public firm is always more efficient than a private one, except in the trivial case when both of them are equally efficient.[5]

Let us now turn to the empirical aspect of the issue. Some early surveys of empirical studies on efficiency comparisons between private and public firms enthusiastically reported that the evidence was in favour of private sector performance. For instance, Bennett and Johnson (1980) argued that the empirical findings suggest that the same level of output could be produced at lower costs in the private sector compared to the public sector – but in many of the later studies, such a strong judgement could not be passed.

In their survey, Borcherding et al. (1982), came to the conclusion that when public and private producers operated in the same environment, they

20 *Industrial policy and performance*

tended to show similar unit costs. It is not so much the difference in the ownership, but the lack of competition, and often the difference in operational environment, which could be responsible for often observed less efficient production in the public sector firms. Some of the surveys – for instance, by Millward and Parker (1983) – arrived at the conclusion that there is no systematic difference between performance under public and private ownership. But superior performance was found in Canadian railways, Australian airlines and US electric power. Estrin and Pérotin (1987) made a comparison between Britain and France, and concluded that the public sector firms in France were more cost efficient than the public sector firms in Britain, and that there was no significant difference in performance between the public and private firms in France.

Boardman and Veining (1989) compared the efficiency of 409 private companies, 57 public enterprises, and 23 enterprises in mixed public-private ownership from the list of the Fortune 500 largest non-US manufacturing and mining corporations in the world in 1983 to obtain robust evidence that public enterprises and mixed enterprises are less profitable and less efficient than private enterprises, so the empirical evidence on the productive efficiency of public versus private enterprise is inconclusive.

An important study by Hutchinson (1991) compares relative performance of public and privatized firms in the UK for the period 1970–87. The findings are striking. Publicly owned firms showed higher levels of growth in labour productivity, while private firms showed higher levels of profits. This evidence obviously suggests that privatization of state enterprises in the UK made firms more profitable, while also – in all probability – negatively impacted labour productivity.

A United Nations Development Programme (UNDP) review finds no conclusive evidence that any particular type of ownership (i.e. public, private, or mixed) is inherently more efficient than the others. The review also suggests that efficiency most often is dependent on the sector or type of service (health, education, etc.) and other specific contextual factors. Efficiency under all types of ownership depends on common factors such as competition, regulation, financial, legal, and institutional environment, and also on some firm-specific factors (UNDP 2015).

Government-owned companies are very often natural monopolies or are monopolies by virtue of government industrial policy, and performance of monopolies is generally weak. A robust comparison of performance of government-owned companies vis-à-vis privately owned companies would be possible only when both type of companies are operating in the same market and facing a similar policy environment. But these conditions are difficult to satisfy.

Then there is another situation: when a government-owned company is privatized. A comparison of pre- and post-privatization performance might not give a clear picture, as the market or industrial environment is also not static. In the Indian context, of course, many otherwise poorly performing firms were taken over by the government with the hope that the government will be able to

Industrial policy and performance 21

turn them around. However, when we judge performance of an industry in an economy from a long-term sustainable growth perspective, such comparisons are almost meaningless, particularly in the context of a developing country where the degree of industrialization is low and it is trying to industrialize.

The importance of the public sector, however, cannot be judged by a static efficiency framework only. In several developing countries, public investment was called for, as it was perceived that private investment will not be forthcoming in some sectors due to lumpiness of investment required, high gestation lag, and high risks. The private sector in developing countries might also be reluctant to invest in such sectors, as they have to compete with well-established transnational corporations (TNCs). There have been several instances globally when government came forward to establish companies even if they were not in sectors that have strong public interest dimensions, and handed over them to private ownership in due course (Chang 2007). POSCO of South Korea (Box 2.2) and Embraer of Brazil are the classic examples of such a policy. It is true that they became more efficient after privatization, but it was unimaginable for a private company to establish such companies in South Korea and Brazil.

Box 2.2   History of POSCO

During the 1960s, the government of the Republic of Korea held extensive deliberations and came to the conclusion that self-sufficiency in iron and steel was essential to Korea's economic development. As a result, the Pohang Iron & Steel Company was established in 1968. The World Bank refused to fund it, on the grounds that the project was not viable as "Korea did not have reserves of coking coal and iron ore, and its companies were exporting fish and clothes". Hence, the government decided to construct the first steel works at Pohang in 1970 with the money it received from Japan as compensation for Japanese colonial rule in Korea.

Until 1988, when it issued its first public offering, the Ministry of Finance and the government-owned Korea Development Bank jointly owned POSCO. In 1994, it got itself listed in the New York Stock Exchange. In 1997, it established its base in China, as well. By 1998, POSCO became a leading steel maker of the world. It went on expanding its operations in foreign countries. By 2000, it was completely privatized.

Despite the fact that it imports all the raw materials it needs to make steel in Korea, in 2010, it became the most competitive steel maker of the world; at the end-2015, it still remained the most competitive steel maker, and with about 42 million tonnes of crude steel production, it was the fourth largest steel maker in the world, though it made losses for the first time in its history due to slowdown in China.

Sources: Chang (2007); www.posco.com.

22 Industrial policy and performance

Over the last couple of decades, the importance of public sector enterprises (PSE) has increased in the global economy, mainly due to the emergence of China as a global economic power. In 2000, there were just 27 PSEs in the Fortune500 list of companies, which increased to 102 in 2017, accounting for more than 20 per cent of their number and 22 per cent of their combined revenue. Out of these 102 PSEs, as many as 75 were from China, compared to only 9 Chinese PSEs in the Fortune500 list in 2000 (Lin et al 2020). In 2017, only 115 Chinese companies were in the Fortune500 list, indicating that only 40 private companies were in the list. In that sense, the Chinese economy is still being led by PSEs. In this context, the study by Estrin and Pelletier (2018) assumes crucial significance. It reviewed the recent empirical evidence on privatization in developing countries and found that privatization does not automatically bring economic gains in developing countries. Very often, developing countries do not have the preconditions like regulatory infrastructure and good corporate governance to make success out of privatization, and as a result, privatization often created adverse social impacts. While it is possible to have efficiency-enhancing privatization that also promotes equity, it requires substantial capability and absence of corruption, which are often not the case in developing countries. In a country with well-developed capital markets, divestment through public offering can deal with the issue of corruption and can also ensure that the process is not captured by the elites.

2.4 Technology and IPR policy

An essential requirement for industrialization in an economy is promotion of innovation, access to knowledge, and learning, and government policy plays an important role in this (OECD 2004; Stiglitz and Greenwald 2014). Since developing countries have been latecomers to industrialization, the innovations that took place in advanced countries often become the "moving targets" for developing countries (Pérez 2001). It is also to be noted that it is not just about getting one particular advanced technology that will put a developing country on a path of sustainable industrial development. If adoption of new technology from abroad does not create wide linkages, its initial innovative effect will soon be exhausted. While strong learning, as well as strong linkages, could offer the best possible scenario, even a weak learning but strong linkages can provide a systemic advantage (Ocampo 2017). Hence, along with transfer, diffusion of knowledge and technology is important for sustained industrial performance. Since most of the existing knowledge and technologies are protected by some form or another of IPR, related policies can have implications for industrialization of developing countries.

The issue of fair access to patented knowledge has always been a matter of concern since the beginning of the history of modern intellectual property rights. The public good nature of intellectual property has been considered

Industrial policy and performance   23

to be the main reason for according state protection to the creator in the form of legal rights to exclude others from using it. The nature of intellectual property is such that once created, others can easily free-ride on as the cost of recreating it, or the marginal cost is almost zero. In a competitive market, there would not be any incentive for creation of knowledge or innovation, as the market determined price of innovation will be zero. Thus a system of legal protection of intellectual property rights evolved to make innovation free of free-riding.

However, such an approach to promoting innovation has an inherent limitation. Since a monopoly market is inherently inefficient, production and sale of an IPR-based product is likely to be not only inefficient but also less than optimum. Hence, there would not be enough diffusion and use of knowledge. Thus, the question is raised if the state should promote a system if the innovation that it creates does not serve the society at large. While a lack of access to innovation by the poorer people has always been a concern, with the internationalization of IPR, in particular due to the adoption of a legally binding commitment in the form of the WTO Agreement on Trade Related Aspects of Intellectual Property Rights (TRIPS), developing countries are finding it difficult to access patented knowledge, as innovations mostly happen in developed countries (Maskus 2000; Giannakas 2001). This has implications for industrial performance in developing countries.

In more recent times, another such issue has received attention. This is about the effectiveness of the IPR-based innovation promotion system itself, mainly on two grounds. First, a rational monopolist will invest in R&D only up to the point where profit is maximized, which is much less than what could be the case in a competitive environment. Hence, resources invested by a monopolist will be much less compared to what could be socially optimal. The second ground relates to the fact that creation of knowledge is cumulative, in the sense that it depends on existing knowledge that has been created in the past. If the access to existing knowledge becomes difficult in an IPR-based system, which is likely to be in the absence of free flow of knowledge, creation of knowledge or innovation itself can become the casualty.

The fact that developing countries are finding it difficult to access patented knowledge came to the limelight in 1998, when South Africa, trying to deal with the problem of AIDS by importing drugs from Indian companies which were not authorized licensees to produce these drugs, got sued by 39 big pharmaceutical companies. This triggered a global movement, as actions by these companies were believed to be undermining the efforts to combat the AIDS crisis, which eventually led to an amendment to TRIPS making it easier to access patented medicines in the case of public emergency (IEGBIIP 2008). However, developing countries need access to patented knowledge – not just in medicine, but in a whole range of industries – in order to industrialize.

Given the current state of affairs, for most developing countries, the major concern is not about incentivizing innovation but rather access to technologies owned by foreign players. In 2017, the value of cross border payments

24 *Industrial policy and performance*

of royalties and license fees for use of IP was about US$367 billion, out of which an overwhelming $336 billion (representing 92 per cent) went to OECD countries.

The trade in IPRs is largely dominated by or rather limited to OECD countries (Table 2.1). Even the upper middle–income countries are making significant payments ($52.76 billion), but receiving very little ($7.07 billion). China's payment of charges for use of IPRs amounted to $28.66 billion in 2017, but in the same year, it received just about $4.78 billion, which was meagre $0.89 billion only in 2013. So was the case even with the Republic of Korea, which is considered to be at par with developed countries (and a member of the OECD), made IPR-related payments of about $9.25 billion, and received only about $7.14 billion in 2017. India paid about $6.52 billion on this account in 2017, but received only $0.66 billion in the same year.

While developed countries receive substantially more than what they pay on account of royalties, the upper middle income countries are paying more than seven times what they receive, which is more than ten times in case of the lower middle–income countries. The case of the least developed countries is striking. While it is well expected that they are unlikely to create IPR and hence hardly receive any royalties, they are not even paying much in terms of royalties, indicating that they are simply unable to use IPRs in any significant measure. Poor countries might be finding it difficult to access technology due to high costs. Given this scenario, resource-starved developing countries might find it difficult to access knowledge and technology to promote industrialization in their territories.

Royalty payment is, however, not an appropriate indicator of the extent of technology flow or the payments made to access technology. When a developing country firm accesses a particular technology from a developed country, the technology transfer is normally incomplete. While part of the technology could be transferred in the sense that the acquiring firm receives production capability, such capability may not be achieved in the entire range of products or components that might be required to put a particular product on the market. The acquiring firms may be producing a few components; many other components are imported from the seller firm mostly on an exclusive basis. Hence, the payments made for imported components are actually due to the technology embedded in the components. Hence, a substantial part of IPR-related payments are hidden in import bills (Nanda and Srivastava 2011).

While several countries are known to follow a rather weak IPR regime during their early stages of development, it is also important to note the kind of technological change that usually occurs in a developing country. A uniform IPR policy across the globe is being promoted now with the premise that this will promote innovations everywhere and will accordingly promote economic and industrial development everywhere.

While advanced developed countries take pride in introducing new products in the market, later industrializers make efforts to adapt products

Table 2.1 Payments for Use of IPRs by Country Groups (BoP, current billion US dollars)

Country	Indicator	2006	2008	2010	2011	2012	2013	2014	2015	2016	2017
OECD members	Payments	117.85	159.64	166.92	180.00	182.29	191.49	289.10	317.33	290.75	303.24
	Receipts	151.79	191.86	205.92	235.46	235.33	245.77	320.8	315.08	317.39	336.15
Upper middle–income countries	Payments	15.91	21.80	25.68	28.53	33.01	38.06	48.83	45.06	46.24	52.76
	Receipts	2.03	1.96	2.36	2.40	2.76	4.67	2.38	3.04	2.99	7.07
Lower middle–income countries	Payments	3.25	5.09	6.22	6.77	8.23	8.33	9.66	9.42	9.93	11.31
	Receipts	0.53	0.44	0.47	0.68	0.67	0.81	1.06	0.85	0.88	1.01
Low-income countries	Payments	0.06	0.08	0.07	0.07	0.07	0.11	0.09	0.10	0.27	0.08
	Receipts	0.06	0.14	0.10	0.06	0.11	0.10	0.06	0.06	0.04	0.01

Source: World Development Indicators Databank (https://databank.worldbank.org/source/world-development-indicators).

26 Industrial policy and performance

developed elsewhere in their own production process and improve them in the process. German firms boast of their "engineering" capabilities rather than their innovation capabilities. This has also been the approach in other coordinated market economies like Japan and Korea (Amable 2000; Chadwick and May 2003). It has also been observed that while a liberal market economy focuses more on product innovation, a coordinated market economy focuses more on process innovation (Huo 2015). However, in the current IPR framework adopted everywhere, following such a strategy is difficult. In essence, the current IPR framework could be more appropriate for developed countries that are technologically advanced and devote substantial resources towards product innovation, whereas in developing countries, the focus should be more on process innovation and adaptation of technologies that already exist elsewhere.

It is often argued that in the current scenario, developing countries can get technologies through FDI where foreign companies can transfer technologies to their local subsidiaries. However, this can also have its costs, as it might involve transfer of substantial financial resources as royalties to parent companies. Developing countries with limited supply of capital and most often having adverse balance of payments situation can also find such option prohibitively expensive.

2.5 Foreign investment

The biggest challenge of any poor country in the process of industrialization is the issue of accumulation of investible funds. An abrupt rise in savings might not be the answer, as that might lead to suppression of demand, which in turn will affect industrial growth adversely. Historically, the advanced countries have been exporters of capital, with the exception of colonies with European settlers, but advanced countries had access to resources which enabled them to invest more than what they could otherwise.

According to an estimate, about 7.0 per cent of GDP of Bengal and Bihar were being transferred to Britain annually during 1793–1807 in the form of land revenue. In addition, revenue from India was also being used to finance war for capturing new colonies. This was happening at a time when Britain was investing approximately about 7.0 per cent of its own GDP for its own industrialization and India was going through deindustrialization through which the share of manufacturing sector in its GDP fell from about 20 per cent to about 10 per cent. The total amount extracted from India and Burma from 1871–1916 could be between £3,199 million and £3,799 million, which were more than three-fourths of the estimated total of British foreign investment world-wide of about £4,000 million (Bagchi 2002). According to a recent estimate, during 1765–1938, Britain transferred about $45 trillion from India (Patnaik 2019). Apart from financial resources, advanced countries also had inexpensive access to natural resources.

However, foreign investment is now often welcome as it is believed to supplement domestic investment resources required to thrust economic growth. For capital-scarce developing countries, FDI is often considered to be one of the easiest ways to access capital from outside the country without any associated risks that are linked to debt (Demirhan and Masca 2008). Borensztein et al. (1998) contend that FDI brings with it modern technologies, management practices and skills that often spread to other local industries.

FDI is also seen as a major source of foreign exchange which not only helps to ease the balance of payment constraint, but also helps developing countries import capital goods that they need badly for their industrialization. However, it is debatable if such an approach can be effective even in the long term. Even theoretically speaking, FDI is unlikely to have any long-term impact on economic growth, as growth depends on technological change, which is considered to be exogenous in theoretical models (Solow 1957). There is now significant empirical evidence that FDI cannot have an independent impact on growth performance of a host country.

Such a possibility was recognized in the Korean growth strategy, as it is believed that unconditional acceptance of FDI can have an adverse impact on long-term development in the country. It was thought that there is the risk that foreign investors could sell their assets and take their money out of the country at any point in time. They could also raise money from the domestic banks and take the money out of the country. The chaebols, which had a strong influence on the government, played their part in making government take such a view (Nicolas 2003).

Since existence of a value chain is an important feature of modern industrial production, FDI also creates backward and forward linkages. Foreign companies help domestic firms that are linked to them through such linkages to improve technology and productivity (Blomström et al. 2000). While vertical integration has long been recognized as a channel of technology transfer, there is now evidence that this can happen through horizontal integration, as well (Wang and Zhao 2008). A study in the context of India, however, shows that while foreign firms promote beneficial horizontal linkages with local suppliers, they make relatively less effort to develop vertical inter-firm linkages and to create appropriate technologies for local markets (Ray and Rahman 2006).

Some studies, however, argue that spillover of technology and skills from foreign firms to local industries is not automatic. Such benefits can accrue only if the local industries already have the capacity to absorb such technologies (Blomstörm and Kokko 2003). Moreover, there are some studies that also recognized the potential negative effects on economic growth that FDI can bring in developing countries (Singer 1950; Griffin 1970). Herzer (2012), after a careful analysis of FDI and growth data of 44 developing countries over the period 1970–2005, found evidence that FDI impacted growth rate adversely. In a study on FDI experience in Pakistan, Saqib et al. (2013) found that FDI had a negative impact on Pakistani economic performance over the

28 Industrial policy and performance

period 1980–2010, and that domestic investment is more beneficial to the economy compared to foreign investment.

In case of transition countries, Lyroudi et al. (2004) concluded that FDI did not have much impact on economic growth. Haddad and Harrison (1993) also concluded that foreign firms did not have much of positive spill-over effects on domestic firms in the Moroccan manufacturing sector. Even though faster productivity growth in domestic firms was observed, the same could not be attributed to higher FDI.

In the case of Vietnam, Hoang et al. (2010) found that even though foreign firms brought advanced technology and knowledge, the same did not have much impact on its economic growth. Blomström and Kokko (2003) found that FDI does not necessarily bring positive impacts, as local firms' adoption of foreign technologies and skills is influenced by local conditions. Kotrajaras et al. (2011) analyzed the experience of 15 East Asian countries to conclude that the extent of positive impact of FDI on growth depends on several local factors, including the level of financial market development, institutional development, governance, and macroeconomic policies, and as such, low-income countries find it difficult to absorb new technologies from developed countries.

In the current context, access to technology could be one reason to look for foreign investment. Empirical evidence, however, is quite mixed. It is noteworthy that in the post-TRIPS world, access to technology has become even more difficult. In developing countries, where firms are already behind their developed country counterparts, these firms improving their technology and competing in a globalized market has become even more difficult. FDI as a source of technology, hence, has become more significant now.

The moot question, however, is whether FDI necessarily brings better technologies or if such an outcome is contingent upon other factors, and if industrial policy can have a role in this regard. One important aspect that has often been highlighted is that the type of FDI is also important. FDI that comes through acquisition route might not be as beneficial as FDI that comes for a greenfield project. In fact, there is also a possibility that acquisition FDI can be outrightly harmful, as there have been several cases when acquisition took place essentially to thwart competition rather than for expansion (Nanda 2009b).

An important distinction that was also observed in China was that a higher share of its FDI inflow came through greenfield routes as compared to other developing countries (Nanda 2009b). China also a got a relatively higher share of FDI inflows into its manufacturing sector compared to global inflow that has come to be dominated by the service sector. This was not by accident. Before China joined the WTO, it received about 60 per cent of FDI inflow into manufacturing, largely because it allowed too little FDI in other sectors (OECD 2000).

Tintin (2012) analyzed the experience of 125 countries of different categories and came to an interesting conclusion. While FDI fosters economic growth, the impact is quite insignificant in the cases of developed and least-developed countries compared to developing countries. However, Lund (2010), on the basis of analysis of 128 countries over the period 1980–2003, argued that that FDI does not promote much growth in developing countries. He argued that foreign companies come essentially to exploit cheap labour, abundant natural resources, lower taxes, etc., but protect their knowledge vehemently, limiting technology and skill spill-overs.

Asheghian (2011) did not find much of evidence in support of FDI-induced economic growth in the developed-country setting of Canada. On the contrary, domestic investment played the major role in TFP growth, as well as economic growth in the country. In a study on FDI in Nigeria, Uwubanmwen and Ajao (2012) could not find any significant impact of FDI on economic growth and development. Kolster (2015) found a positive impact of FDI on welfare improvement in North Africa, but also argued that such benefits cannot come automatically and that the governments should try to channelize FDI in certain sectors to maximize benefits from it.

One important characteristic of FDI that has been highlighted in the context of development impacts of FDI is the primary motivation with which a foreign company enters a host country. It has been argued, with some evidence, that efficiency-seeking FDI is generally more beneficial compared to market-seeking or resource-seeking FDI (Nunnenkamp and Spatz 2004). It has also been argued that development impacts often depend on the origin or the home country of FDI. It has been argued that Asian FDI could be pro-trade and, therefore, efficiency seeking, while American FDI could be market-seeking (Kojima 1973). This could be due to the historical context, as Asian MNCs have generally been export oriented from the very beginning.

2.6 Regulation and public support

State participation in the production process is only a small part of the potential role that a government can play in the industrialization process or economic development of a country. Historically, the state played an important role in industrial development, not only in socialist countries, but also in several capitalist countries. For example, the East India Company that ruled India for about a century and played an important role in enabling the British economy to achieve better access to resources enjoyed substantial royal patronage. Obviously, even though Britain might have followed "liberal" economic policies in its own way, one cannot claim that the state had no role to play in the process of industrialization.

Such options were not available to developing countries like India, which embarked on the path of industrialization after gaining Independence. Additionally, they had to compete now with the established industrial powers, a challenge that early industrializers did not have to face. Protectionism is now used as a word to describe a type of policy that is followed only in a country that rejects all forms of modernity, but most nations that are considered to

30   *Industrial policy and performance*

be developed today historically used such tools in some form or other at their initial stages of development (Chang 2002). Kumar (2018) has also argued that present-day developed countries have used several strategic intervention measures like industrial policy, infant industry protection, and public procurement in their development process which have been successfully emulated by East Asian countries.

The experiences of some countries in Africa and Latin America are often cited as the proof that import-substituting industrialization policy based on protectionism did not work. As against this, the experiences of East Asian countries are cited as the success of the so-called export-led industrialization. However, this is also misrepresentation of facts. The industrialization strategy of East Asian countries was not based on free trade. These countries realized quite early that there are limits to what infant industry protection can achieve. Protection cannot help beyond a certain point, as firms in a protected but small market cannot enjoy economies of scale. The beauty of the Korean industrialization strategy was that it promoted them with subsidies rather than just protecting them with tariffs. Moreover, subsidies were also linked to some measure of performance to foster competition and improve efficiency. The import-substituting industrialization strategy and export-led growth strategy need not be mutually exclusive, and they can be pursued simultaneously.

As a matter of fact, the industrialization strategies followed by countries like Korea and Taiwan were a combination of both import-substituting and export-promoting policies. An interesting example is the case of the automobile industry in Korea. In 1995, it exported more than one million cars, yet its share of imports in domestic automobile market was below 1 per cent in the same year. Korea had a policy in which import license was linked to export performance, similar to what even India also followed in its automobile industry in 1990s. This was the basis on which Paul Krugman coined his famous phrase, "import protection as export promotion" (Krugman 1984). Korea maintained relatively low tariffs, but that does not mean that it followed a free trade policy. Getting an import license was quite difficult, and it was granted only for inputs or capital goods after the importing firm could demonstrate that the item in question was not easily available. Such a policy ensured that local manufacturing was encouraged; at the same time, the user industry was not adversely affected due to non-availability of necessary inputs or equipment.

The mainstream economists, the free trade enthusiasts in particular, now reluctantly accept that successful industrialization in East Asian countries has not been due to free trade policy in a classical sense. Nevertheless, it has been argued that they created what Bhagwati called "simulated free markets" (Berger 1979; Bhagwati 1988). Such simulated markets were created as import-substituting measures, and export-promoting measures cancelled each other. While it is difficult to imagine how these two types of "distortions" can cancel each other and create a system that is free of distortions on balance, rather than creating a system of "double distortions", some neo-classical economists now prescribe that export subsidies may be used along with import restrictions, rather than following a neutral regime (Bustelo 1996; Nanda 2008).

However, it is noteworthy that liberal trade policy and absence of state intervention are not necessarily linked in practice even in developed economies. Such a perception has been generated largely due to the fact that World Bank-IMF–sponsored economic reforms in developing countries largely came as the so-called LPG (liberalization, privatization and globalization) package. Liberal market economies, in the sense that the role of state is at a minimum, are difficult to find outside the Anglo-Saxon world. Hence, the US, the UK, Canada, Australia, and New Zealand are the major developed liberal economies, though they also had their own spheres of state intervention.

However, it is also noteworthy that except US and UK, other economies are not industrial powers, as even today their major exports are primary commodities. Most other developed economies, including Germany, Japan, Sweden, and Austria, are known as what are often called coordinated market economies. Newly industrialized countries (NICs) like South Korea, Taiwan, Hong Kong, and Singapore are often characterized as state-led capitalism. Even Japan had similarities with the policies and strategies followed by the NICs. Hong Kong and Singapore are quite exceptional, as they followed highly liberal trade policies, yet their industrialization process was facilitated by an active state.

Germany adopted what is called organized capitalist model or coordinated market economy (CME), not only in the post-war reconstruction period but also during its initial industrialization in the late nineteenth century in the Bismarck regime. Such an industrialization policy was a combination of dynamic institutions and visionary ideas in the context of state building or re-building (Hall and Soskice 2001; Pierson 2004; Thelen 2004). It was believed that the free market model was inappropriate for the country as it made efforts towards industrialization in the late nineteenth century then engaged in post-war reindustrialization in the mid-twentieth century. Early industrializers like Britain and France tended to follow relatively free market polices, as their early lead allowed them easier access to markets, raw materials, and capital. However, countries like Germany and Japan, which arrived late in the scene, had to face very different situation, and hence, made very different choices (Wolfgang and Yamamura 2001).

As a late industrializer, it had to move very fast, and hence, Germany decided to avoid a trial-and-error approach. It also did not have ready access to resources in terms of colonies that some other industrial economies had. Hence, cooperation rather than competition became its preferred approach. Similarly, when General Park Chung-Hee came to power in South Korea in 1961, he followed five-year development plan, and by 1979 when he was assassinated, per capita income had increased ten times. For him, a free

32 Industrial policy and performance

economy was a luxury that South Korea could not afford, and economic development was considered to be a matter of national security.

In South Korea, many state-owned companies were established while many were provided subsidies from the state budget. Economic development was centred on exports, and many companies were given export targets. Export performance was linked with import licenses and tax exemptions for import of machineries and raw materials only.

While during the rule of Bismarck, the state became a pseudo entrepreneur in Germany, the option was not politically feasible in the post-war reconstruction period. First, there was significant foreign pressure on Germany not to follow a policy regime that may look like a socialist or a communist style rule. Second, the pervasive abuse of state power during Nazi rule meant that even the Germans did not want a state that was omnipresent. However, two things were common in both the regimes: a highly regulated universal banking system and coordinated actions by major producer groups (Loungani and Assaf 2001). While they were actually called cartels in the earlier regime, cartel became a dirty word by the time of World War II, and they hence were called Verbände during the reconstruction period. The Verbände played a significant role as the members did not see themselves as competitors of one another; rather, they acted in a coordinated manner and viewed foreign companies as their common and principal competitors. Germany also established a system of democratic management of corporations whereby labour had an important stake as trade union representatives were allowed to sit in the boards of all large corporations (Eichengreen 2007).

An important side effect of such rapid economic transformation was that the growth process was iniquitous where ordinary people had very little stake. Both Bismarck, who led the initial industrialization, and the captains of the social market economy, Adenauer and Erhard, who led the post-war reconstruction efforts, were acutely aware of this. Hence, they paid substantial attention to protective social policies. If the German framework looks different now, it is because of the pressure of globalization that also came through the expansion of the European Union (EU) and the stresses of unification.

In 1953, Taiwan adopted its first four-year plan. By 1993, it had ten such plans and it already became one of the Asian tigers. Three important steps were taken, in stages, to achieve this. First, it conducted agrarian reforms that improved productivity in the sector and freed labour for industrial development. Second, the state established export-oriented enterprises in heavy industry. Third, after 1970, the government directed private investment towards high-tech sectors. In 1973, the government launched ten major development projects to improve physical infrastructure, including in railways, freeway, airports, and nuclear power plants. Five years later, it launched 12 major development projects to develop social and cultural infrastructure, along with physical infrastructure.

Industrial policy and performance   33

The latest example of a successful industrialization over a short period of time is that of China. which is now very often characterized as "state-led capitalism", indicating a major role of the state in the process. China's industrialization strategy included enormous government support for infrastructure-building and continuation of a mixed-economy approach rather than wholesale privatization. While private and foreign companies were expected to play a bigger role, the government-owned companies were also to retain an important role (Wen 2016). In 1978, the PSEs accounted for 77.6 per cent of industrial output in China, which dropped to 28.8 per cent in 1996 and further to 19.75 per cent in 2017. In the same year, PSEs' total investment in industrial fixed assets accounted for 38.5% of all domestic companies but accounted for about 52 per cent of the market capitalization of the two stock exchanges in China (Lin et al 2020).

China also followed a bottom-up approach in terms of encouraging different sectors. It started from agricultural development and moved up the industrial ladder, from light to heavy industries, from manufacturing to financial capitalism, and established its first stock exchange only in 1990. The PSEs were engaged in heavy industries to provide critical materials for industries and infrastructure development (Wen 2016). However, now it is a global leader, even in emerging sector like solar photovoltaics, which was developed with substantial state support. The National Development and Reform Commission (NDRC), the government planning agency, took up a mission-oriented programme in 2007 for industry involvement in technology development and facilitated firms' entering into production of raw silicon and accessing finance from government banks (Hopkins and Li 2016).

2.7   Access to Finance

Historically, access to finance and the role of banks have been considered important in industrial development (Schumpeter 1934, Gerschenkron 1962). Banks can act as "catalysts" for industrialization by mobilizing large financial resources and playing a coordination role (Rin and Hellmann 2001). While financing through formation of joint-stock companies played an important role in the UK, it must also not be ignored that many of the joint-stock companies were actually banks. Moreover, in the continental Europe, banks played a central role in nineteenth century industrialization (Schumpeter 1934). Gerschenkron (1962) examined the industrialization process in Europe and came to the conclusion that the role of banks was central in the countries that were left behind by industrializing England. Singh and Weisse (1998) examined the long-term development implications of less-developed countries of emerging stock markets and portfolio capital flows as sources of finance for industrialization, and came to the conclusion that a bank-based system would work better for them.

Historically, banks not only facilitated capital accumulation by serving as intermediaries between lenders and investors, they also provided other

34 *Industrial policy and performance*

financial services including providing means of payments. In this context, the issues of regulation of banks and their ownership have been a subject of intense debate and discussion. The passage of the National Banking Acts in the US stabilized the existing financial system and helped the national banks attract more deposits by raising people's confidence in banks, and it was also found that the states with higher concentration of banks could see more manufacturing activities (Jaremski 2013).

Germany created a universal banking system, as it thought that the large sums of money required for industrial development could not be raised by newly created firms from the stock markets that were relatively underdeveloped at that time. By virtue of large loans, banks that were aided by the state, held ownership of company stock, and often had their representative in the board of directors hence played a significant role in the management and direction of these firms. In the post-war model, Germany also evolved a unique form of framework regulation (*Rahmenbedingungen*) that was *ex ante* in nature, in contrast to the American-style regulation, which focuses mainly on market failure issues in an *ex post* manner. An important example of such regulation was that the banks had to maintain high capital adequacy reserves (Dyson 1992).

The role of banks was important in the industrial development in South Korea as well, The government established full control over institutional credit not only through regulation but also by nationalization. If private firms were reluctant to invest in sectors that were considered important, the state would invest to create capacity in the sector. If private firms were not performing well, the state would take control, restructure it, and again hand it over to private ownership and management (Westphal 1990; Loungani and Assaf 2001).

While some studies have shown that private banks are associated with higher profits, it has been pointed out that such evidence does not necessarily imply that state-owned banks are inefficient, as this low profitability might be due to the fact that they finance projects that could involve low private return but high social return that the private banks tend to avoid. There is also no clear evidence that countries with more state-owned banks have lower growth and financial development (Yeyati et al 2004). The experience of China shows that the state-owned banks played a crucial role in industrial development in the country in recent decades (Wen 2016). A recent study in Brazil has shown that while both private and state-owned banks played equally important role, after the global financial crisis, credit from state-owned banks and its growth became more pronounced (Silva et al 2019).

An important aspect of state support has been the creation of development finance institutions (DFIs) in most countries that followed coordinated market economy type of development framework. In countries that are late comers to industrialization, accessing finance for industrialization is generally difficult, but it is more difficult to get financing for industrial projects that have longer gestation period and also need relatively larger amount

Industrial policy and performance 35

of finance. The problem is further exacerbated when such investments are characterized by lumpiness. Since regular commercial banks did not have the expertise or the compulsion to finance high technology projects with long gestation periods, development finance institutions were instrumental in filling this gap (Nayyar 2015).

Not only did development banks fill a gap in domestic financial systems by offering loans with longer maturities and lower interest rates, other industrial policy instruments, including grants, equity investments, technical support, and all the financial instruments targeted at micro, small, and medium enterprises played an important role in the industrialization of many countries. In many countries, DF institutions made it possible for domestic firms to launch and expand operations and to enter strategic industries which would not have been possible otherwise (Guadagno 2016). DFIs have received wide attention in recent years, mainly due to their counter-cyclical role, particularly in dealing with financial crisis. A Deutsche Bank research paper also observed that DF has been an important feature of banking and financial markets in Europe for a long time and played a crucial role in promoting economic growth and structural change. The financial and economic crisis of 2008 led to more reliance on DF institutions, and they are likely to play an important role in future (Wruuck 2015).

However, this is their secondary role; their main function has been to take care of market imperfections that often lead to a missing market situation for long-term finance (Ferraz 2017). Historically, DFIs played an important role not only in countries like South Korea, Brazil, and China, but also in developed countries like Germany and Japan. Moreover, they can have a role in developed countries even now (Griffith-Jones and Cozzi 2017). While DFIs have often been criticized for political interference, cronyism, adverse selection, and the related inefficiency, it has also been suggested that such risks can be mitigated with appropriate institutional designs (Ferraz 2017).

2.8   Global economic scenario

The fact that the global economic environment impacts economic growth and industrial performance in an economy did not receive adequate attention until recent times. In most literature on the subject, while trying to analyze growth or industrial performance of a country, its own trade policy is taken as a possible factor, but hardly anyone looked at the trade policy in the rest of the world. The literature on Indian growth performance is no exception. Even in the pre-1991 years, though India followed a relatively protectionist economic policy, by no means was it a closed economy.

While the impact of trade policy on industrialization and industrial performance is a debatable issue, there is no debate that the trade policy followed in the rest of the world has significant impact, and the more open that trade policy is, the more positive is the impact on a country's industrial performance. For any country that is linked with the outside

36 *Industrial policy and performance*

world, which is the case for most developing countries, economic growth in the rest of the world, *ceteris paribus*, will augment the demand for its products in the outside world, regardless of type of trade policy it follows. This also means if the rest of the world adopts a more open trade policy with reduced tariff and non-tariff barriers, the industrial development of the country will get a boost – and vice versa. Hence, the global economic context is an important factor in industrial development – and accordingly, industrial policy needs to keep pace with the changing global context (Andreoni 2017).

That economic growth and trade policy in the rest of the world will impact industrial performance of a country is rather easy to understand. But that is not all. An important factor in this regard is also the technological changes and structural changes that take place in the rest of the world. The product cycle hypothesis put forward by Vernon (1966) is worth noting in this regard. According to this hypothesis, an innovation generally happens in a developed country, and to start with, its production generally happens in the country of innovation. After the product establishes substantial presence in the major world markets, its production gradually spreads from the country of origin to other developed countries. When the product becomes standardized, its production gradually moves to developing countries. Eventually, the country of origin ends up importing the product.

It is also important to recall in this context what economists have called the "flying geese" pattern of development. In this hypothesis, once wages start rising in a country, it becomes difficult to sustain labour-intensive activities. It moves to capital- or technology-intensive industries, while some other developing countries – where wages are still low – adopt the labour-intensive industries. In essence, the product cycle hypothesis and the flying geese hypothesis are complementary to each other. In a product that is matured or standardized, maintaining high price is difficult – and hence, it is difficult to produce in a country with high wages.

Due to high wages and the advent of technologically advanced products in advanced countries, they move away from relatively low technology and labour-intensive industries and start importing them. This gives an opportunity to developing and low wage countries to catch up with industrialization. In the process, advanced countries move away from industry to the service sector, giving further opportunity to developing countries. Understanding these dynamics is important in analyzing the industrial performance of a developing country.

While the importance of market structure in influencing industrial performance has been duly emphasized in the literature, in the context of industrial policy, it is also important to understand the role of global industrial structure as distinct from market structure. It is not how different companies in a country are related to each other, but how different companies in a country are related to their main competitors in the global market. While the global context itself is changing, it is also important to note that at different stages of development, a country experiences different industrial structures (Andreoni 2017).

2.9 Conclusion

Among all the relevant policy domains, trade policy has been discussed most widely for its role in promoting industrialization, as well as industrial productivity and efficiency. However, the linkage between trade policy and industrialization is neither one-dimensional nor clearly established. While trade – exports in particular – played an important role, by no means does this indicate that a liberalized trade policy automatically ensures industrialization, economic growth, or efficiency. Most countries that have achieved economic development followed a strategic interventionist trade policy during at least some period of their development experience.

While foreign investment hardly played any role in the economic development of the countries that are now developed countries, especially the early developers, the current situation is quite different. While early developers had colonies that helped them mobilize and access resources, late developers do not have such options. Hence, FDI can play an important role in complementing domestic capital formation. Moreover, until the late twentieth century, there was no strong global IPR regime, and hence, accessing technology was relatively easy. In the post-TRIPS world, not only has accessing technologies from developed countries become difficult, but even developing new technologies is more difficult now. Given this context, foreign investment can be a conduit of technology transfer to developing countries.

That said, free flow of foreign investment to developing countries does not automatically bring growth and development benefits to them. Global experience shows that FDI can also be harmful in some cases involving acquisition of existing business by foreign firms. With some generalization, it can be said that while greenfield foreign investments are likely to bring benefits, acquisition-type FDI brings very little benefit, if any.

One important factor that influences industrial development of a country is the prevailing global economic situation, and how a particular country is positioned therein. While it is difficult to imagine that a country can industrialize quickly when the global economy is not growing fast enough, the development experience of Asian economies also shows that the position of a country in the global process of value addition is also important. This region followed a flying geese pattern of development in the sense that when a country achieved a particular level of development, the resulting wage increase facilitated industrialization of another country, particularly in labour-intensive sectors. This is how countries like Japan, South Korea, Taiwan, Malaysia, and Thailand took turns in industrialization. However, the entry of China into the chain has changed the scenario. China, being a large country with a huge army of reserve labour, did not experience much

38 *Industrial policy and performance*

of wage increase as observed in other countries, making it difficult for any other country to take the turn.

Broadly speaking, while the state played an important role in almost all economies in their early stages of development, late industrializers generally followed more interventionist economic policies. In general, state-led economic development using interventionist economic policies are often considered to be associated with the East Asian growth experience. However, the so-called Asian model is not purely Asian, as one can also argue that Germany is the actual birthplace of such an economic model. The visionary ideas that informed the post-war coordinated model of development in Germany came from a group of economists who were known as the Freiburg School.

East Asian countries embraced the model, of course, with their own modification to suit the local conditions. In most countries, economic policy "models" are characterizations of institutional arrangements that are not created *ex ante* with absolute clarity, but are developed through a trial-and-error process recognized as such after their creation, sometimes many years later. An economic policy model has to be an iterative, experimental, trial-and-error process, rather than being a pre-determined fixed model, and the key to its success lies in the innovative capacities of the economic and political actors, and their ability to adjust to the changing economic and political reality.

Notes

1 For a detailed discussion on the SCP paradigm see Scherer (1980), or Waterson (1984). A review of the studies on structure-performance can be found in Geroski (1988).
2 In the present context, the "vent for surplus" theory of trade would be of some interest. The theory, not widely discussed in the recent years, assumes that, because of internal immobility and specificity of resources, a non-trading country is not able to fully utilize all of its potential productive capacity. The opening up of trade may then increase the demand for those sectors in which it can expand, so output and employment may rise as trade begins. But this argument relies greatly on inflexibility of productive capacity. In the longer run, the inflexibility and inadaptability of resources may inhibit sustained development, or it may disappear. For details on the "vent for surplus" theory, see Myint (1958).
3 For examples, see Westphal (1982) and Pack and Westphal (1986).
4 Assumptions and arguments are skipped for the sake of brevity, wherever necessary.
5 Although it seems to be surprising, de Fraja gives an intuitively simple explanation for such a result. The fact that consumer welfare enters the government utility function, and not that of the private shareholders, implies that the government (principal) has higher incentive to bring improvement in the firm's efficiency, and therefore it will be prepared to pay more for it than the owners of a private firm.

3 The Indian context of industrial policy and performance

3.1 Introduction

Most literature on industrial performance viewed it as the performance of various sectors within the industry. Further, since the seminal work of Bain (1956) linking performance with market characteristics like market structure, there have been a large number of studies to link performance with factors like import protection through measures like tariff barriers. In the Indian context, a substantial number of studies have attempted to examine the difference in industrial performance before and after the economic reforms of 1991. However, this is quite problematic, as several studies have pointed out that economic growth or industrial growth picked up one full decade before liberalization was introduced in 1991, and more importantly, another pick up, probably even of higher magnitude, was experienced in the early 1950s (Nayyar 2006).

It could be dangerous to get into a simple binary of "before and after" 1991 kind of analysis. Economic or industrial policy evolved over time, and a set of policies adopted in 1948 or 1951 did not continue until 1991. Neither is it the case that the economic or industrial policy regime that India has today is the same as what was adopted in 1991. It is, therefore, important to recognize that industrial policy is an evolutionary process and not an event that happens at a point in time.

Industrial performance, if influenced by macroeconomic or industrial policy, therefore, is unlikely to remain similar for four decades when the industrial policy evolved through time. Once this is recognized, industrial policy and performance can bring some new dimensions for analysis. It is also not difficult to see that similar economic or industrial policies produce very different industrial performance over time, and also that similar policies can produce different industrial or macroeconomic performance in different countries during the same period.

This opens the door for recognizing that economic and industrial policies are not the only factors that impact economic or industrial performance, but that several non-economic factors can also influence them. These can be political, social, cultural, historical, or geographical circumstances (Lensink

DOI: 10.4324/9781003047490-3

40 *The Indian context*

and Kuper 2000; Acemoglu and Robinson 2012). Neither is it the case that economic policies are entirely delinked from these factors; rather, economic policies are adopted keeping such contexts in mind.

Obviously, it is also expected that the economic or industrial performance of a country will be influenced by not only what happens inside the borders but also by what happens in the rest of the world. Any discussion of economic or industrial performance, therefore, needs to keep all such factors in view, even though one single study cannot do justice to analyzing all such factors.

The next section briefly reviews the evolution of industrial policy in India after it attained Independence in 1947. The third section gives a special focus on export and import policy in India (though this is discussed in the second section, as well) until 1991 in the light of whether India followed an export-led or import-substituting industrialization policy. The fourth section looks at the performance of industrial sector along with the growth in GDP and other sectors, and attempts to examine its links with industrial policy and other possible factors that might have influenced the industrial performance at the aggregate level, along with a brief review of literature on the issue. The fifth section provides a review of industrial policy and macroeconomic growth performance in India. The sixth section concludes the chapter.

3.2 Evolution of general industrial policy in India

The first Industrial Policy Resolution of India was announced by the government of India on April 6, 1948. The Industrial Policy Resolution, 1948 identified roles for both public and private sectors for industrial development of the nation, and classified industries into four categories. The first category was the exclusive monopoly of the central government and included defence and strategic industries such as manufacture of arms and ammunition, production and control of atomic energy, and ownership and management of railways.

In the second category were basic industries such as coal, iron, and steel, as well as some important industries like aircraft manufacture, shipbuilding, etc. In these industries, only the state was given the right to set up new units, but the existing units were to continue to be run by the existing entrepreneurs for the next ten years, after which their ownership status was to be reviewed.

In the third category, there were industries in which private entrepreneurs were expected to take lead in investment and production but the state was to exercise regulation and control. Automobiles and tractors, sugar, cement, cotton and woollen textiles etc. were kept in this category.

The fourth category included the rest of the industries which were to remain primarily the domain of the private sector, and the government was not to have much regulation or control except some general oversight.

The next milestone in this regard was the Industries (Development & Regulation) Act, 1951. The primary objective of the Act was to regulate the

The Indian context 41

direction of investment and pattern of industrial development in view of scarcity of resources. It was also to ensure that industrial development could promote public interest which possibly meant that resources were allocated to ensure socially desirable outcomes. The Act enabled the government to establish full control over:

- Capacity, location, and expansion, as well as manufacture of new products.
- Use of foreign exchange which was primarily meant for importing plant and machinery.
- Terms of foreign collaboration.

The Industrial Policy Resolution of 1956 which was not much different from the earlier one gave an explanation for adopting such a policy:

> the need for planned and rapid development, require that all industries of basic and strategic importance, or in the nature of public utility services should be in the public sector. Other industries which are essential and require investment on a scale which only the State, in the present circumstances, could provide have also to be in the public sector.

The 1956 policy classified industries into three categories. The first category was the exclusive domain of the state and included 17 industries. In the second category of industries, the state was to play the dominant role, while private enterprises could also operate – but with substantial government regulation. Twelve industries were identified for this category. All basic and strategic goods and infrastructure services were put either in the first or in the second category. The third category was primarily left for the private sector that included the rest of the industries.

Following such policies that kept a substantial role for the state, as well as government regulation and control, also raised some concerns. Accordingly, it became imperative for the government of India to examine the existence and effects of concentration of economic power in private hands, and hence it established the Monopolies Inquiry Commission in 1964. The Commission recommended a new law to regulate concentration of economic power and to ensure that it does not harm public interest, and the Monopolies and Restrictive Trade Practices Act, 1969 was enacted. It also intended to regulate monopolies and curb monopolistic and restrictive trade practices. Interestingly, monopoly was defined not in terms of market power (e.g., share in market) but rather in terms of absolute size of the enterprise.

In the same year, the government also appointed the Industrial Licensing Inquiry Committee to examine the effectiveness of the licensing policy. The committee observed that the licensing policy did not succeed in ensuring development of industries according to announced licensing policies. Moreover, licensing policy also could not prevent investment in non-priority

42 *The Indian context*

industries. As a result, a new licensing policy was announced in 1970 which put a few new restrictions on large industrial houses. Meanwhile, the government reserved 47 products exclusively for manufacture by small-scale industries.

Another policy measure that could be a game changer was adopted in this period. In July 1969, the 14 largest private commercial banks were nationalized. These banks controlled about 85 per cent of deposits and hence could play an important role in allocation of resources. Until then, the State Bank of India (along with its subsidiaries) was the only public sector commercial bank.

An amendment was made to the Foreign Exchange Regulation Act (FERA), and as a result, a restriction was put on foreign equity participation. Only industries that required large investments and advanced technology, or were making exports, could be considered for foreign equity participation. Foreign equity participation in excess of 40 per cent became even more difficult and was allowed only in industries that required sophisticated technology, but with a limit of 51 per cent. The companies with foreign equity participation were brought under stricter restrictions, including on expansion and introduction of new products.

The Industrial Policy Statement of 1973 put substantial emphasis on small and medium entrepreneurs, particularly in the production of mass consumption goods. It also prepared a list of industries that required advanced technologies to be started by large industrial houses. These were the priority sectors where small and medium enterprises were also encouraged. The large industrial houses were also encouraged to go into rural areas to promote local development and that of ancillary units. The government set up the Secretariat for Industrial Approvals (SIA), which was given the responsibility of dealing with industrial licenses, capital goods, import licenses, and foreign collaboration. Keeping in line with the overall emphasis, the number of products reserved for SSI was also increased substantially.

The Industrial Policy Statement of 1977 brought some relaxation of regulations as it announced that if FERA companies diluted their equity to bring it below or up to 40 per cent, they would be treated at par with Indian companies. However, it also issued a list of industries where indigenous technology was already available, and accordingly kept them out of new foreign collaboration. Fully-owned foreign companies were allowed only in cases of sophisticated technologies or highly export-oriented areas. However, as with the previous policy statement, the 1977 policy also put emphasis on cottage and small-scale industries (SSIs). Also to promote decentralization of industrial development and its spread into rural areas, the District Industries Centres were established in each district to provide necessary support and services required by SSIs. The policy also expanded the list of reserved items for SSI from 504 to 807.

The Industrial Policy of 1980 provided substantial relaxation in licensing conditions as it allowed an automatic expansion of capacity up to

The Indian context   43

5 per cent per annum, particularly in industries with export potential. It was also announced that setting up of 100 per cent export-oriented units and for expansion of existing units for purposes of export would be considered sympathetically.

By this time, India was already hit by two instances of oil price shocks. Keeping this in view, the policy put emphasis on promoting technologies for improved energy efficiency and exploitation of alternative sources of energy. The government, however, continued to exercise full control over foreign exchange use. The thrust of small-scale industries also continued as the number of items reserved for them was increased further to 834.

After Rajiv Gandhi became the prime minister in 1984, some perceptible changes happened. Substantial delicensing was announced in 1988; all industries were exempted from licensing, subject to investment and locational restrictions, and a negative list of 26 industries that still required licensing. Restrictions on foreign currency, foreign investment and imports, and foreign travel were also relaxed to some extent. More emphasis was placed on science and technology, and telecommunications and automation in particular. Tax rates were also reduced, and the concept of modified value added tax was introduced in the excise tax system.

In the area of small-scale industries, however, the earlier trend was maintained. Not only was the number of reserved items increased further to 873 in 1985, but in 1988, the government announced the Growth Centre Scheme under which 71 Growth Centres were to be set up throughout the country. The Growth Centres were expected to have all basic infrastructure facilities such as power, water, telecommunications, and banking that were often not readily available.

The so-called New Economic Policy of 1991 made some drastic changes as the government also initiated a macroeconomic stabilization programme entailing a reduction of fiscal deficit and a major devaluation of the currency. Several other changes were also made in other areas of economic policy management. In July 1991, licensing requirement was abolished, except for 18 industries which were considered to be strategically or environmentally sensitive or had very high import content.

The private sector was encouraged to play a much bigger role as the number of areas reserved for the public sector was reduced from 17 to only six that involved strategic and security concerns. Sectors like iron and steel, electricity, air transport, shipbuilding, and heavy machinery industries, such as telecommunication cables and instruments, which were earlier considered to be "core industries" and reserved for the public sector, now became open to all.

Import licensing was virtually abolished and import regulation became subject to a negative list rather than a positive list. Almost all capital goods and raw materials became freely importable subject only to import duties. Import tariff rates were also reduced drastically. The MRTP Act was amended and the provision that required the "monopoly firms" to procure separate

44 The Indian context

permission for investment and expansion – including through mergers and acquisitions – was removed altogether.

The FDI regime was also liberalized substantially. Automatic approval of up to 51 per cent foreign equity holding was allowed in 35 specified, high-priority, capital-intensive, and high technology industries, subject to the requirement that the foreign equity would take care of the foreign exchange requirements. To consider the cases involving foreign equity participation over 51 per cent, the Foreign Investment Promotion Board (FIPB) was set up. More importantly, India moved from a regime of "foreign investment regulation" to a regime of "foreign investment promotion".

To accord greater operational flexibility to firms with foreign equity participation, the Foreign Exchange Regulation Act of 1973 (FERA) was also liberalized. This included removal or relaxation of various restrictions on such companies with regard to borrowing and raising funds in India, as well as taking over or investing in Indian companies. Substantial reforms were also undertaken to ease the operations of Indian firms on foreign soil.

In 1991, the government initiated wide-ranging reforms, and the reforms were followed up by several similar measures in the succeeding years. While the rupee was devalued substantially in 1991, by 1992–93 it was made partially convertible. Further, by 1993–94, the rupee was made fully convertible on trade accounts, and by the next year, it became fully convertible on current accounts. The trade regime was progressively liberalized by different governments and the quantitative restrictions were removed in 2002. Similarly, the FDI regime was also liberalized over time.

Even though the 1991 industrial policy remained in force, in 2011, the government announced the National Manufacturing Policy (NMP). By then, it was clear that two decades of liberalized policy had not been able to strengthen its manufacturing sector; hence, the objective of this policy was to enhance the share of manufacturing to 25 per cent of GDP within a decade from the then-existing share of 16 per cent. The NMP divided industries into three categories. In the first category were strategic industries like aerospace, shipping, IT hardware, electronics, telecommunication equipment, defence equipment, and solar energy, in which capacity was proposed to be built in a mission mode. In the second category were the industries where India traditionally enjoyed a competitive advantage, like textiles and garments, leather and footwear, gems and jewellery, and food processing, in which adequate support was to be provided. In the third category were the capital goods industries like machine tools, heavy electric equipment, heavy transport, and earth-moving and mining equipment, which were to be given special attention.

The NMP proposed to create a Technology Acquisition and Development Fund (TADF) for acquiring appropriate technologies and a patent pool for emerging technologies. SMEs were proposed to be supported in the areas of manufacturing, management, information technology, skill development, and access to capital; and to that end, the equity base of the National Small

Industries Corporation (NSIC) was proposed to be broadened. The NMP proposed creation of land banks, digitization of land and resources maps, and a scheme to make available land that previously was not productively used available. By that time there were already concerns about the possible adverse impacts of FTAs that India signed; nevertheless, NMP stated that India would continue to encourage free trade agreements but would also ensure that they did not impact domestic manufacturing adversely.

The NMP also proposed creation of National Investment and Manufacturing Zones (NIMZs) that would be developed as greenfield industrial townships, with the state-of-the-art infrastructure using clean and efficient energy technology and facilities for skill development, and they would compete with the best industrial hubs in the world. As also announced in the NMP, the Manufacturing Industry Promotion Board was set up in 2012. However, not much is known about what this board has been doing. Similarly, almost a decade later, only one NIMZ has been approved, and the work for the same has not yet started. The NMP was an action-oriented policy and seems to be rich in promises and proposals but lacks a comprehensive approach and has not made any visible impact on the ground.

In September 2014, the government announced the "Make in India" programme with the objective of making India an important manufacturing hub. Companies across the globe were invited to make investment and set up factories and expand their facilities in India. It focused on eliminating unnecessary laws and regulations and on time-bound project clearances through a single online portal. It also proposed to launch skill development programmes for people from rural areas and poor ones from urban cities. It intended to create industrial infrastructure along the Dedicated Railway Freight Corridors (DFC). It retained some of the proposals from the NMP, such as NIMZ and TADF.

As a part of this programme, the government brought substantial reforms in terms of regulatory clearances, making them much easier and faster. The government also liberalized the FDI regime substantially, and as a result, FDI in most sectors are allowed at 100 per cent under the automatic route, and only a few sectors need government approval. Even the strategic sectors such as manufacture of defence equipment have been opened up now. Nevertheless, Make in India is a programme of actions, and there has not been much change in the industrial policy, except that the government has raised the tariffs for some products and encouraged public procurement of domestically manufactured products.

In 2017, the government released a discussion paper under the title "Industrial Policy–2017" for consultation with the stakeholders. The objective was to finally adopt an action-oriented and actionable industrial policy. The paper briefly discusses the important provisions of the 1991 Industrial Policy and their implementation. The paper identified some constraints to industrial growth, such as inadequate infrastructure, restrictive labour laws, a complicated business environment, low productivity, challenges for trade,

46 *The Indian context*

and inadequate expenditure on R&D and innovation, and also outlines some of the broad objectives of the proposed policy. It does not, however, elaborate much on how these constraints can be overcome and how the objectives could be met. It raises concern that FDI that came to India did not help much, as their value addition is quite low but did not give any indication of how this concern could be addressed.

3.3   Export-import policy

The Indian policy regime has often been characterized by import-substituting industrialization policy rather than an export-led growth strategy. Indeed, in the beginning of the planned era, export promotion did not receive much attention as India had inherited a substantial amount of sterling balances at Independence accumulated mainly during World War II. Hence, while the first plan was being prepared, the government did not anticipate any foreign exchange constraints, and as a result, export promotion policies were not considered to be important. However, as the implementation of the plan started, India started importing capital goods in substantial measure, and hence the need for export promotion was recognized.

At the end of the First Five Year Plan, India established the State Trading Corporation of India in 1956. While it was expected to engage in both exports and imports, its focus was on organizing exports and channelizing import of raw materials for promoting exports. Similarly, Minerals and Metals Trading Corporation was established in 1963. Meanwhile, to provide adequate export finance and export insurance facilities to Indian exporters, Export Risks Insurance Corporation Private Limited (ERIL) was set up in 1957; it was later reconstituted and renamed as Export Credit and Guarantee Corporation Ltd. (ECGC) in 1964.

The Export Inspection Council, a statutory body, was set up in 1964 to ensure quality of various exportable commodities. In the same year, Indian Institute of Foreign Trade was established to create trained personnel for promoting exports from India as well as to create and disseminate knowledge on export potential. The Indian Institute of Packaging was also created in 1964 as it was recognized that good packaging was essential for promotion of exports. The Indian Council of Arbitration was established in 1965, primarily for settling commercial disputes among the traders, particularly those engaged in international trade.

In 1965, India established its first export processing zone (EPZ) in Kandla in the state of Gujarat. Subsequently, six more EPZs, spread over different parts of the country, were set up. These were Santa Cruz (near Mumbai) in Maharashtra, Falta in West Bengal, Madras (now Chennai) in Tamil Nadu, Noida in Uttar Pradesh, Cochin in Kerala, and Visakhapatnam in Andhra Pradesh. For each of these export processing zones in the country, an office of Development Commissioner was established that was responsible for the

The Indian context 47

administration of the zone. These EPZs, however, did not see much success. Some of them did not even take off.

Over time, more than two dozen export promotion councils were established covering almost all types of manufactured goods. Commodity boards were established for coffee, tea, spices, coir, rubber, and tobacco to promote exports. Similarly, the Marine Products Export Development Authority was established in 1972. To encourage exports of agricultural and processed food products, the Agricultural and Processed Food Products Export Development Authority was also established in 1986.

Realizing that the access to finance was hindering exports, the Export-Import Bank of India was established in 1982. The EXIM Bank, in coordination with the existing commercial banks in India, started issuing guarantees in foreign currencies on behalf of Indian exporters in favour of foreign importers. In 1983, it introduced a scheme known as the EXIM Syndication Facility to attract greater participation in export credit by commercial banks. The EXIM Bank provided funds and syndicated the credit risks to commercial banks, which earned a commission on account of assuming the risk. In due course, the EXIM Bank also started providing information and advisory services.

As mentioned earlier, export promotion received attention since the Second Five Year Plan as the trade deficit widened during this plan largely due to imports of capital goods and raw materials. Hence, a series of measures were introduced including organizational changes, increased facilities and incentives. The Third Plan, however, recognized the need for making export promotion schemes an integral part of planning.

To promote exports, several fiscal incentives like drawback of import duty, refund of excise duty, and income tax concessions were introduced. The institutional framework was also strengthened. A special scheme was introduced that gave exporters some import entitlement in a number of manufactured and processed products. Another scheme was introduced that provided direct export subsidies in 22 specified products.

Immediately after the Third Plan, a major step was taken on June 6, 1966 when the Indian rupee was devalued by a whopping 36.5 per cent, followed by withdrawal of schemes like import entitlement and cash subsidy for exports. However, the imports were liberalized. Exporting units and industries were given specialized treatment in respect of imports and credit arrangements for exports.

In a landmark decision, the government of India announced the Export Policy Resolution in 1970 to encourage exports. It was expected that with presentation of this, the export effort will be viewed as one of the highest national commitments. During the 1970s, substantial growth in exports could be achieved despite the fact that overall industrial growth performance did not improve. During the 1980s, industrial and import policies were liberalized to encourage production of goods for exports, more export processing zones were set up, and 100 per cent export-oriented units were promoted.

48 *The Indian context*

The Seventh Five Year Plan (1988–93) put emphasis on identifying sectors, industries, and products with high export potential. The government identified 14 broad sectors for giving a special thrust to exports. These included not only traditional items like tea, but also items like capital goods and consumer durables, electronic goods, and consumer software. But even before the plan period could end, the government devalued the Indian rupee twice in July 1991 – first on July 1 against the major currencies, including the US dollar, by 7–9 per cent; and again on July 3 by 11 per cent – and introduced a series of liberalization measures.

While imports were quite restricted through both quantitative and qualitative measures, except for raw materials and capital goods that were not readily available in India, it was hardly the case that such a restrictive policy was followed with a protective intention. Successive budget speeches of the finance ministers indicated that high import duties were imposed on what governments thought to be luxury items rather than to promote production of those items within India. Import duty was seen more as a source of revenue rather than an industrial policy tool. High import duty was introduced not to promote domestic production, as through the licensing procedure, government also restricted flow of domestic capital into production of such luxury items. However, over time, the government also imposed high tariffs with a view to promote domestic production in some cases.

Hence, neither did India ignore the role of exports, nor were its import restrictions imposed exclusively for import substitution. At a broader level, its trade policy was quite similar to that of South Korea. There were two differences when it came to matter of details. First, in the initial years, India's export push was primarily to earn foreign exchange so that it could finance import of raw materials and capital goods for its own industrialization. This, however, changed by the 1960s as it pushed for exports of almost all types of manufactured goods. Second, while South Korea encouraged export of luxury goods like electronics and automobiles while discouraging their domestic consumption, India not only discouraged their domestic consumption but also domestic production.

Overall, however, it can be said that India's trade policy was a combination of export promotion and import substitution, broadly in line with the strategies followed in countries like Korea and Taiwan.

3.4 An assessment of macro performance

The GDP growth rate of India accelerated in the early 1980s, yet it remained unnoticed for almost a decade. Encouraged by its economic reforms since 1991, the global community started taking interest in the Indian economy in the mid-1990s, and in the process it was discovered that India had found its place among the fastest growing economies of the world. Several economists, particularly the advocates of the economic reforms, were quick to attribute

The critics of the reforms, however, questioned this as reforms initiated in
this growth to the economic reforms initiated in 1991(Ahluwalia 2002; Srinivasan and Tendulkar 2003).

The critics of the reforms, however, questioned this as reforms initiated in
1991 could not, by any stretch of imagination, be the cause of superior growth
performance that started in the early 1980s (De Long 2003; Rodrik and Subramanian 2004).[1] The advocates, however, shifted their stance to argue that
the growth acceleration could have been caused by limited economic reforms
undertaken in the 1980s. Critics, however, found this argument also to be
unacceptable as the limited reforms that the advocates referred to came only
in the late 1980s, which could not have stimulated acceleration of economic
growth in the early 1980s. Another view was put forward to make a distinction between pre- and post-1991 polices. It was postulated that in the 1980s,
the growth process was stimulated by a "pro-business shift" in the economic
policy regime, while the 1991 economic reforms could be characterized by a
"pro-market shift" in the policy framework (Kohli 2006).

Even the architects of 1991 reforms now concede that the growth rate
during the first decade after the reforms was not markedly higher than the
growth rate in the 1980s, though they point out that reforms did not bring
the economic deceleration feared by many at the time of reforms (Ahluwalia
2016). A quarter century on, the sustainability of the growth process is being
questioned partly due to conditions created by the reforms. Crises confront
the economy in agriculture, infrastructure, industrialization, education, and
social inequality as constraints on the country's future prospects. Faster
industrialization, which was a key goal of the reforms in 1991, remains unat-
tained with the share of manufacturing sector virtually remaining stagnant
(Nagraj 2017; Nayyar 2017).

What remains relatively unrecognized is the fact that India achieved a
reasonably high growth rate, particularly in the industrial sector, right from
the beginning of its experience with planned economic development. This is
due to the fact that economists tended to look at GDP growth rates as the
measure of economic performance rather than the industrial growth rates.
This is rather strange, as most of the economic policy debates in the country
centred on industrial policy rather than policies for agriculture or services
particularly before the mid-1960s, when food crisis forced the government
to give more attention to agriculture, yet the issue of industrial growth performance did not receive enough attention.

Nevertheless, the so-called Hindu rate of growth got strongly etched in the
minds of the economic academic community, and the view that the growth
performance of the Indian economy was quite poor during the first three
decades of Indian planning is now widely accepted. Naturally, economic
planning – along with the policies like emphasis on heavy industries, industrial licensing, prominence to public sector enterprises, high tariffs, and
regulation of foreign investment – were held responsible for such a "disap-
pointing" growth record. The first prime minister of India, Jawaharlal Nehru,
is often personally blamed for the so-called poor performance.

50 *The Indian context*

In a marked departure from such an understanding, (Nayyar 2006) argued that even the first three decades of the planned era was not really bad in terms of economic achievements, particularly when looked at from the overall global scenario and achievements, in the developing world in particular. When India is generally compared with the East Asian countries, and condemned as a failure, it must not be overlooked that India did not go the African way. Moreover, from a longer term perspective of the entire twentieth century, India witnessed a massive structural break in its economic growth in the early 1950s. In fact, this break was substantially stronger than the break that was seen in the early 1980s.

The occurrence of structural break in early 1950s was also supported by a study that applied econometric test for structural break (Hatekar and Dongre 2005). An earlier study applying econometric test (Wallack 2003) concluded that the year 1980 was the most significant time for a break in GDP growth, and it was only in some sub-sector of services like trade, transport, storage, and communication that a break could be observed. This study, of course, did not look at pre-1950 growth experience or a possible break around 1950. Roy Choudhury and Chatterjee (2017) econometrically tested for multiple structural breaks, and found that there were indeed multiple breaks during the post-1950 period depending on which sectors and subsectors were considered, with the first break coming as early as 1964–65 with a negative impact. Similar observations were also made by Nanda (2009a). Mazumdar (2010) suggested three turning points – namely, the mid-1960s, 1980, and the mid-1990s – and, accordingly, four phases of growth in the post-1950 period.

Let us ignore the GDP growth for the time being, and look at how different sectors of the economy performed in different periods. The industrial growth rate achieved during the Nehru regime at 6.60 per cent appears to be the highest, followed by 6.30 per cent during 1991–2014, which is closely followed by 6.23 per cent during 1980–2014. Even if one compares the post-Independence industrial growth rates in two periods, namely pre- and post-1991 reforms, the difference is not really stark as they are 5.46 and 6.30 per cent, respectively, particularly due to the fact that the former period, as discussed later, experienced several internal and external shocks.

Even in case of the agriculture sector, the pre- and post-1991 growth rates (2.75 and 3.16 per cent, respectively) are not different enough for one to claim that there was a substantial jump. It is only in case of the services sector that the growth rates (4.97 per cent and 8.12 per cent, respectively) are vastly different. However, it may still be difficult to claim that the structural break in this sector was achieved in 1991, as the growth in this sector also picked up in 1980s itself.

Now, as suggested by (Nayyar 2006), if we look at the growth rates in the pre-Independence period, it may well be argued that in the entire twentieth century, there was just one structural break that occurred in the early 1950s, as the difference between pre- and post-1950 growth rates was much higher

The Indian context 51

compared to the difference between pre- and post-1980 growth rates. Moreover, the proposition that a significant break occurred around 1980 is also questionable, as the "possible break" could be observed only in the services sector growth rates, compared to "break" in all sectors in the early 1950s. It is indeed also quite strange that when economists tried to analyze the causes of the "possible break", they mostly emphasized the industrial policies or other polices that were expected to impact industrial performance; yet, instead of trying to look at growth rates in industrial sector, they looked at the GDP growth rates.

In popular perception, of course, post-1980 or post-1991 would look much brighter compared to the earlier periods as people, in their lives, experience the reflection of the growth in per capita income rather than the growth in GDP. Post-Independence, due to better medical care, population growth started increasing and continued to increase until 1981, and started falling thereafter.[2] Post-1981, India experienced relatively higher per capita income growth also due to lower population growth. However, from the perspective of economic performance, particularly in a context where labour supply is not a constraint, GDP growth is a better measure.

3.4.1 The three phases

The popular narrative is that India had a long period of bad industrial growth starting from the beginning of the planned era, and then suddenly in the 1980s or 1990s, it picked up. However, a closer look at the growth rates would reveal that this is far from the truth. Figure 3.1 provides the Hodrick-Prescott[3] trends of growth rates of GDP and those of the different sectors of the economy.

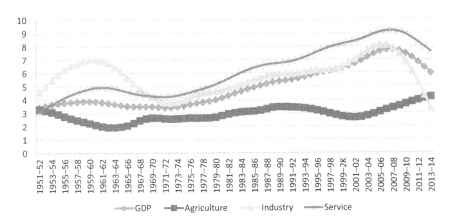

Figure 3.1 Hodrick-Prescott Trends of Growth Rates (per cent)

Source: Created by the author based on data from the National Accounts Statistics, Central Statistical Organisation, Government of India, New Delhi.

52 The Indian context

Looking at the trend in the growth rates of the industrial sector, it is quite clear that an acceleration in the industrial sector started with a bang right in the 1950s, but then the growth rate fell sometime in the 1960s. The same is true for the services sector, as well. The GDP growth rate also shows a similar trend. The fluctuation in it is less sharp, and hence, the higher growth rate of 1950s is not so obvious. This is largely due to the higher share of the agricultural sector in the GDP which did not do so well.

Given this, if one accepts that there was a structural break in Indian growth performance in the early 1980s, then it would be a folly to ignore that there was also a structural break in the mid-1960s, and the latter was probably stronger than the former. There is no rule that a "structural break" has to imply a change for a better; it could be a change for the worse as well, which was the case in mid-1960s.

As Table 3.1 shows, right at the initiation of the planned economic development, the industrial sector embarked on a high growth path that averaged 6.60 per cent between 1950 and 1965. However, the industrial growth rate slowed down substantially thereafter, and could post an average growth rate of 4.27 per cent only between 1965 and 1980. The industrial sector growth picked up again in the early 1980s, and 1980–2014 recorded an average industrial growth rate of 6.23 per cent. It is interesting to note that the average growth rate of the period 1980–2014 is significantly lower than what was achieved during 1950–65. While one can argue that the 1950–65 average growth rate could appear high due to lower base, it is also worthwhile to note that India attained Independence along with substantial social and economic disruption due to partition. Even the average growth rate of the period 1991–2014 at 6.30 per cent was significantly lower than that of 1950–64.

Given the two possible breaks in growth trends, H-P trends were worked out for the three periods – namely, 1950–1964, 1964–1980 and 1980–2014 – separately, which are shown in Figure 3.2.

Looking at Figure 3.2 and Figure 3.3, it is quite obvious that there were structural breaks in industrial and services sectors growth, as well as GDP growth, in the mid-1960s and early 1980s. Agriculture appears to be an exception. Fluctuations in agricultural growth rates, however, had more to do with the weather rather than government policies or other economic factors. Considering this, Indian industrial growth experience in the post-Independence era can broadly be divided into three phases. The first phase was the period between 1950 and 1965, the second phase spanned between 1965 and 1980, and the third phase was of the period after 1980.

It appears that the industrial sector embarked on a growth trajectory in the 1950–65 period, which is higher than even the one experienced during 1980–2014. The average growth rate in the services sector was higher during 1965–80, yet the growth trajectory of the 1950–65 period seems to be higher and the growth trajectory of 1980s seems to be similar to that of 1950–65. Even the overall GDP growth rates in the 1950–65 were reasonably good, even though it was lower than what could be achieved during the post-1980 era.

Table 3.1 Growth Rates of GDP and Different Sectors

Period	1900–1947		1950–2014	1950–1965	1965–1980	1965–2014	1980–1991	1991–2014	1950–1991	1980–2014	1992–2003
	Sivasubramonian	*Maddison*									
Agriculture	0.40	0.80	2.90	2.92	1.42	2.90	4.37	3.16	2.75	3.55	2.70
Industry	1.70	1.10	5.76	6.61	3.91	5.52	6.10	6.30	5.46	6.23	5.96
Service	1.70	0.80	6.12	4.58	4.23	6.56	6.48	8.12	4.97	7.59	7.66
GDP	1.00	0.80	4.96	4.09	2.94	5.21	5.56	6.52	4.06	6.21	5.92
Population	0.8	0.8	1.99	1.98	2.12	1.99	2.15	1.77	2.1	1.89	1.88
Per capita GDP	0.2	0	3.97	2.11	0.82	3.22	3.41	4.75	1.96	4.32	4.04

Note: Post-2014, the methodology of GDP estimates changed, which means that post-2014 data are not comparable, and hence, have not been considered here.

Sources: For 1900–1947, Sivasubramonian (2000) and Maddison (1995). For 1950–2014, National Accounts Statistics, Central Statistical Organisation, Government of India, New Delhi.

54 *The Indian context*

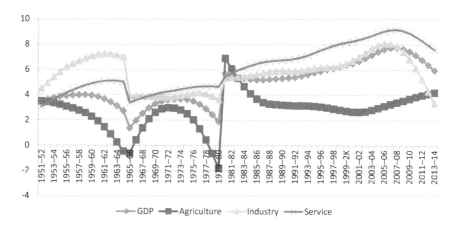

Figure 3.2 Period-wise Hodrick-Prescott Trends of Growth Rates (per cent)
Source: Created by the author based on data from the National Accounts Statistics, Central Statistical Organisation, Government of India, New Delhi.

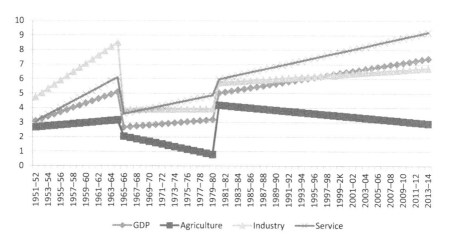

Figure 3.3 Period-wise Linear Trends of Growth Rates (per cent)
Source: Created by the author based on data from the National Accounts Statistics, Central Statistical Organisation.

3.4.2 *The smoke and mirrors of GDP growth*

A defining feature of the Indian growth experience since Independence is that industry and services displayed much higher growth rates throughout. This, when looked at along with the economic structure and its change over time, portrays a picture that has generally been ignored by almost all economic analysts and commentators who worked on Indian growth experience. The

The Indian context 55

economic structure of India changed fast due to these differential growth rates of the constituent sectors. Due to higher growth rates, shares of industry and services in the economy started rising and continued that way, while agriculture, which was the dominant sector in the economy, gradually lost its importance as a contributor to GDP (Figure 3.4). It is not unreasonable to argue that if all the three sectors of an economy – namely, agriculture, industry, and services – show different growth rates but they remain the same over time – for instance, say agriculture, industry and services grow at a constant growth rate of 2 per cent, 6 per cent, and 7 per cent, respectively – then the economy is not showing any change in its growth performance. However, even with this kind of growth dynamics, the overall GDP growth will become higher and higher with time.

In the Indian economy, the primary reason why the GDP growth showed higher rates in later years is that industry and services, with their higher growth rates, improved their shares in the economy, which, in turn, also made GDP growth rate higher. Lowering of the share of agriculture that always showed relatively poorer performance compared to industry and services gradually lost its ability to pull down the overall GDP growth rate with its poorer performance. In the process, bad monsoons ceased to be an important factor determining GDP growth rate in India.

Given the economic structure of the 1950s and 1960s, bad monsoons not only pulled down the overall GDP growth through its low growth rates and higher weight, but also through their depressing impacts on industrial and service sector growth rates through forward and backward linkages.

To get a better understanding of the picture, let us assume that the economic structure of India remained the same, i.e., the shares of different sectors in GDP in 1991 were the same as they were in 1950 (Figure 3.4). Under this assumption, we get the estimated GDP growth rate during 1991–2014, calculated as the weighted average of actual sectoral growth rates with shares

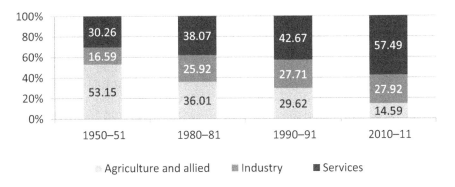

Figure 3.4 Share of Different Sectors in GDP (per cent)

Source: Created by the author based on data from the National Accounts Statistics, Central Statistical Organisation, Government of India, New Delhi.

56 The Indian context

of the respective sectors as weights, as $(3.16 \times 53.15 + 6.3 \times 16.59 + 8.12 \times 30.26)/100 = 5.18$ per cent. This is far below the actual GDP growth rate of 6.52 per cent during 1991–2014, but not exceptionally high compared to the actual growth rate of 4.09 per cent during 1950–1965.

Alternatively, if we assume that in 1950–51, India had the same economic structure as it did in 2010–11, and calculate the GDP growth rate by using the sectoral growth rates of 1950–64 and 2010–11 shares as weights, the GDP growth rate becomes 4.90 per cent. This is substantially higher than the actual growth rate of 4.09 per cent, and pretty close to the actual GDP growth rate of 5.52 per cent achieved during the period 1980–91.

Looking at Figure 3.2 and Figure 3.3, one might not see much difference in growth performance between the two periods 1950–1965 and 1965–1980, if only judged by the GDP growth trends. However, if one looks at the trends of sectoral growth rates, the differences become stark. It is well recognized that an average can be deceptive and misleading. GDP growth rates are, after all, averages of sectoral growth rates and hence are no exception. Looking at Figure 3.2 and Figure 3.3, it is quite obvious that the trajectory of industrial growth rates achieved in the 1950s was quite spectacular and the performance could not be matched even in the 1980s and 1990s. It was only around the turn of the century that the industrial sector could show similar dynamism.

While judging the performance of the Indian economy in terms of GDP growth in the 1950s and 1960s, it must also be noted that the savings rates were relatively low. An interesting feature of the East Asian economies that are considered to be the success stories in the second half of the twentieth century is that high growth rates and high savings rates went hand in hand in all these countries. Curiously, these countries believed that too much reliance on foreign investment, while it could complement domestic savings, could have had adverse and potentially destabilizing impacts, a sentiment echoed in the Indian planning process, as well – even in the post-1991 era.[4]

In the 1950s, the total domestic savings rate in India was less than 10 per cent of GDP, which increased marginally in the 1960s and remained less than 13 per cent. It started showing somewhat better growth in the 1970s and crossed the level of 30 per cent to reach 33.12 per cent in the 2000s (Table 3.2). This was still lower than the better-performing economies of the East Asian countries, but comparable to some of them. The abysmally low savings rate in India during the 1950s was largely due to high incidence of poverty, though some institutional issues could have played a role. Given this scenario, it was impossible to increase the savings rate substantially in a short period and, to that extent, achieving high growth rate was extremely difficult since growth cannot happen without acceleration in capital formation. One can also argue that despite the savings rate being much higher in the 1980s and 1990s compared to what they were during 1950s, a commensurate acceleration in economic growth was not observed. In fact, one study has argued that the growth trajectory

The Indian context 57

Table 3.2 Savings and Capital Formation in India (per cent)

Period	Total domestic savings	Household savings	Private corporate savings	Public Sector savings	Gross domestic capital formation
1950–51 to 1959–60	9.97	7.16	1.01	1.80	11.17
1960–61 to 1969–70	12.66	8.40	1.49	2.77	14.66
1970–71 to 1979–80	17.51	12.2	1.57	3.74	17.63
1980–81 to 1989–90	19.41	14.6	1.76	3.05	21.23
1990–91 to 1999–2000	23.13	18.44	3.72	0.97	24.55
2000–01 to 2009–10	33.12	25.00	6.76	3.31	30.63

Source: National Accounts Statistics, Central Statistical Organisation, Government of India, New Delhi.

after 1991 implied that India failed in utilizing its full potential in capital accumulation rather than improving its efficiency of capital use (Mazumdar 2008).

While it is well recognized that the oil shock of the early 1970s impacted the Indian economy adversely, it had a positive side, as well, that showed up in a few years. This led to a boost in economic activities in West Asia, which attracted substantial migration from India, making foreign remittance an important factor in Indian economy. Foreign remittances were less than $100 million a year during the 1950s and 1960s, but started picking up in the mid-1970s. From the level of 0.18 per cent of GDP in the 1960s, foreign remittances rose to 1.15 per cent of GDP in the 1980s. Remittances reached even higher levels of 2.65 per cent and 3.46 per cent of GDP in the 1990s and 2000s, respectively (Nanda 2009a). Thus, since 1980s, higher foreign remittances played an important role in achieving higher GDP growth, either by complementing domestic savings, or by boosting the demand in the economy.

As noted before, development finance has played an important role in industrial development in several countries, not only in developing countries but also in many developed countries. Such development finance institutions were created in India, as well. It is interesting to note that the first phase of the evolution of the development finance institutions in India as discerned by Nayyar (2015) roughly coincides with the first phase of economic or industrial growth of India from the beginning of the plan period to the mid-1960s. The second phase of heightened activities of the DFIs started in the early 1980s, which also saw a higher growth trajectory for the economy and industry. The post-1991 industrial development of India is characterized by India falling behind in new age industries like information technology (hardware) and mobile phones (Mazumdar 2008). Decline of DFIs in India could be one of the reasons for this.

58 *The Indian context*

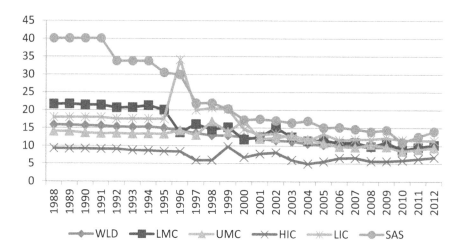

Figure 3.5 Falling Tariffs: Income Group Wise, 1988–2012 (per cent)
Source: Created by the author based on data from World Development Indicators, World Bank.
Note: WLD = World, LMC = Lower Middle Income Countries, UMC = Upper Middle–Income Countries, HIC = High-Income Countries, LIC = Low Income Countries, SAS = South Asia. Tariff figures zero indicate data are not available.

The growth performance of Indian industry in the 1990s might look further dampened if one also looks at the changing global scenario. While many have attributed the slightly better performance in the 1980s and 1990s to falling tariff barriers, it would be interesting to look at the tariff scenario in the rest of the world (Figure 3.5).

It is observed that the world as a whole started reducing tariffs since the early 1990s, but they fell drastically in the mid-1990s. This trend was observed not only for the world as a whole but also for all groups of countries – income group–wise, as well as all regions of the world including countries like the US and the UK. While the impact of falling tariffs at Indian borders on industrial performance is uncertain, the falling tariffs across the world are most likely to have impacted the Indian industrial performance positively.

3.4.3 *The period of crises*

The question that arises is why the growth momentum achieved during the period 1950–65 was not sustained. Was there something built into the system or the economic policy regime that made it unsustainable? Before one can venture to provide answers to these questions, it is imperative to examine the prevailing political, economic, and social environment in the country during the 1960s and 1970s. Indeed, this was a period when India went through a

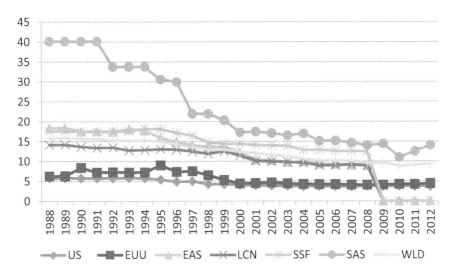

Figure 3.6 Falling Tariffs: Region/Country Wise, 1988–2012 (per cent)

Source: Created by the author based on data from World Development Indicators, World Bank.

Note: US = United States, EAS = East Asia and Pacific, EUU = European Union, LCN = Latin America and Caribbean, SSF = Sub-Saharan Africa, SAS = South Asia, WLD = World. Tariff figures zero indicate data are not available.

series of crises of all types. Unfortunately, this aspect of the history did not receive adequate attention by economic analysts, neither the apologists of the "planned model" nor its critics. The economic crises were largely due to some shocks, both internal and external, but not really linked to the prevailing economic or industrial policy of the country. Even the critics of the so-called planned model concede this (Klein and Palanivel 2002).

India had to face a war with China unexpectedly, and naturally India was least prepared for it. The humiliation that India received from the Chinese changed the entire security and development perspective India followed. India did not think that spending a huge sum of money on defence preparedness was important, and rather, it was prudent to spend the money on development and nation building. However, the war changed this perspective entirely, and India started spending much higher resources for defence preparedness diverting from development activities that received the priority earlier. However, even before India could overcome the shock of the Chinese war, it had to face another war with Pakistan in 1965. This war not only meant a drain of resources to unproductive use; it also meant some dislocation, as after the war, some of the transport links that it had through and with Pakistan were snapped. Around the same time, it suffered two consecutive droughts, in 1965–66 and 1966–67. Since agriculture contributed about half of the national GDP, the droughts had high impact on the economy.

60 *The Indian context*

On the domestic political front, this period witnessed huge instability. Jawharlal Nehru and Lal Bahadur Shastri, both serving prime ministers, died in 1964 and 1966, respectively, leaving a political vacuum and power struggle within the ruling party which continued even after Indira Gandhi took up the leadership, and eventually it split vertically in 1969. This period also saw the emergence of the Naxalite uprising in West Bengal that affected the state, then among the most industrialized ones, almost for a decade.

In 1971, India had to deal with a huge influx of refugees from what was then East Pakistan, and a war with Pakistan. Even though India had a convincing victory, a large proportion of the refugees did not go back, putting substantial burden on the economy, and India's security perception also changed, forcing India to spend even more resources on defence. Another two droughts, in 1972 and 1974, and the first oil shock in the intervening year of 1973 badly damaged the economy. Such a time of economic crisis prepared the ground for political unrest and Indira Gandhi's response to it by declaring internal emergency fuelled the political instability further. Political movement in the wake of the emergency hit the entire north of India and Gujarat hard, affecting the economy of the country, as well. While political instability continued even after the emergency was ended and the newly formed Janata Party came into power in 1977, due to power struggle within the ruling party leading to its fall and the return of Indira Gandhi into power in 1980, India had to face another round of economic hardship due to a severe drought and the second oil shock in 1979.

This is also the period when the green revolution programme was launched in India. However, as can be observed from Table 3.1 and Figure 3.2, it could not make much of positive impact on the economy or the agricultural sector, which performed much better in the 1980s compared to in the 1970s. Maybe the programme took some time to show results. Agriculture remained (as it is still) crucially dependent on the monsoons. The decline in industrial growth performance in this period could partly be due to a shifting focus away from industry to agriculture. However, agriculture, by its very nature could not show a growth performance similar to that achieved in the industry in the previous years.

While it may reasonably be argued that that some internal and external shocks that did not belong to the domain of economic policy or measures impacted the economic performance in this period, some policy changes that occurred during this period should also be scrutinized for their possible adverse impacts, even though it was also the case that the 1980 growth recovery took place without any major policy changes. Apart from the launching of the green revolution programme, three major policy changes can be identified. These are: enactment of MRTP Act, nationalization of major commercial banks, and expansion of public sector enterprises, particularly into areas that were not demarcated to be priority areas for the public sector.

While the primary objectives of the MRTP Act were to control growth of monopolies and restrict monopolistic and restrictive trade practices, it had

The Indian context 61

some serious design and implementation issues. While monopoly is generally defined with respect to market share and market position, India chose to define it in terms of absolute size of the firm. As a result, companies with turnover that could be considered small by global standards, and occupying market shares that were far from giving any position of dominance in the market, which itself was quite small, would be treated as monopoly and would be denied further growth and put under severe controls. The provisions on restrictive trade practices were reasonably good but they were hardly implemented, as that would have required substantial investigative capabilities that were seriously lacking. The fact that the authority had the power to issue "cease and desist" orders only, and that the relevant provisions were *ex post* in nature, ensured that they remained largely unenforced. In contrast, the monopoly related provisions were *ex ante* in nature, and required very little investigative capability, and hence, they were enforced almost automatically (Nanda 2009a). As a result, the companies were forced to ventures into new areas in which they hardly had experience or competence as they could not invest further in their existing business (Das 1998). This was certainly a recipe to promote inefficiency in the system. Interestingly, the very idea behind the licensing policy which was still in operation was that limited available resources should not go into undesirable or inefficient use. In this sense, the MRTP Act might have worked counter to the objective of the licensing policy.

As mentioned before, this was also a period that saw mushrooming growth of public sector enterprises. Between 1969 and 1979, the number of central public enterprises almost doubled with similar growth in the capital investment in real terms (Table 6.1). To put the issue in perspective, between 1956 and 1961, the number of public sector enterprises also doubled, but the size of capital invested rose by more than nine times in real terms. What was more problematic, however, is that they entered into several non-priority areas where private enterprises were doing reasonably well. There was some kind of competition among the different ministries of the government to have their own enterprises (Das 1998). Many sick enterprises were nationalized rather than finding any alternative or efficient solutions, primarily to protect employment. Such initiatives sucked up substantial capital without actually reviving these enterprises (Ahluwalia 1993). This tendency might have led to misallocation or inefficient allocation of resources, as well as inefficiency in production.

Half a century later than when the banks were nationalized, it might be quite obvious to criticize the move. However, any evaluation of this action would require a critical evaluation of the existing banking system prevailing in 1969, rather than simply comparing the performances of public sector and private banks of today.[5] Unlike today's private banks, the existing banks at that time were not professionally managed, and loans were granted without proper evaluation. Not just the average employees, but even top executives lacked expertise in bank management. While many banks were working

62 *The Indian context*

simply as an arm of existing business houses to collect deposits and invest in their own business, even others were serving sectarian interests and preferred to support conventional trading activities rather than manufacturing industries. More importantly, the banks were operating only in big cities and urban areas, and as a result, potential deposits from rural and semi-urban areas could not be channelized for industrial development of the country, apart from the fact that people in such areas were also deprived of banking facilities and their entrepreneurial ambitions would be nipped in the bud due to lack of capital (Narayana 2000).

Post-nationalization, the banks spread their branches rapidly into rural and semi-urban areas, along with bringing professionalism and modern techniques in their management. Since the household sector was the predominant source of savings in India, expansion of banks into rural areas brought banks within the reach of millions of rural households, which resulted in faster growth of savings rate in the country (Table 3.2).[6] Nationalization of banks was, of course, not an isolated Indian socialist misadventure. Even South Korea, often considered the poster child of the export-led capitalist model of development, also nationalized its banks in 1961, almost a decade ahead of India. Even in Germany, publicly owned banks were instrumental in promoting fast economic growth, particularly during post-war reconstruction.

3.4.4 Recovery and the 1991 crisis

The argument that the Indian industry recovered in 1980s even without significant changes in the policy regime has been contested. Panagariya (2004), for example, argued that the 1980 growth recovery was driven by substantial fiscal expansion and growth in external borrowing, a strategy that was unsustainable and was also responsible for the 1990–91 economic crisis in India, as against this, the growth process in the 1980s was sustained due to economic reforms that removed the structural imbalances to a great extent.

It would, however, be a misjudgement to attribute the 1980 growth recovery entirely to the fiscal expansion that indeed occurred to some extent. Fiscal expansion very often leads to higher trade deficits. However, in the 1980s, export growth rates exceeded import growth rates, while the general trend for other decades has been just the opposite. Hence, the decline of the Soviet Union that severely affected Indian exports and the disturbances in the Gulf that affected the import bill and remittances could be the direct reasons for the crisis, which is well recognized by now. It is also worth noting that the year 1991–92 was not bad just for industry but for agriculture, as it also experienced a decline.

It is important to understand how the government utilized the fiscal space that was created due to limited fiscal expansion in the 1980s. This was neither used to enhance government investment to boost productive capacity in any significant way, nor used to generally boost the aggregate demand within the Indian economy. A major share of this was used to acquire weapons from abroad. In five years between 1983 and 1988, India increased its defence bill by 85 per cent to become among the largest defence importers, procuring one-fifth of the arms exported to Third World countries. When fiscal expansion is used to buy such huge quantity of arms from abroad, it might boost the income of arms exporters – but not the domestic economy.

Throughout the 1980s, however, the issue of high defence imports and their potential impact on the balance of payments were ignored, which in a way was responsible for the 1990–91 economic crisis in India. Defence import figures were not publicly available, as they were closely guarded by the ministries of defence and finance. What made it more opaque is the fact that defence procurements were made largely on credit. Such huge defence import came into public knowledge when a huge gap was discovered between the import figures provided by the Ministry of Commerce and the Reserve Bank of India.[7] On an average, the gap was about $500 million a year during 1980–1985, which increased to about $4 billion in 1990 alone. During 1985–1990, the cumulative gap rose to $14.2 billion, and it was predominantly accounted for by defence imports (Kaushal 1995).[8]

Contrary to popular perception, the 1980 economic recovery was accompanied by the highest phase of agricultural growth ever achieved in India, as it clocked a decadal growth rate of 4.37 per cent. It is important to mention here that the 1980–91 period also saw a high growth rate in the industrial sector. One may tend to conjecture that in this period, agriculture and industry could have complemented each other's growth performance. At 6.48 per cent per annum, even the service sector recorded substantial expansion. Hence, 1980–91 is probably a period when the economy recorded a balanced growth performance. It is questionable if excessive reliance on the service sector is an effective growth strategy, as there is some evidence that exports of intermediate services offer some potential, but still remain small, as such services and manufacturing activities have a tendency to collocate (Kuan 2017; Nanda 2019).

3.5 Review of policy and performance

J. K. Galbraith once reportedly observed that if India was considered a socialist country as it had a large public sector, then the US was more socialist than India as its share of the public sector in GDP was even higher. The government's share in the US gross national expenditures had expanded from 10 per cent in 1929 to 27 per cent in 1952. While this share did not decline in 1960, it at least still stood at 27 per cent. Similarly, in 1960, the government share in GDP was about 31 per cent in West Germany. If the social security contributions and the war damage related taxes were taken into account, the public sector in West Germany could occupy as high as 42 per cent of its GDP in 1960 (Brandt 1963). Nobody ever claimed West Germany to be a socialist country; rather, it was often considered to be among the most important free-enterprise economies of the world.

64 *The Indian context*

India, with much less share of the government in the national economy, was considered a Soviet-type planned economy! West Germany also followed a universal banking system and the government coordinated activities of major producers' groups. In South Korea, also, several state-owned companies were established, companies were given export targets, and export performance was linked with imports licenses and tax exemptions for imports – and since banks were planned to have a major role in this, the government nationalized the banking sector and established full control over all forms of institutional credit. In contrast, in India, banks were largely in the private sector during the 1950s and 1960s, as India nationalized the Imperial Bank to establish State Bank of India in 1955, and other major banks were nationalized only in 1969. It seems characterization of the Indian economy was just a matter of semantics rather than an analysis of its economic attributes.

The term socialist entered the constitution only in 1976, largely as a political move, essentially to please the Communist Party of India which was the only party that supported the emergency imposed by the Indira Gandhi government. It did not make any impact on the economic policy or structure. The Second Plan document had the term "socialistic pattern of society", but it was clarified by the Planning Commission that it meant egalitarian outcomes of the development planning in terms of income and wealth, which was very different from socialistic pattern of economy which could mean all means of production, except labour, being under state ownership and control.

The Industrial Policy of 1948 envisaged a "mixed economy" whereby the public sector would engage in production, as well as side by side with private enterprises and operating in pre-identified priority areas. However, the term mixed economy is a vague concept, as it only indicates that public sector also engages in production, it does not say anything about the character of the state or the orientation of the economic system in place.

The industrial policy emphasized that the state should invest in industries that were essential and required investment in too huge a scale for the private sector to be able to handle. This gives an indication that socialism was far from the agenda. Yet the inclusion of the term "socialistic pattern of society" in the Second Plan document raised confusion. When pressed for a precise definition of the term, the then-prime minister merely equated it with welfare state (Dasgupta 1957).

It is also noteworthy that the Planning Commission used the term "socialistic pattern of society" rather than "socialistic pattern of economy". The latter would mean that the means of production except labour will be under state control, while the former, as also clarified by the Planning Commission, was to mean egalitarian outcomes of development planning in terms of income and wealth. As one of the prominent economic commentators of that time observed,

> The prognosis indicated here will perhaps be unpalatable to those who have some kind of an implicit faith in the realization of a socialistic

The Indian context 65

pattern of society through the operation of our present Plan [Second Five Year Plan]. Yet the broad facts are there to show that whatever the Plan may achieve – and its achievements are not to be inconsiderable otherwise – it has very little of socialistic content in it.

(Dasgupta 1957, p. 91)

It is worth mentioning here that the 1948 Industrial Policy was announced by the then-Minister of Industries, Dr Shyama Prasad Mukherjee, who remained the president of Hindu Mahasabha, and in 1951 went to form the new right-wing political party called Bharatiya Jana Sangh. As a politician holding diametrically opposing views from that of the Indian National Congress and Jawaharlal Nehru on several issues, it was unlikely that Mukherjee adopted such a policy entirely on Nehru's bidding. Thus, the industrial policy adopted by India immediately after Independence was unlikely to be an outcome of Nehruvian socialist ideas but represented a broader consensus.

The economic and industrial policy of the country was largely influenced by the Bombay Plan that was prepared by the leading industrialists and technocrats of India in 1944–45. The Bombay Plan – that had Ghanshyam Das Birla, Ardeshir Dalal, Kasturbhai Lalbhai, John Mathai, Sri Ram, Ardeshir Darabshaw Shroff, Jamshedji Ratanji Dadabhoy Tata, and Sir Purshottamdas Thakurdas as the signatories – argued for state intervention in the post-Independence economic development of the country. The economic development model introduced after Independence was, thus, not just Nehru's brainchild but had much broader consensus, including from the leading Indian industrialists of that time. In fact, the Bombay Plan's targets were more ambitious than what the Planning Commission tried to achieve. The size of the Bombay Plan allocation planned for 15 years was much higher compared to the total allocation over the first three five-year plans, and there were striking similarities in allocations across different sectors – except that the Bombay Plan provided more emphasis on social sectors and less emphasis on transport and communication (Sanyal 2018). At most, one can also argue that even Indian industrialists were influenced by the views of political leaders like Nehru (Chhibber 2018). But then, that also indicates that there was broad consensus on the kind of economic and industrial policies that India was to adopt during the time around India gained Independence.

Similarly, in a "mixed economy", planning can have a very different purpose compared to a socialist economy. Planning can be used not only as a nudge to channelize resources to a desired direction, but also to guide all market players on where and how the economy and the markets are expected to move. There is enough uncertainty and private enterprises find it difficult to make decisions on projects that involve long gestation periods, even in a free market economy where planning can help (Bagchi 1987). While planning was used to allocate government budget into different sectors, it was also used to assess future infrastructure needs, including the demand for power. It was also through planning process that the need for trained

66 *The Indian context*

technological manpower was recognized and the technical institutes like the Indian Institutes of Technology were established.

Contrary to popular perception, as per the Industrial Policy of 1948, foreign investment was encouraged – provided that there were no strings or conditions attached. It also emphasized that foreign capital would be allowed in joint participation with Indian capital and that a majority in management and control should remain in Indian hands. Not only in Industrial Policy of 1948, but then-Prime Minister Nehru also gave a statement in the Parliament on April 6, 1949 (cited in Dhar 1988), emphasized that India,

> with low level of domestic savings rate, needs foreign capital to undertake larger investments for rapid industrialization. Foreign private capital was also important because in many cases scientific, technical and industrial knowledge and capital equipment can best be secured along with foreign capital.

He also clarified that the government was not against foreigners being employed in India if they brought technical experience and skills that were required but not available in India, a policy that is followed in all developed countries even today. Foreign entrepreneurs were, however, expected to give importance to training of local people for such jobs in the quickest possible manner. Interestingly, many Indian entrepreneurs complained that foreign capital was given too much of encouragement and demanded that the sphere of foreign capital should be limited so that domestic industry could develop (Dhar 1988). It was only in the late 1960s that serious restrictions were imposed on foreign capital (Balasubramanyam and Mhambere 2003; Sen 2010). Another feature of the Industrial Policy 1948 was that it emphasized the role of cottage and small-scale industries in economic development. These industries were encouraged because they make use of local resources and provide larger employment opportunities.

Table 3.1 and Figures 3.1–3.3 indicate that the reforms of 1990s did not have much of impact on the overall growth performance of India. However, when looking at different sectors closely, it appears that there was a slowdown in the industrial sector which was more or less offset by an acceleration in the services, maintaining the overall growth at the similar level. Across the world, economic reforms generally involved some adjustment costs, particularly in the short term. In comparison, India performed much better as there was not much adjustment costs in terms of slowdown in the economy. This had been possible mainly because of the fact that the reforms process followed a gradual and staggered approach, and also because of the strong economic foundations built over the four preceding decades. But it is also worthwhile to recognize that immediately after the 1991 reforms, service sector growth fuelled the overall GDP growth for which the reforms played a limited role at best. The reforms of 1991 were largely intended to impact the industrial sector which slowed down since the reforms and it took more than a decade to catch up with pre-1991 growth momentum which might have been the adjustment costs in the Indian context.

At the time of adopting its development model, India was a resource-scarce country with a savings rate lower than 10 per cent which justified that there was some restriction on how available resources could be used. The situation, however, changed drastically by the 1990s and there was far less need to channelize resources into desired direction through licensing. Hence, abolition of industrial licensing in 1991 could be considered to be endogenous to the Nehruvian model itself, as the economy no longer had resources as scarce as in 1948 that forced policy makers to introduce industrial licensing (Singh 2008). However, licensing requirement was done away with in 1988 itself for most industries except a negative list of 26 industries. In effect the 1991 reforms amounted to a pruning of the negative list from 26 to 18.

As argued before, the MRTP Act, particularly its provisions on monopoly, was against the spirit of efficient use of resources. Hence, scrapping of the "monopoly"-related provisions from the MRTP Act was also necessary. In any case, it became anachronistic with the scrapping of the licensing requirements. The amendment to the MRTP Act also meant liberalization of FDI regime which was also intended in the New Economic Policy.

Given the balance of payments situation, devaluation of the rupee was possibly unavoidable. It had to be done sooner or later. Moreover, a developing country may need to maintain an undervalued currency as a part of its industrialization strategy to make a dent in the global market, as has been done by several other countries, including China in most recent times (Nayyar 2013).

However, it is doubtful if the dismantling of trade barriers – or the way it was done – can be given similar assessment. It can be the case that the industry was enjoying protection far in excess of its requirements and the ongoing Uruguay Round negotiations under the General Agreement on Tariffs and Trade (GATT) indicated that maintaining such high levels of tariffs would be difficult. Given this, some degree of trade liberalization was essential and inevitable. It is, however, a completely different issue as to how far the country should have gone along with its trade liberalization. In most products, India's applied tariffs are far below the levels that India committed to at the WTO. Given this, question may be asked if India's not-so-good performance in the industrial sector could have been caused by the fast and excessive dismantling of trade barriers.

Support to domestic industry has played an important role in industrial development of several countries, more visibly in countries like Germany, Korea, and China. There were, however, three main ways in which India differed from Korea in terms of industrialization policy and strategy. First, India went for excessive expansion of public investment, not so much in terms of capital invested but in terms of the range of areas that it entered into disregarding the boundaries drawn at the time of planning. As against this, in South Korea, public investment was limited to infrastructure and

68 *The Indian context*

strategic industries only. A related aspect of this is that Korea also had "exit" as a strategy for its public enterprises when the private sector became capable of managing the needs; in case of India, an entry by a public enterprise meant that it would be there for all time to come. Second, while India's export promotion efforts did not involve much subsidy, subsidies played an important role in both Korea and China in devising an effective mix of export promotion and import substitution strategies. Theoretically speaking, both tariffs and subsidies are considered to be distortionary in nature and better avoided to avoid build-up of inefficiencies. In terms of industrial strategy, however, they can bring different outcomes. While tariffs can give protection, it also discourages the domestic companies to go beyond national borders and thereby limits the scope of economies of scale; subsidies can encourage them to explore global market and help enjoy far better economies of scale. Since subsidies are revenue depleting, a government cannot use it beyond a point, and hence, it becomes more selective and efficient; tariffs, being revenue generating, can encourage a government to go overboard and beyond the efficient level (Nanda 2008). Third, while countries like Germany, Korea, and China made huge efforts in promoting "national champions" and encouraged them to venture into foreign markets and compete with the global players, India restricted the growth of its domestic companies through the MRTP Act, and may be even by licensing beyond what could be optimum.

By the 1980s, it was well recognized that the public sector expanded far beyond what was desirable and it was necessary not only to put a brake to its expansion but to withdraw from the non-priority areas. Accordingly, new policy towards the public sector, as mentioned in the Industrial Policy Statement of July 24, 1991 – namely, "Portfolio of public sector investments will be reviewed with a view to focus the public sector on strategic, high-tech and essential infrastructure" – was quite appropriate. In reality, however, the infrastructure needs did not receive adequate attention, as the government expected the private sector to satisfy them.

Private sector investment does not materialize without a guaranteed return, which is the case in many infrastructure sectors. As result, it is not easy to attract adequate private investment for delivering these services. Many infrastructure sectors are also prone to market failures, and hence, even with private investment taking place, ensuring these services with the desired quantity and quality is always a challenge. Some studies (e.g., Kirkpatrick et al. 2006) argued that it is difficult to find evidence where private ownership produced better outcomes in delivering infrastructure services, even with regulation. It is, however, interesting to note that even though achieving regulatory objectives through private firms in delivering infrastructure services poses enormous challenges, even public ownership may not negate the need for regulation (CEMT 2004). In delivering many such services, however, publicly owned service providers may be preferred over private firms (Williamson 1998).[9]

The Indian context 69

Private investment did not come up for infrastructure at the desired scale. Consequently, the lack of adequate infrastructure services emerged as the major constraints to a higher, sustainable growth path (Srinivasan 2006).[10] The fact that development finance institutions generally ignored the needs of infrastructure sectors, which were generally funded from state resources, ensured that private players could not manage enough finance to fill the gaps created by the withdrawal of the state in this sector (Nayyar 2015). This was indeed recognized way back in the early 2000s, and the government accorded priority to upgrade infrastructure services, including with an increase in public investment, but one full decade was lost in the process. Nevertheless, the idea of mobilizing private investment did not die down, and the idea of public-private partnership gained ground. Nevertheless, private investment in infrastructure still remains much less than what was expected.

Most importantly, much of the accelerated GDP growth after 1980 can be explained by the fact that different sectors performed differently throughout post-Independence history, changing the economic structure in the process. This manifested in terms of higher GDP growth. The higher growth of later years was primarily due to an increase in the share of high growing sectors like industry and services, and decline in the share of the low-growing agriculture sector. This, along with the fact that savings rates became more than double in the 1980s and 1990s compared to the 1950s, indicate that changes in economic policies could not have been responsible for boosting the growth performance of the economy, in particular, they failed to boost the industrial sector, though some of the changes might have been the need of the time.

3.6 Conclusion

Though the Indian economy has often been characterized as a "mixed economy", as the term has not been used elsewhere so widely, it could easily give in to misinterpretation. It means that the public and private sectors coexist in an economy, but concluding beyond this is difficult. It is quite odd to characterize India's development planning with the term "centrally planned economy". The fact that India became politically quite close to the communist bloc, and also used technologies from the Soviet bloc – particularly in state-owned enterprises in steel and oil and gas sectors – and also developed close trade linkages with the bloc could have also been responsible for such a perception.

However, these were, to a large extent, a political necessity for India and also due to the fact that these were the countries that could give India their technologies easily at low costs. In the Western world, technologies are generally held by companies and not the government, and hence, it is quite difficult to access technologies at cheaper costs from there, even if the governments were willing. Hence, it would be more appropriate to characterize India's development planning with a coordinated market economy like Germany, South Korea, or Taiwan, rather than a Soviet-type centrally planned economy

70   *The Indian context*

While Jawaharlal Nehru is held responsible for introducing the "Soviet socialist-type planned economy", the first industrial policy of the country was introduced by the then-industries minister Dr Shyama Prasad Mukherjee. The main opposition party of that time was the Communist Party of India, which never believed that India was anywhere near being socialist.

Similarly, it is also difficult to characterize Indian economic policy in terms of the pre- and post-1991 binary. Major course changes took place in the Second (1956–61) and Third (1961–66) Five Year Plans in terms of putting emphasis on the heavy industry in the former and export promotion in the latter. A major policy intervention took place in 1969, when all major commercial banks were nationalized.

If devaluation of the Indian rupee is considered a major component of 1991 economic reforms, a similar measure was adopted even in 1966. If delicensing is seen as a hallmark of 1991 industrial policy, then delicensing actually happened in 1988 in case of all industries subject to a negative list of 26 industries. In 1991, delicensing was done for all industries except 18 industries specified in the negative list; hence, in effect, delicensing of 1991 was essentially for eight industries that were removed from the negative list. If liberalization of imports is considered a defining feature of the1991 economic reforms, then reduction in import duties did not happen only in 1991, but it happened in 1988, as well. More importantly, a more drastic cut in import duties took place 1995 onwards when the Uruguay Round of trade agreements came into effect and the WTO was established. Moreover, a reduction in import duty continued gradually, even after that and the quantitative restrictions on imports were removed in 2002. India abandoned its product patent regime in pharmaceuticals and agrochemicals in 1970; the same policy continued until 2005, when the product patent regime was re-introduced.

While India was made more open to foreign direct investment in 1991, by no means was it a one-time event: the gradual liberalization of FDI regime continued well after 2014 when the new government made substantial liberalization in this regard (Table 3.3). It is possibly in case of public sector enterprises that one can claim to have pre- and post-1991 differences, as the number of public sector enterprises stopped growing since 1991, remained almost the same for more than 15 years and increased marginally again afterwards (Table 3.4).

Similarly, the industrialization strategy of India has been characterized as an import-substituting one, in rather a facile manner. In any case, it is extremely difficult to describe an economy or industry as import substituting or export led (Westphal and Kim 1977). At most, the decade of the 1950s can be characterized with such a term, as exports were indeed not a priority then, though some measures to encourage exports already existed even then. Since the Third Five Year Plan, export promotion became an important part of planning. Several measures were introduced including linking export performance with import entitlement around the same time when South Korea

The Indian context 71

Table 3.3 Milestones in Economic Policy Reforms Since 1980

1980	Automatic capacity expansion up to 5 per cent per year Setting up of 100 per cent export-oriented units
1988	Most industries were exempted from licensing, except 26 Limited trade liberalization
1991	Devaluation of the Indian rupee Reduction of import duties Delicensing, except 18 industries Some major sectors opened for the private sector Limited liberalization of FDI regime
1995–97	Drastic fall in import duties Full convertibility in current accounts
1997–2000	Further fall in import duties
2002	Removal of quantitative restrictions on imports Removal of performance requirements for foreign enterprises
2005	End of the Multi-Fibre Arrangement in textiles Re-introduction of product patent regime

Source: Author's compilation.

Table 3.4 Growth of Central Public Sector Enterprises

Date	Number of enterprises	Cumulative net investment* (Rs crore)	Cumulative investment at constant (2004–05) prices	Growth over the previous level as indicated (%)	Growth over 1951 level (%)
April 1, 1951	5	29	795		
April 1, 1956	21	81	2,360	197	197
April 1, 1961	47	948	24,678	945	3,003
April 1, 1969	84	3,897	49,508	101	6,126
March 31, 1979	169	15,534	101,866	106	12,710
March 31, 1990	244	99,329	256,107	151	32,107
March 31, 2002	240	324,614	346,349	35	43,455
March 31, 2007	247	421,089	329,756	–5	41,368
March 31, 2015	298	1096057	438137	33	54998

Source: Department of Public Enterprises, Annual Report, various issues, Government of India, New Delhi.

* Investment is defined as the sum of paid up capital, share application money and long-term loans.

72 The Indian context

introduced similar measures. India was among the pioneers to conceptualize and establish an export processing zone in 1965, ahead of South Korea, Taiwan, and China in this regard. The next year, India devalued its currency substantially to boost its exports.

Despite this, the pre-1991 economic policy regime in India is linked with import-substituting industrialization strategy as against the export-led industrialization strategy linking the post-1991 period, even though the country tried its best to promote exports for a full three decades before 1991. One could think this is possibly due to what happened in reality, rather than what was the policy intent. But even that is problematic, as there is no clear example of the growth of any industrial sector that was driven by exports to any substantial extent after 1991, except probably the pharmaceuticals industry.

On the other hand, there is a clear example of the growth of the automobile industry in India after 1991 that was driven by domestic demand under import-substituting trade regime, as the import tariff is still high in this sector. Clearly, it is quite problematic to term the industrialization strategy before 1991 to be import-substituting and that of post-1991 to be export led. Rather, as many economists have pointed out in case of South Korea, India also followed a combination of export-led and import-substituting industrialization strategies all along. Overall, it would be more appropriate to describe the Indian economic structure as a coordinated market economy, rather than a centrally planned one, where the degree of coordination is substantially diluted since 1991.

If the binary of pre- and post-1991 is not valid for economic and industrial policy regimes, it is quite natural that such a binary is unlikely to hold good for economic growth or industrial performance. The fact is that the Indian economy, as well as Indian industry, indeed took off around 1950 but it could retain the momentum only until the mid-1960s. It continued to perform poorly until around 1980, and improved thereafter. It is also to be noted that the poorer performance in the interim was largely influenced by political factors and some economic factors that were beyond the control of Indian policy makers. It would be improper to attribute this poorer performance to economic or industrial polices.

Second, the lower GDP growth rate during the 1950s and 1960s is more a reflection of changing shares of different sectors in GDP – namely, agriculture, industry and services – rather than acceleration in sectoral growth rates. When India started its development planning exercise, the share of agriculture was more than half, with industry and services sharing the rest. An important characteristic of the growth process is that agriculture always showed a lower growth rate, and by and large, industrial and service sector growth rates were much higher. This meant that the share of agriculture fell drastically along with substantial gain for industry and services. Hence, even if the growth rate of agriculture was still relatively low in the 1980s and 1990s, its depressing impact on the overall GDP growth rate became much lower, and on the other hand, high growing sectors of industry and services started showing much higher elevating impact on the overall GDP growth rate due to their higher share of GDP.

Such simple issues have not been adequately highlighted in the literature on Indian economic growth experience, largely due to the fact that the recent studies in this regard always centred on the pre- and post- 1991 binary. The Hindu growth rate narrative caught the imagination of most researchers so much that, they did not venture to say that there was no such thing as Hindu rate of growth.

When India adopted its development planning exercise around 1950, its initial conditions were much worse compared to where it was in the 1980s and 1990s. Investment required for faster growth was limited by low savings rates, and poorer agricultural performance meant that it was a net food importing country, which meant that a substantial part of its investible fund had to be diverted to meet food imports. Hence, one can also argue that in fact there was only one structural break, taking place around 1950.

Notes

1 It is quite difficult to group economists purely as advocates and critics of economic reforms. Some of them supported the economic reforms in general but were critical of some aspects or the process. On the other hand, some critics of the reform process wanted reforms, but of entirely different kind. It may also be noted that many of the advocates of reforms were of the view that the GDP growth rate experienced a structure break in the early 1980s.

2 The exact year might be different, but we are constrained to accept this year as the year of plateauing of population growth as the census of Indian population was conducted this year.

3 The Hodrick-Prescott (HP) filter is a mathematical tool that is used as data-smoothing technique to remove short-term fluctuations and to get a long term trend of a variable. As against the linear trend, it retains the medium term turns and twists in the trend which helps understand the path of a variable better. The technique was popularized in the field of economics in the 1990s by Robert J. Hodrick and Edward C. Prescott.

4 See the Approach Paper to the 11th Five Year Plan (2007–2012).

5 Several reports of RBI, however, indicate that there was no reason to believe that public sector banks were less efficient compared to the private sector banks, including the foreign banks operating in India. Some of the criteria used for such comparison were operating profits, cost of funds, rates of return on advances and on investments and reduction in non-performing assets. See for example, RBI (2020)

6 To illustrate this in more concrete terms, the commercial banks at the time of nationalization in 1969 had in the aggregate less than 5,000 branches and had mobilized total deposits of Rs. 53 billion for the entire banking system. After nationalization, the bank branches swelled over 50,000 in the 1990s, with a considerable spread in rural and semi-urban centres, and deposits crossed Rs 5,000 billion and further doubled to Rs 10,000 billion in the year 2000 (Nanda 2009a).

7 RBI import figures include defence bill, as well, whereas the Commerce Ministry figures do not include defence imports.

8 In a 1993 RBI report, the governor, C Rangarajan, identified defence imports during 1985–1990 as among the major contributors to the balance of payments crisis of 1990–91.

74 *The Indian context*

9 This is quite important, as Williamson wrote the paper when he was the chief economist for the South Asia Region at the World Bank – and hence, the region, India in particular, could have been his intended target for such suggestions. He argued, "it is conceivable that public ownership could offer a preferable way of achieving the objectives of regulation. Water in England is a case where I am still unconvinced that privatization made sense".

10 For example, electricity generation capacity witnessed a growth of 8–10 per cent per year in the 1980s but fell to just 4–6 per cent a year in the 1990s (Nagaraj 2003), which affected industrial expansion of the country.

4 India's industrial performance
Assessments and policy linkages

4.1 Introduction

There is no universally accepted definition of industrial performance. Performance is very often measured as profitability or price-cost margin, but other indicators have also been used. Each firm holds a unique position in the market and the firm's position influences its behaviour and performance. The performance of the whole market is considered to be the aggregate of individual firms' performances. Industrial performance is often also understood to be the rate of industrialization or the rate of growth of the industry – an approach used in the previous chapter.

In a developing country context, measuring performance in terms of profit has its problems, particularly at the initial stage of industrialization when the market is quite small. In a small market, even if there are just a few firms, they might find it difficult to post even a reasonable rate of profit due to absence of scale economics in such markets. In a country like India, however, the situation might be different as it is a reasonably large country, and hence, it can sustain a number of firms in a particular industry and at the same time allow them to enjoy sufficient scale.

Moreover, a lower price margin may indicate higher efficiency in a static sense but not in a dynamic sense. The kind of influence the market structure has on dynamic efficiency or technological progress is not yet adequately understood, even at the theoretical level. The evidence that comes from empirical studies is also mixed. It is often argued that a perfectly competitive market is most suited for technological progress as the firms are always under competitive constraints to improve quality or reduce costs, forcing them to invest in technology development. A larger market share can make firms complacent and ignore the need to invest in technology.

However, Schumpeter (1950) is of the view that a large share or monopoly power is good for inventive activities. He visualized an economy which goes through a process of "creative destruction" which is like an organism with cells whereby some of the cells are constantly dying and being replaced with improved ones, and in the process, it grows and flourishes. Hence, replacement of existing products, processes, and organization by their upgraded

DOI: 10.4324/9781003047490-4

76 India's industrial performance

versions through innovations is an essential feature of a capitalist economy. The motivational force behind innovation is to earn extraordinary profits.

Innovation can happen only in a market that is not highly competitive, as it requires a sizeable deployment of resources which can be mobilized only in a market that gives some power to the firms. Moreover, a potential innovator will also expect to earn some abnormal profit post-innovation, even though competitors may soon imitate the technology and bring the profits back to the normal level. Hence, a market that might not be competitive in a static sense may well be competitive in a dynamic sense, as long as there is threat for imitation and rival innovation.

Industrial performance in a marketplace need not depend on the market structure of an individual country, as no country in today's world is a closed economy. Hence, the performance of firms or an industry in a country cannot be assessed in isolation, regardless of what happens to firms and industries in other countries. Better performance might mean firms or industries in a country being able to compete well in the global market.

However, in the global market, firms do not compete only through costs or prices of a product, but also because of goodwill or reputation that has been built over the years. Hence, an emerging industry in a developing country might find it difficult to compete with well-established firms in the global market, particularly those from the developed world. Due to adverse perceptions about their quality, they will need distinct price advantage. Such an advantage can come from the fact that they have lower costs of labour. The question is whether they can utilize this advantage to acquire prominence in the global market.

The next section discusses the measurement issues in industrial performance. The third section reviews the literature on market structure and performance in the context of India. The fourth section explores some alternatives in measuring industrial performance. The fifth section provides some estimates of industrial performance in India. The sixth section analyzes the industrial performance of India in the context of the key polices that might have influenced the performance of industries that showed relatively better performance. The seventh section concludes the chapter.

4.2 Measuring performance: the popular methods

Performance of an industry has generally been measured using three approaches: profitability, productivity, and efficiency. Profitability can be measured by using two different methods, rate of return and price-cost margin. Price-cost margin has been more popular in the literature, owing to difficulty in measuring capital stock which is an essential component in measuring the rate of return. Price-cost margin is also problematic, as it tends to underestimate price effects that might occur in the markets (Scherer 1980; Schmalensee 1989). Neither one can expect, *a priori*, any strong correlation between the two measures (price-cost margin and rate of return). For example, if a low rate of return is associated with a high capital output ratio, there can be a high margin; similarly, a high rate of return can be associated with a low margin in a sector using little capital. So the two measures are not perfect substitutes.

It is, however, questionable if profitability – whether measured in terms of rate of return or price-cost margin – is an appropriate indicator of performance. If a firm enjoys monopoly power, it will reap high profits which might come not just from market power but also from an efficient production process.

Productivity is another measure that has been used extensively in the literature. Most studies have used a measure of total factor productivity (TFP). The methodology is based on a model of production and technical change derived from the theory of production. TFP is a measure of increase in output that is not explained by increase in inputs, and is estimated by the difference between the time derivatives of output and inputs. If there exists a transformation function relating inputs (denoted $X_1, X_2, \ldots, X_m$) and outputs (denoted $Z_1, Z_2, \ldots, Z_n$), and the transformation function satisfies the appropriate differentiability and curvature properties, and if a scalar index of the m inputs and the n outputs at time t and the time derivatives are denoted as X_t, Z_t, $\dot{Z}/Z$, and $\dot{X}/X$, respectively, then the index of TFP is computed as:

$$TFP = \dot{Z}/Z - \dot{X}/X \tag{4.1}$$

Another measure of performance is efficiency, which is often considered to be the most important goal pertaining to industrial performance. There are three types of efficiency: technical, allocative, and distributive. Technical efficiency relates to the extent to which goods are produced with the least-cost combination of inputs. Allocative efficiency is concerned with the optimum input mix for a given output as dictated by the marginal rates of technical substitutions and the factor price ratio. Distributive efficiency is concerned with how any particular aggregate output would be reallocated between individuals in order to maximize welfare, but economists often consider this to be irrelevant in the context of industrial performance.

Measuring technical efficiency involves estimating a frontier production function and seeing how an average firm deviates from it. There has also been an effort to capture both TFP and technical efficiency in the same model. The stochastic frontier production function approach can be used also to break up these two components, and to quantify how much of the productivity growth is due to increased efficiency and how much is due to technical progress.

These approaches to measuring productivity and efficiency suffer from serious limitations. Since data for inputs and outputs are available in value terms, estimates are highly affected by changes in prices. While it is theoretically possible to factor in all price changes, it is practically quite impossible. Very often, studies have measured TFP to see the impact of trade liberalization

78   *India's industrial performance*

on productivity, ignoring the fact that if input and output prices have not changed in the same proportion, then the estimates will be misleading. TFP is a measure of productivity that cannot be explained by changes in different factors of production; hence, it is essentially a residual measure. While, generally, it has been interpreted as the reflection of technological improvements, some economists have also jokingly said it amounts to a measure of our ignorance (Jorgenson and Griliches 1967).

Another deficiency is the way material inputs are treated in such models. Such inputs are either ignored, subsumed in capital, or taken as another factor of production, along with capital and labour. However, as Georgescu-Roegen (1971) has pointed out, capital or labour are not substitutes for material inputs. In a normal situation, such material inputs will be consumed directly in proportion to output. Above all, measurement of capital itself is hugely controversial. Magdoff and Sweezy (1980) argued that there is no such thing as a straightforward or "true" measure of productivity.

Moreover, Block and Burns (1986) hugely unsettled the measures of aggregate productivity by examining the human, institutional, cultural, political, and ideological factors involved in the development of such measures. They explored how the invention of sophisticated measures of productivity was essentially a part of political developments concerning trade unions and collective bargaining, whereby the unions would try to demand higher wages justified on the basis of productivity gain while the capitalist would try to point out that there has been a productivity crisis. Hence, linking productivity with industrial performance, no matter how sophisticated the methodology, can be misleading (Foster 2016).

Measures of productivity and efficiency try to assess the performance of domestic industry in isolation. For example, the estimate of frontier production function is based on the input-output combination of the most efficient firm within the country, but if all firms are far behind the most efficient firm globally, then the estimation of technical efficiency will be a huge underestimate. Hence, in the trade literature, there has been an attempt to assess performance based on how a country does in the global market.

International trade literature is dominated by the concept of comparative advantage, which is considered to be the driver of trade among countries. The concept of revealed comparative advantage, or RCA (Balassa 1965), is based on the comparative advantage theory, which in turn is based on the assumption that the relative costs of products in countries determine the pattern of trade. This, of course, ignores the later theoretical developments that several other factors can influence the pattern of trade, including economies of scale, consumer preferences, natural resource endowments, and several other factors.

Even with this limited construct, comparative advantage is measured indirectly as it is difficult to measure relative costs empirically. RCA is an indirect measure where trade performance of individual sectors is assessed vis-à-vis the trade performance of the whole economy to identify the sectors that

India's industrial performance 79

might enjoy a comparative advantage. The RCA for a particular product is defined as the ratio of its share in the total exports of the country to the country's export share in total global exports. The estimated value of RCA can range between 0 and $+\infty$. When the estimated value of RCA is greater than 1, the product in question is believed to have comparative advantage. While it is well recognized that RCA does not capture several factors that influence the flow of trade, it does not even capture the comparative advantage in the true sense, as RCA is based on observed values of trade which are likely to deviate from what comparative advantage pattern might dictate, due to existence of trade barriers. RCA is computed as:

$$RCA = (\Sigma_d x_{isd}/\Sigma_d X_{sd})/(\Sigma_{wd} x_{iwd}/\Sigma_{wd} X_{wd}). \ldots \tag{4.2}$$

Where i and s are the product and country of interest, respectively, d and w are the set of all countries in the world, x is the export flow of the product of interest and X is the total export. The numerator represents the share of good i in the total exports of country s, while the denominator represents the share of good i in the total global exports.

However, the measure has a serious conceptual difficulty which is inherent in the theory of comparative advantage itself. Theoretically speaking, a country is expected to export a good that enjoys comparative advantage and import otherwise, until the point at which one of the countries will reach its full capacity in a product. In reality, countries are engaged in intra-industry trade. Thus, the competitive situation of a country vis-à-vis a particular good cannot be assessed through a measure like RCA which is based entirely on exports. The fact that comparative advantage theory is unable to explain most of world trade is well accepted, and it is this acceptance that gave rise to alternative trade theories.

It is quite possible for a country to have an export share of a particular good in its total exports that is higher than that good's share in global export, while at the same time, its import share in total imports of the country is also higher than its share in total imports of the world. A country might engage in both export and import of a particular product in substantial quantity. Looking at high exports, one can consider it to have comparative advantage, but in that case, why should the country import the same product in substantial quantity? In an open economy, if the domestic demand has increased, and if the domestic producers have been able to capture the additional demand, and at the same time exports have not increased, then of course domestic industry has become stronger. RCA will not be able to capture this as well.

4.3   Existing estimates of productivity and efficiency

There have been a large number of studies that attempted to assess the performance of the manufacturing sector of India with the help of total factor productivity and efficiency estimates.[1] Goldar (1986), Ahluwalia (1991),

80 India's industrial performance

Aggarwal and Kumar (1991), Balakrishnan and Pushpangadan (1994), Upender (1996), and Mohan Rao (1996) are among the earlier studies that measured the productivity trends and growth of Indian manufacturing sector. These studies have estimated TFP growth rate at an aggregate level, as well as for individual sectors of Indian manufacturing.

By using panel data involving 15 states and 17 two-digit level industries, Mitra (1999) studied the increase in technical efficiency and the growth in TFP over the period 1976–77 to 1992–93. By estimating frontier production function, the study arrived at estimates of TFP of the selected states and India. The estimates indicate that in most of the states, the TFP declined in the cases of food products, beverages and tobacco products, basic metals, and metal products over the period 1985–86 to 1992–93 compared with the previous years. In the rest of the industries, an increase in TFP growth was observed in most states between 1985–86 and 1992–93.

Some other estimates (Goldar and Kumari 2003; Goldar 2004), however, showed that the rate of growth of productivity in Indian manufacturing declined from 1991 onwards. They also observed that this slowdown in the productivity growth was largely due to lower level of capacity utilization during the 1990s, compared to the 1980s. However, they also indicated that a decline in level of protection tends to have a positive impact on productivity growth.

Using sector-level data, Madheswaran et al. (2007) examine TFP growth and technical efficiency change (TEC) in manufacturing sector in India from 1979–80 to 1997–98. Their estimates suggest that, for most industries, TFP growth has accelerated during the period. It also finds that the TFP growth is mainly driven by technological progress, and not by increase in technical efficiency.[2] This, of course, could imply that a substantial number of firms operate below optimal level.

Singh (2012) analyzes TFP growth trends in 16 major states and at all-India level for the period 1979–80 to 2007–08. By calculating the Malmquist productivity index, the study finds that the TFP in the manufacturing sector of India has been growing at 9.1 per cent per annum. Out of 16 states, there are five states – namely, Uttar Pradesh, Madhya Pradesh, Gujarat, Orissa and Rajasthan – where double-digit TFP growth has been noticed, with Uttar Pradesh showing the highest growth rate of 12.8 per cent. It was also observed that the productivity growth was driven by both technical progress and increase in efficiency, but at the all-India level, improvement in efficiency made a higher contribution.

Kathuria et al. (2013) estimated the TFP growth of both formal and informal sectors of the Indian industry for the period 1994–95 to 2005–06 by using methods like stochastic frontier, semi-parametric, and non-parametric models. The resulting estimates suggest that productivity in the formal sector varied widely from that in the informal sector. The estimates were also found to be sensitive to the method used, and hence, it is difficult to draw any clear inference on productivity growth in India since 1991.

Deb and Ray (2013) made an attempt to compare pre-1991 manufacturing performance with that of post-1991 period, with the help of TFP growth, to find that the productivity growth rate improved during the post-reform period. Moreover, the states tended to converge in terms of rate of productivity improvement after 1991.

Sharmila and Hosamane (2014) tried to assess the performance of the organized manufacturing sector in the state of Karnataka for the period 1980–81 through 2010–11. The study compares the performance in terms of TFP growth in the pre-1991 reform period separately from that of the next two decades during the post-reform era. It concludes that the TFP growth rate was lower during the decade immediately succeeding the reforms, but it improved in the second decade of the post-reform period.

Parida and Pradhan (2016) estimated TFP growth and technical efficiency separately for all and labour-intensive industries, and for the pre- and post-reforms periods. They used three different approaches belonging to three different genres – namely, non-parametric, semi-parametric, and parametric, represented by growth accounting, production function with correction for endogeneity (Levinsohn-Petrin) and stochastic production frontier, respectively. Their estimates based on the data for the period 1980–81 to 2007–08 indicate that the labour intensity declined faster in the labour-intensive industries, and that the labour-intensive industries experienced productivity decline for the entire period. All three methods show similar results, but some variations are observed depending on the method used, and also to a certain extent between TFP growths at the aggregate and disaggregated levels.

Goldar et al. (2016) estimates TFP in the formal and informal sectors of Indian industries for the period 1980–81 to 2011–12, which indicate that the productivity growth in the informal sector was substantially lower compared to the performance of the formal sector. They also observe that the productivity growth declined in both the sectors during 1994–2002 vis-à-vis the performance during 1980–93, but accelerated once again during 2003–11. The faster productivity growth in the formal sector since 2003 was largely driven by superior performance in the petroleum refining industry, whereas textiles and leather products, wood and wood products, and chemicals and chemical products, were the key drivers of superior performance in the informal sector. They also observed that the formal segment of Indian manufacturing performed much better that the Korean manufacturing during 2003–11.

There have also been a good number of studies to understand the competitiveness performance of manufacturing industries in India by using the estimates of revealed comparative advantage. Agrawal et al. (2000) and Ganesh-Kumar et al. (2002) are among the earlier studies to assess competitiveness of Indian exports in the global market. Ganesh-Kumar et al. (2002) computed the revealed comparative advantage of Indian manufacturing exports for each year over the period 1971–96. They found that Indian products were not competitive enough in export markets as the RCA was found to be less than 1 for most export items. In the post-1991 period, the

82 *India's industrial performance*

increase in RCA was most prominent for jewellery, followed by carpets. Some other items like grain mill products, wearing apparel, and leather products also experienced increasing RCA. Made-up textile goods other than wearing apparel were among the items that showed a declining RCA in the study period.

Batra and Khan (2005) found that there is a similarity in the structure of comparative advantage in India and China, but despite that, there is no convergence between their performances in the global economy. The two countries show competitive relationships in sectors that are known to be capital-, skill-, technology-, and scale-intensive, but also in some sectors with low capital, skill and technology but having high resource intensity. However, some labour-intensive sectors like textile yarn, fabrics, and articles of apparel and clothing accessories showed complementary relationship.

Burange and Chaddha (2008) analyzed the trends of comparative advantage in Indian industries for the period 1996–2005 with the help of RCA estimates. The study found that labour-intensive items like textiles and scale-intensive items such as chemicals and iron and steel had substantial comparative advantage over the entire period. Mukherjee and Mukherjee (2012) evaluated India's export performance and analyzed the various factors underlying such performance. The study also analyzed the performance of three important export items – namely, gems and jewellery, cotton textiles, and electronic goods – with the help of RCA.

Anand et al. (2015) tried to explore the products that can drive India's export growth, particularly in the context of the government's "Make in India" campaign, and also used RCA to identify products that have comparative advantage. Mann et al. (2015) used RCA to understand the nature of changes in the technology intensity of India's exports in the post-1991 period. They found a noticeable shift in favour of medium-low technology–intensive products from low technology–intensive products. However, Indian exports were still dominated by low technology–intensive products, despite the entry of even medium-high technology items in the export basket.

Chaudhary (2016) analyzed the export potential of Indian textiles industry on the basis of competitiveness assessment for the period 2005–14. This is the period after dismantling of the Multi-Fibre Arrangement, and hence, a substantial increase of exports was expected. Using RCA, it found that the industry has strong comparative advantage in this item and has strong export potential that has been improving over the years.

The existing studies do not establish any clear pattern and throw up rather mixed evidence. One of the studies noted that results depend on the type of method (functional form of production function) chosen in estimating the TFP or technical efficiency. Another study finds that while reduction in effective rate of protection tends to impact TFP positively, in the post-1991 period, Indian manufacturing industry also showed a decline in capacity utilization, and that if this is factored in, TFP growth shows an increasing trend. This also raises the question if the observed higher productivity is due

India's industrial performance   83

to some firms going out of business. In essence, the existing literature has neither been able to establish a trend in performance over time, nor any pattern of performance across different sectors/sub-sectors.

4.4   Alternative measures of performance

As discussed before, measures like profitability, price-cost margin, and productivity have both conceptual as well as empirical difficulties. While RCA is relatively easy to estimate, as it is estimated traditionally, it cannot reflect the competitive strength of a country vis-à-vis the product in question. It might thus be better to look for a modified version of RCA which can discount for the imports that a country might be making as import means absence of comparative advantage unless it is the case that it cannot meet its demand of the commodity even after devoting all its resources.

$$
\text{MRCA} = \{(\Sigma_d x_{isd}/\Sigma_d X_{sd})/(\Sigma_{wd} x_{iwd}/\Sigma_{wd} X_{wd})\}/
$$
$$
\{(\Sigma_d m_{isd}/\Sigma_d M_{sd})/(\Sigma_{wd} m_{iwd}/\Sigma_{wd} M_{wd})\} \tag{4.3}
$$

Where m stands for commodity import flows and M stands for total import flows and other symbols are the same as in equation (4.2).

We can assume that the world export of a commodity is the same as the world import of the commodity, and world export is the same as world import, and hence:[3]

$$
(\Sigma_{wd} x_{iwd}/\Sigma_{wd} X_{wd}) = (\Sigma_{wd} m_{iwd}/\Sigma_{wd} M_{wd})
$$

We can thus write,

$$
\text{MRCA} = (\Sigma_d x_{isd}/\Sigma_d X_{sd})/(\Sigma_d m_{isd}/\Sigma_d M_{sd}) \tag{4.4}
$$

The numerator is the share of good i in total exports, while the denominator is the share of good i in total imports of country s. In this measure, if MRCA is greater than 1, the sector might be considered to have competitive advantage and if it is less than 1, then it might have competitive disadvantage. This is, of course, the relative performance of a sector, as the performance of a particular industry judged vis-à-vis how all other sectors in the economy are doing. If a country is having a large trade deficit and all sectors of the economy are showing large deficits, then one can argue that no sector is showing good performance, even though MRCA can be higher than 1 in some sectors. Hence, even MRCA can have serious limitations.

If we assume that that global export is equal to global import, we will get $\Sigma_d X_{sd} = \Sigma_d M_{sd}$. The MRCA can thus be written as:

$$
\text{ACA} = \Sigma_d x_{isd}/\Sigma_d m_{isd} \tag{4.5}
$$

84 *India's industrial performance*

This is nothing but absolute competitive advantage (as against comparative advantage).

Judging industrial performance on the basis of trade performance can have its own problems, particularly in the context of a large economy. A large country has a large domestic market, and if its domestic industry is able to hold on to its domestic market without being protected through trade measures, then surely the domestic industry is performing quite well. In such a situation, if one has to look at the performance of a particular sector, then it can be judged by the share of sectoral production in a particular country in total global production or consumption. If the share is increasing, the performance is considered to be improving.

We call this global competitiveness ratio, which is written as:

$$GCR = P_{ij}/\Sigma_i P_{ij} \tag{4.6}$$

Where P_{ij} is the production of jth commodity in country i.

However, if the share is constant or increasing due to protection given to domestic industry, or export subsidy, then the performance may not be considered to be so good. Hence, the measure of performance needs to be adjusted to the degree of protection given to domestic industry or the degree of openness to which the industry is subjected. Measuring the degree of openness in a country is quite difficult, as trade barriers are not only tariff barriers, but there can be several non-tariff barriers.

While GCR can be a useful tool for assessing performance of an industrial sector (provided that trade barriers do not change over time), it may not be useful to compare competitiveness of performance of two different sectors in a particular year. Given this, it might be useful to bring the concept of competitive performance index (CPI), which is the ratio of the share of an individual sector in global production of that sector and the share of total industrial production of the country in question (India, in this case) in total global industrial production, which is written as:

$$CPI = (P_{ij}/\Sigma_i P_{ij})/(\Sigma_j P_{ij}/\Sigma_{ij} P_{ij}) \tag{4.7}$$

This is similar to the RCA that has been used widely in the literature, but it reflects absolute advantage rather than comparative advantage. Unlike RCA, however, this does not suffer from the limitation of being based only on exports. In this formulation, if the ratio is more than 1, then the performance of the sector is above average, and if it is less than 1, then it is below average. While GCR, CPI, and ACA do not suffer from the several limitations that other measures have, they also have one of the limitations similar to RCA, as they are also not able to factor out the impacts of trade barriers that might be prevailing.

The notion of competitiveness has also been criticized. Paul Krugman (1994) called it a dangerous obsession. He was particularly opposed to measuring the competitiveness of an economy as nations do not compete, but corporations do. It may, however, be interesting to note the warning of Michel Foucault as he said that it is "not that everything is bad, but that everything is dangerous, which is not the same as bad. If everything is dangerous, then we always have something to do" (Foucault 1997, p 256). At the cost of some generalization, one can explore competitiveness at sectoral level that can be in line with the notion of absolute advantage. In any case, this is not about measuring the competitiveness of an economy.

It is also important to note that Lall (1987) observed that technological capability and the effort of an industry in a developing country can be evaluated, simply and effectively, by the criterion of competitiveness, even if the techniques that it might be using are vastly different from those used in advanced countries. More recently, Reinert (2007) made similar observations. According to him, it is trivially true that every economy has comparative advantage in some sector or other; however, what really matters is absolute advantage or technology gap, which determines the distribution of world income.

4.5 An assessment of industrial performance in India

This section tries to understand how Indian industry and its different sectors performed vis-à-vis the rest of the world. This will require a departure from the methods that have been used widely, like measurement of total factor productivity and efficiency. The choice here is based on the fact that not only do they have some limitations, but also because they have already been used so much that further use might not add much of value. These methods have not been able to settle some of the key issues in industrial performance. Since RCA also has some serious limitations, GCR, CPI, and ACA are used here for an assessment of the industrial performance of India.

4.5.1 Measuring competitive performance (GCI and CPI)

An attempt is made first to measure the GCRs (share of India in global production) and CPIs by using UNIDO industrial statistics. The ACAs of different sectors are measured essentially to validate the findings from the estimates of GCRs and CPIs. For GCR and CPI, the data is sourced from INDSTAT 2 2017, ISIC Revision 3. This data is at two-digit ISIC level. INDSTAT provides different variables of which industrial value added was taken for this analysis. While data are available at four-digit level as well, they come with huge data gaps. Even at two-digit level, data for sufficient period were available only for a small number of countries. Data for the period 1980–2010 were available only for 56 countries. Hence, it was not possible to get exact figures for global production; however, the data covered most of the major countries with manufacturing strength. Among the major countries, Argentina, Brazil, and Germany could not be included for the analysis,

86 *India's industrial performance*

as data for these countries were not available for a sufficient length of time. It is, however, expected that despite this data limitation, a picture may be available that will be pretty close to the reality, and the aggregate production of these 56 countries will be referred to as the global production. Since Germany is a country with substantial manufacturing capability, its exclusion could introduce bias into the results. For the shorter length of time for which data are available for Germany, however, they show that the share of Germany in global production has not changed much in most commodities, reducing the chance of such bias occurring.

As can be seen from Figures 4.1a–d, in most sectors, the Indian share of global production remained quite stagnant until about the mid-1990s, after which it kept on rising slowly. To start with, the Indian share was also quite low in 1980, and was less than 1 per cent except in textiles, chemical and chemical products, and basic metals. India's overall share was also quite low at less than 1 per cent, which remained so until the turn of the century. While the three sectors that had relatively better share even in 1980 continued to do well and improved their shares, few other sectors also improved their shares. These are: petroleum products, wearing apparel, leather goods, non-metallic mineral products, electrical machinery, and, of course, motor vehicles.

Even among these, not all sectors performed equally well. To understand this better, CPI, the share of an individual sector in the global production, was compared to the share of total industrial production of India in total global industrial production (Figures 4.2a–d). Textiles, chemicals and

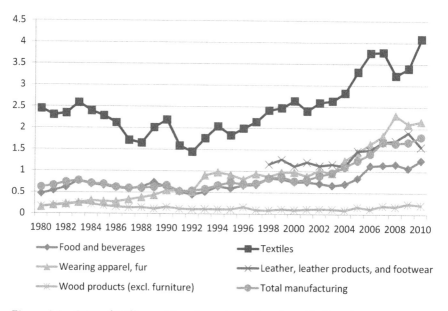

Figure 4.1a GCR of Different Manufacturing Industries of India (1/4)
Source: Created by the author based on data from the UNIDO.

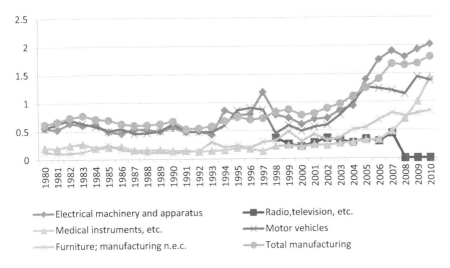

Figure 4.1b GCR of Different Manufacturing Industries of India (2/4)
Source: Created by the author based on data from the UNIDO.

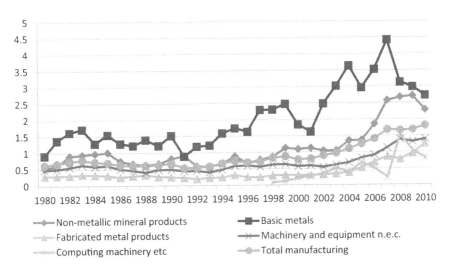

Figure 4.1c GCR of Different Manufacturing Industries of India (3/4)
Source: Created by the author based on data from the UNIDO.

chemical products, basic metals, and non-metallic mineral products showed above average performance almost throughout the period. However, the relative performance of textiles declined substantially.

In petroleum products, wearing apparel, electrical machinery, and motor vehicles, the performance was below average to start with, but improved

88 *India's industrial performance*

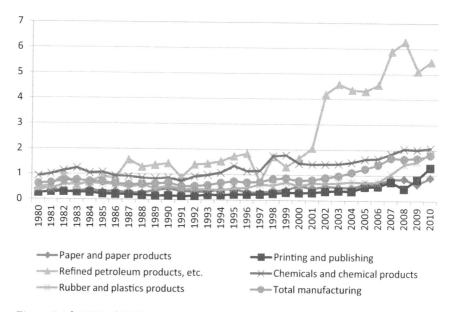

Figure 4.1d GCR of Different Manufacturing Industries of India (4/4)
Source: Created by the author based on data from the UNIDO.

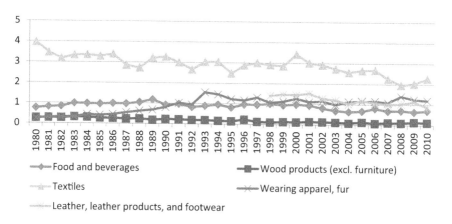

Figure 4.2a CPI of Different Manufacturing Sectors of India (1/4)
Source: Created by the author based on data from the UNIDO.

substantially to become above average. While the performance of motor vehicles and electrical machinery became above average in the mid-1990s, the same for petroleum products became above average in the mid-1980s. The motor vehicle industry, however, could not retain this performance on a consistent basis. Wearing apparel jumped into the above average category in the early 1990s.

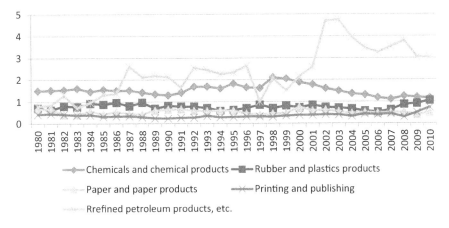

Figure 4.2b CPI of Different Manufacturing Sectors of India (2/4)
Source: Created by the author based on data from the UNIDO.

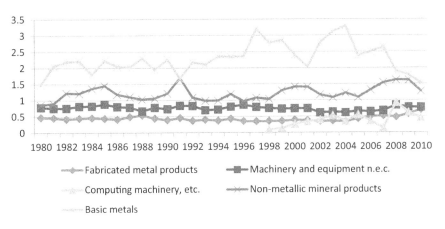

Figure 4.2c CPI of Different Manufacturing Sectors of India (3/4)
Source: Created by the author based on data from the UNIDO.

4.5.2 The global context

Some of the industrial sectors experienced increasing GCR since mid-1990s. Does this necessarily mean that the Indian industry, in general, has been showing improved performance since 1990s? Not really. An important dimension to consider is the nature of the industry and the global scenario, including structural change at the global level. If the industry in question is a mature or sunset industry and the developed countries are exiting them to focus more on new or sunrise industries, then the performance measured in terms of the share in global production may not be good enough.

90 *India's industrial performance*

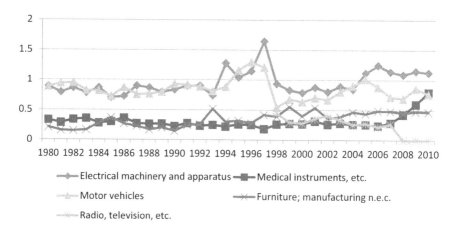

Figure 4.2d CPI of Different Manufacturing Sectors of India (4/4)
Source: Created by the author based on data from the UNIDO.

One way to check for this phenomenon could be to look at the global growth rate of the industry or the sector. If a sector is showing constant or faster growth, then for a particular country, it is desirable to have a greater share in global production. To take this factor into account, the measure may be checked against the growth of the industry globally. Another aspect that needs to be checked is the growth of the industry in developed countries or their share in global production. If the shares of developed countries are declining, it might represent a sunset or declining industry and excessive expansion in that sector might involve some risks.

At the aggregate level, the share of developed countries, particularly the US and Japan in global industrial production, has seen a massive decline (Figure 4.3a). Even other countries like the UK, France, Canada, and Spain have seen a substantial decline in their shares. But only China and South Korea could take advantage of this in a substantial measure. While the share of the US increased in the first half of the 1980s, it fell in the second half of the 1980s then rose again almost until the end of the 1990s, and collapsed afterwards. The share of Japan increased throughout the 1980s and during the first few years of the 1990s, but collapsed thereafter. The share of South Korea increased throughout the period, with a temporary dip around 1997 during the Asian financial crisis.

The general trend in developed countries showed that they vacated the space since the mid-1990s, but India was hardly able to take advantage of it. Even other developing countries, especially the Asian countries like Indonesia and Malaysia, showed a better performance in relative terms (Figure 4.3b).

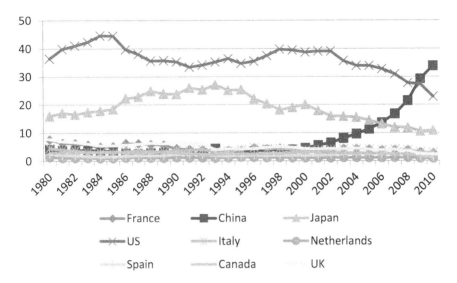

Figure 4.3a Share of Different Countries in Global Industrial Production (per cent) (1/2)

Source: Created by the author based on data from the UNIDO.

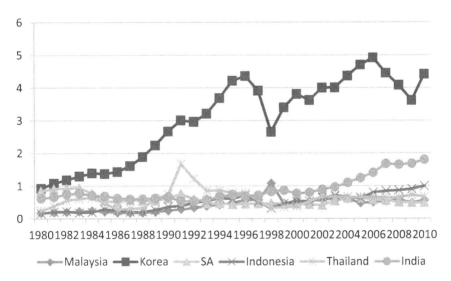

Figure 4.3b Share of Different Countries in Global Industrial Production (per cent) (2/2)

Source: Created by the author based on data from the UNIDO.

92 India's industrial performance

In 1980, South Korea was marginally better than India, but in 2010, it was substantially better. It is also to be noted that not only for all these Asian countries, but also for South Africa, shares in global production increased substantially since the mid-1990s, and hence, there is nothing special about the growth in Indian share since the mid-1990s. It is interesting to note that China was almost stagnant throughout the 1980s and 1990s but it grew in leaps and bounds thereafter. It seems that the entry of China in the WTO in 2001 made a huge difference for China, as well as other countries. The entry of China meant reduced duty for its exports in other countries. This benefitted China hugely, but other countries had to face competitive pressure from Chinese exports.

It is also important to look at how the manufacturing industry and its different components performed in absolute terms. For this, the data were converted from value added in current prices to value added in constant 2009 US dollars by using the US dollar GDP deflator. In both the US and Japan, the manufacturing industry shrunk in absolute terms. While in Japan this declining trend was set in the mid-1990s, in the US, a similar trend was set at the turn of the century (Figure 4.4). It is also interesting to note that while in Japan, such a declining trend was observed in all segments of the manufacturing sector, in the US it was observed in all sectors except chemicals and chemical products (Figures 4.5a–b).

One question that might come up here is if the exclusion of Germany might have distorted the picture. For Germany, data are available for the year 1998 onwards, and hence, it was possible to have an analysis for the period

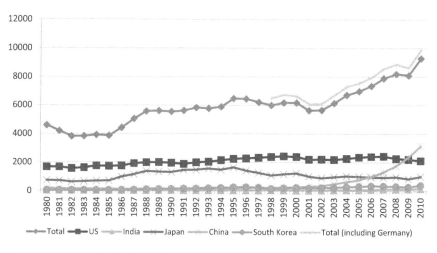

Figure 4.4 Growth of Industrial Production in Different Countries and the World (in billion 2008–09 US dollars)

Source: Created by the author based on data from the UNIDO.

India's industrial performance 93

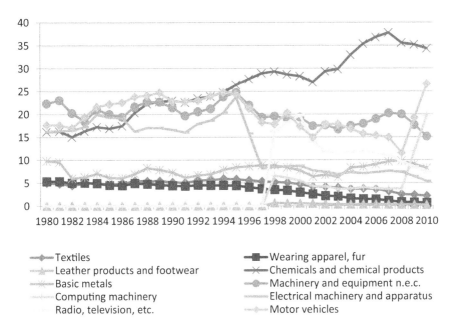

Figure 4.5a Value Added in Select Manufacturing Sectors in the US (in billion US 2008–09 dollars)

Source: Created by the author based on data from the UNIDO.

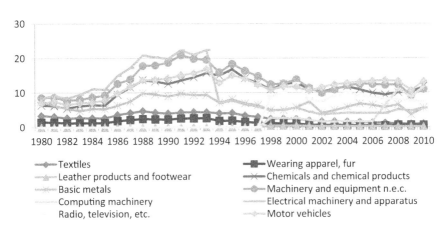

Figure 4.5b Value Added in Select Manufacturing Sectors in Japan (in billion US 2008–09 dollars)

Source: Created by the author based on data from the UNIDO.

94 *India's industrial performance*

1998–2010 with Germany being included in the dataset. For this period, it is observed that Germany had been able to retain its share in global manufacturing value added (Figure 4.6). Hence, its exclusion is unlikely to impact the structural change in the rest of the world in any significant manner. In terms of absolute performance also, Germany did not experience any shrinkage of manufacturing industry as was seen in the US and Japan. Rather, it was able to post moderate growth in its manufacturing industry. The trend was similar in almost all segments of industry (Figure 4.7).

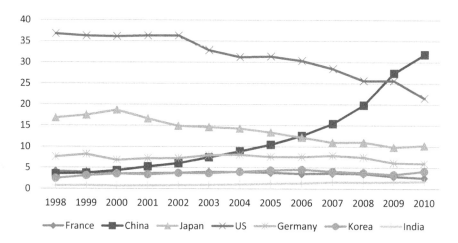

Figure 4.6 Share of Select Countries in Global Industrial Production (including Germany) (per cent)

Source: Created by the author based on data from the UNIDO.

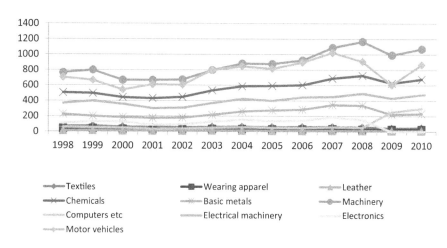

Figure 4.7 Growth of Select Manufacturing Sectors in Germany (in million US 2008–09 dollars)

Source: Created by the author based on data from the UNIDO.

4.5.3 Comparing across countries

Looking at the Indian performance (GCR) in a few sectors in comparison with select countries, it appears that India had an opportunity to make a difference in some sectors but it could not. The textiles industry is one such missed opportunity for India. While India did improve its share marginally, it could not take advantage of the massive decline in the shares of countries like the US and Japan (Figure 4.8a). While South Korea took advantage of it in the 1980s and 1990s, it was China that increased its share in global production particularly since the mid-1990s. India could not make much of a dent even after South Korea started exiting the scene since the mid-1990s. The story of wearing apparel is similar to that of the textiles industry (Figure 4.8b).

In chemical and chemical products, while India did improve its share, it is not comparable to China (Figure 4.8c). Interestingly, in this sector, the US and Japan experienced only moderate cut in their shares, and by and large, they were able to maintain their shares. This is possibly due to the fact that this sector includes pharmaceutical products, as well, in which they were able to maintain their hold due to a stronger IPR regime which might have allowed them to keep control over business in high value medicines.

Electronic goods (radio, television, etc.) is one sector where India's performance has been quite poor (Figure 4.8d). There has been a massive cut in the shares of both the US and Japan but the gainers have been China and South Korea. These two countries pushed down the US and Japan from their dominance in the global market.

In motor vehicles, the US and Japan have lost their shares but only marginally (Figure 4.8e). China has improved its share substantially. Indian performance is relatively good. Along with chemical and chemical products, this is one sector where it has been able to compete respectably with South Korea.

In computers and office equipment, though the US has experienced substantial decline, it remains a major player (Figure 4.8f). Japan has been able to maintain its share. South Korea has improved its share substantially to join the league of the US and Japan. This is one sector in which China, though it improved its share, could not push down the three major players, the US, Japan, and South Korea. India could not make much of dent in this sector.

In petroleum products, Indian performance has been reasonably good, as its share is even higher than Japan and South Korea (Figure 4.8g). As in most other industries, China has improved its share massively, but the US decline in the sector has been marginal, and hence, along with China, it remains one of the two dominant players.

Indian performance in basic metals has also been quite good (Figure 4.8h). Not only has it been able to take over South Korea; it is also competing with the US, Japan, and China.

96 *India's industrial performance*

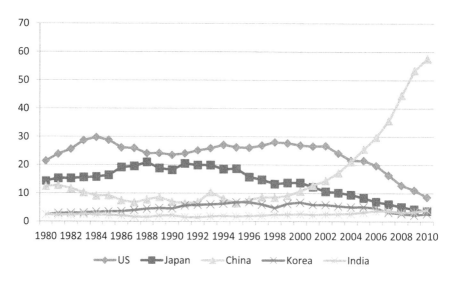

Figure 4.8a GCR of Select Countries in Textiles
Source: Created by the author based on data from the UNIDO.

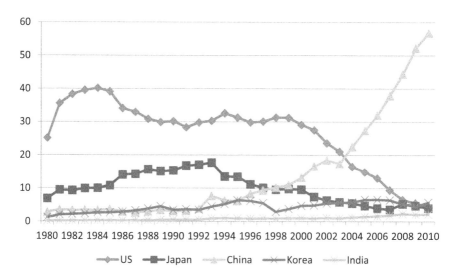

Figure 4.8b GCR of Select Countries in Wearing Apparel
Source: Created by the author based on data from the UNIDO.

India's industrial performance 97

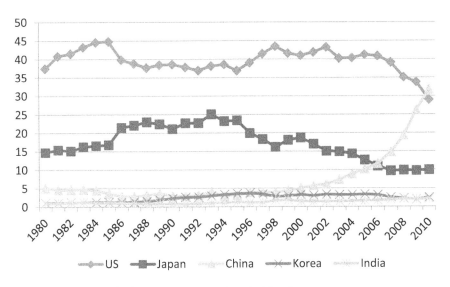

Figure 4.8c GCR of Select Countries in Chemical Products
Source: Created by the author based on data from the UNIDO.

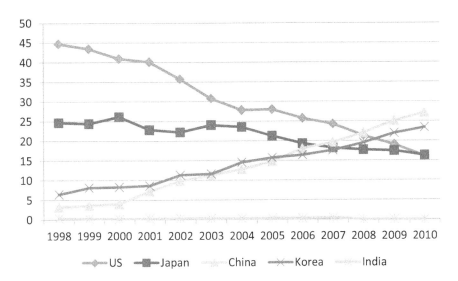

Figure 4.8d GCR of Select Countries in Electronic Goods
Source: Created by the author based on data from the UNIDO.

98 *India's industrial performance*

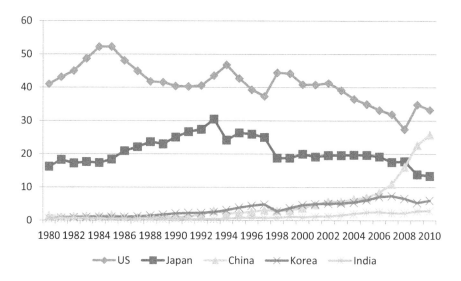

Figure 4.8e GCR of Select Countries in Vehicles
Source: Created by the author based on data from the UNIDO.

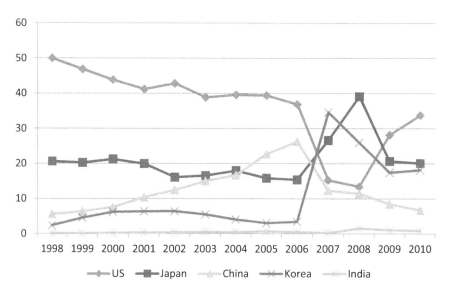

Figure 4.8f GCR of Select Countries in Computers and Office Equipment
Source: Created by the author based on data from the UNIDO.

India's industrial performance 99

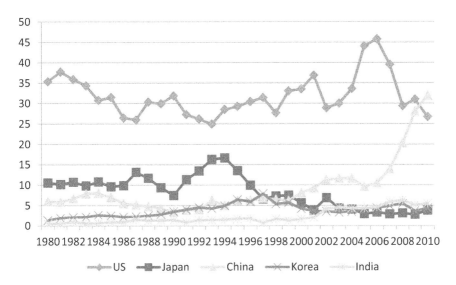

Figure 4.8g GCR of Select Countries in Petroleum Products
Source: Created by the author based on data from the UNIDO.

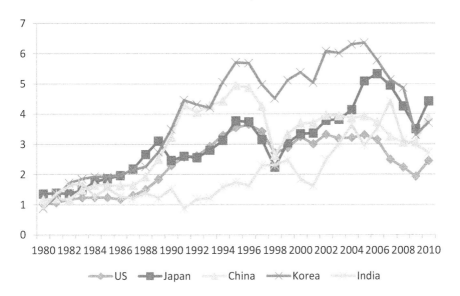

Figure 4.8h GCR of Select Countries in Basic Metals
Source: Created by the author based on data from the UNIDO.

4.5.4 Measuring absolute competitive advantage

As noted earlier, performance measured in terms of share in global production is also compared with performance in international trade as measured through ACA. The data for this is sourced from UN COMTRADE. To keep parity with the estimates of GCR and CPI, data at two-digit level is used here. The data are available for the period 1988–2016. However, since the export-import figures of electrical and electronic equipment are clubbed together at two-digit level, figures were taken at four-digit levels and then were combined into two different categories, electrical and electronic equipment, in line with the UNIDO two-digit level classification.

In this measure (ACA), the textiles industry shows an overall declining trend right from 1988 up to 2016. In wearing apparel, though an increasing trend was seen during 1988–98, a declining trend was seen thereafter. These are quite consistent with the performance trend measured with CPI earlier. The increase in share in global production in these two segments came largely from increasing demand in the domestic market rather than better performance in the global market. The trade performance of leather goods and footwear is also similar to that of the textiles industry.

Chemical products, petroleum products, and motor vehicles sectors have shown relatively better performance (compared to other industries), with an increasing trend in ACA. In absolute terms, ACA varies widely due to the fact that in some industries' export and import figures are comparable, while in other industries, they vary widely. This trend is consistent with their

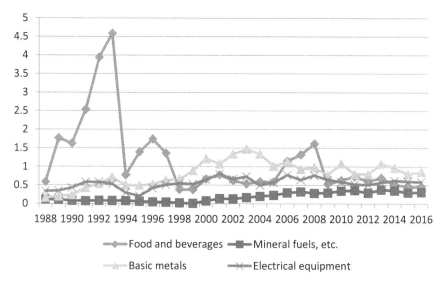

Figure 4.9a ACA of Select Manufacturing Sectors of India (1/3)
Source: Created by the author based on data from COMTRADE.

India's industrial performance 101

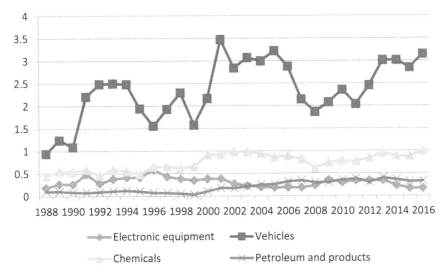

Figure 4.9b ACA of Select Manufacturing Sectors of India (2/3)
Source: Created by the author based on data from COMTRADE.

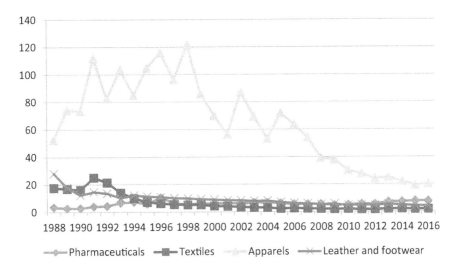

Figure 4.9c ACA of Select Manufacturing Sectors of India (3/3)
Source: Created by the author based on data from COMTRADE.

performance in terms of their shares in global production. In basic metals also, the performance was good with an increasing trend until 2002 but it showed a declining trend since then. In electrical machinery and equipment, a moderate increase in ACA was observed, while in electronic goods, ACA

102 *India's industrial performance*

showed a declining trend. These are also consistent with the trends in GCR and CPI.

4.6   An analysis of performance

The preceding assessment of industrial performance in India based on the estimates of GCR, CPI, and ACA, in particular, when looked at in the context of changing global scenario, as well as what some other developing countries like China, South Korea, Thailand, and Malaysia have been able to achieve, makes it quite obvious that the overall industrial performance in India has been rather subdued. In most sectors, the Indian share in global production was quite stagnant until about the mid-1990s.

Some sectors that performed better are textiles, and chemical and chemical products, and basic metals had an early success. Petroleum products, wearing apparel, leather goods, non-metallic mineral products, electrical machinery, and motor vehicles improved their performance over time.

If competitiveness performance is considered, textiles, chemicals and chemical products, basic metals, and non-metallic mineral products showed above average performance, though the relative performance of textiles declined. Substantial improvement was seen over time in the performance of petroleum products, wearing apparel, electrical machinery, and motor vehicles.

While developed countries vacated space for developing countries in most sectors, India could not take much advantage from the phenomenon. Looking at how some developing countries like South Korea, China, Thailand, Malaysia, and Indonesia occupied this vacated space, textiles, wearing apparel, electronic goods, and computers are cases of missed opportunity for India. India, however, did slightly better in basic metals, chemicals, petroleum products, and automobiles.

As far as ACA is concerned, textiles, wearing apparel, electronic goods, leather goods, and footwear showed declining performance, while chemical products, petroleum products, and automobiles showed markedly improving performance over time. One sector that showed moderate improvement in performance is electrical machinery. Electronic goods, however, showed some improvement in performance during the late 1980s and the early 1990s which could not be maintained for long.

Taking all these into consideration, the sectors that can be claimed to have shown better performance are basic metals, petroleum products, pharmaceuticals and chemicals, electrical machinery, and automobiles. It would be interesting to have a closer look at the sectors that have shown better performance, and in particular, if these sectors operated under some policy regimes that are specific to them and are different from those faced by other sectors. Interestingly, while some earlier studies indicated better performance in petroleum products, chemicals, and basic metals, they did not indicate similar performance in electrical machinery and automobiles. Moreover, some other sectors, like textiles, apparel and leather goods, were found to have performed better in some studies, but the findings here are not quite similar.

It would also be worthwhile to have a closer look at a couple of sectors that held out substantial promise which could not be realized. One such sector is textiles and apparel. This is the sector that was reasonably developed when India got its Independence. Moreover, this industry developed mostly through indigenous entrepreneurship, and technology being relatively standardized, access to technology should not have been a constraint. India is also reasonably well endowed with the basic raw materials and skills needed for the industry.

Another industry that appears to be a good candidate for a detailed analysis is the electronics and information technology industry. In contrast to the textile industry, it was a new kid on the block as it started developing during the 1970s. While the textile industry could have had legacy-related baggage holding back its growth, the electronics industry did not have to suffer such things. The electronics industry was, however, important for one more reason. It was not just a sunrise industry, but also had its growing use in almost all other industries, as all durable goods and machineries were becoming automated. Thus, success in this industry was important for overall industrial development of the country. Taking these into consideration, both textiles and apparel, and electronics and information technology, are also being taken up for a closer look. These are also the two industries that received substantial attention of the government over several decades.

4.6.1 Automobiles

Among the better-performing industries, this is the only sector that did not receive much importance at the beginning of India's planned development era. But today, the automobile industry is one of the most important manufacturing industries of the Indian economy. By virtue of having strong backward and forward linkages, the automobile industry has also become among the key sectors of the Indian economy (Miglani 2019). The industry contributed about 2.77 per cent to Indian GDP in 1992–93, which went up to about 7.1 per cent in 2018, and it constitutes about 27 per cent of manufacturing GDP of India. It offers employment to about 32 million people, including indirect employment that the sector generates. The automobiles sector is one of the biggest metal products consumers. Steel, aluminium, copper, magnesium, and zinc are widely used in the automobile industry. Hence, the industry also gave a huge boost to metal industry in India.

Though cars started plying Indian roads during the nineteenth century, the automobile industry had its beginning in the 1940s as the Hindustan Motors, Premier, and Mahindra & Mahindra were launched in 1942, 1944, and 1945, respectively. After Independence, the government attempted to develop an auto components industry in the country, and in 1953 it imposed restrictions on import of completely built up cars. Since it *de facto* banned

104 *India's industrial performance*

manufacture of cars with purely imported components, some foreign companies like Ford and General Motors which had only assembly plants had to leave India.

During the 1950s and 1960s, the growth of the industry was very slow, but in the 1970s, it picked up a bit due to stricter restrictions on imports – but only in the commercial vehicles and tractors segments. Price controls on cars were lifted but the existing car makers continued with their old models even throughout the 1980s. Interestingly, the modernization of the Indian automobile industry happened through the initiatives of the government of India. In 1981, the government of India established Maruti Udyog Limited, which launched a joint venture with Suzuki Motor Corporation of Japan the following year. In 1983, the company produced its first car in its Gurgaon factory, the Maruti 800, a small 796cc car.

From the very beginning, the company's focus was to source its components locally and it extended generous assistance with technology and know-how to local entrepreneurs, and as a result, a vibrant auto component manufacturing cluster developed around Gurgaon (Khan 2015). In due course, the company launched several models and became the leader in the Indian market. Even now, it captures about 50 per cent of the passenger car market in India, even though most of the global automobile manufacturers are present in Indian market now. The government also established the Ordnance Factory Medak in Andhra Pradesh (now Telengana) that started producing Infantry Combat Vehicles named "Sarath", which is, even now, the only ICV manufactured in India. In 1987, the government established the Engine Factory Avadi in Tamil Nadu to make high-power engines used in ICVs and main battle tanks.

Following the 1991 liberalization of the FDI regime, India conditionally allowed foreign companies to set up factories in India. Foreign car manufacturers had to comply with two requirements that were included in the MOUs that these companies had to sign with the government: (i) an indigenization requirement, meaning that the company had to follow a roadmap for use of India-made components up to certain level as specified; (ii) a trade balancing requirement, meaning that the companies had to export to finance its imports of components.

These two requirements forced companies to buy components from India and assist Indian component manufacturers to produce as per their standards. This facilitated substantial transfer of technologies. In 2000, the US, backed by the EU, launched a WTO dispute claiming India's indigenization and trade balancing requirements to be WTO-incompatible. India lost the case and had to do away with these requirements in 2002. By then, the Indian auto component industry was substantially developed with the capability to produce world-class components at cheaper prices. Hence, it made economic sense for these companies to use India-made components. Moreover, after this, India also increased tariff barriers on several tariff lines, many of which continue even now.

Empirical findings reveal that there are significant variations in technology spillover effects of FDI across different industrial clusters in India. While in some clusters, technology spillover benefits from the presence of foreign firms were limited within the clusters only, in others, such benefits were enjoyed even in other clusters within the region (Behera et al. 2012). It is also interesting to note that the study found the highest technology spillover in the Gurgaon automobile cluster. This was not accidental, as the Indian government had followed a domestic content requirement and import rebalancing policy in automobiles sector which had to be abandoned subsequently due to a WTO ruling.

It is interesting to note that policies related to FDI in automobile industry adopted in the 1990s were similar to those adopted in the 1950s. Yet, the new policies adopted in the 1950s made the existing foreign players leave India, while in the 1990s, several foreign players decided to enter India. This only goes to show that similar polices can produce different outcomes in a country over different time periods. The fact that in the 1950s, the potential size of the domestic market was quite small compared to what it is now could be an important determining factor in this regard.

The Indian automobile industry has enjoyed substantial tariff protection. During 1997–98, this industry had among the highest average tariff. By 2001–02, while there was a decline in the average tariff in this industry, the peak tariff within this industry increased from 45 per cent in 1997–98 to 105 per cent in 2001–02 (Table 4.1). This indicates that the government adopted strategic tariff policy in this sector and accorded a high level of protection to some segments. By 2015, while the average tariff in this sector came down substantially, at 19.4 per cent, it remained the highest among the non-food manufacturing sectors, and the peak tariff in automobile remained as high as 100 per cent.

This industry also received substantial development finance. While it is well known that the revival of the industrial sector in the 1980s owed much to government investment that attracted substantial development finance, it continued to attract development finance at least until the turn of the century. As estimated by Nayyar (2015), this industry, along with machinery, attracted about 12 per cent of total development finance available in the country throughout the 1980s and 1990s, and came down to around 8 per cent by 2002–03.

4.6.2 Basic metals

There are three major groups in the basic metals industry: basic iron and steel, basic non-ferrous metals, and metal casting. The major non-ferrous metals include aluminium, copper, nickel, tin, lead, silver, and gold. These metals are generally more expensive than steel. Among these non-ferrous metals, the widely used are aluminium, copper, zinc, lead, nickel, and tin, although steel is, by far, the most widely used among all metals in the world. In India, too,

106 *India's industrial performance*

the metal industry is dominated by steel. India occupies the third position in steel production in the world, while China and Japan occupy the first and second positions, respectively. In 2016–17, Indian finished steel production was more than 100 million tonnes. The industry contributes about 2 per cent to India's GDP and accounts for about 6 per cent of the total industrial production in India (Ministry of Steel 2018).

The Second Five Year Plan (1956–61) of India put emphasis on the development of basic and heavy industries, and basic metal industry – the steel industry in particular – was at its core. It was also envisaged that the public sector had to play a key role in the development of this industry. Hence, the government established Hindustan Steel Limited (HSL), which was given the responsibility of setting up three steel plants at Rourkela, Bhilai, and Durgapur, each having an ingot capacity of one million tonnes per year. Rourkela and Bhilai plants came into operation in December 1961, and the Durgapur plant was commissioned just more than a month later, in January 1962.

The first modern steel plant in India, however, came into existence with the setting up of Bengal Iron and Steel Company at Barakar in 1875. However, the real beginning of the steel industry took place in 1907 with the establishment of Tata Iron and Steel Company (TISCO) near Sakchi in Bihar (now Jamshedpur in Jharkhand). It launched a major modernization and expansion programme in 1951. Nevertheless, the government thought much more steel would be needed in the country to meet its rising demand. After the three plants were commissioned, the work for the fourth plant in Bokaro started in 1965, which came on stream in 1972. Immediately after this, HSL was renamed Steel Authority of India Limited (SAIL). At present, SAIL has five integrated steel plants, three special steel plants, and one ferro-alloy plant. In 1982, another public sector steel company, Rashtriya Ispat Nigam Limited, was established at Vishakhapatnam. After the liberalization of the sector, several private companies – including Jindal, Essar, and Bhushan – came into this business. However, about one-third of steel is still produced in the public sector.

As against this, Indian aluminium production is just about two million tonnes per annum. It occupies the seventh position in the production of aluminium in the world, occupying about 3 per cent share in global capacity, though it is the fifth largest miner of bauxite in the world, and also holds the fifth position in bauxite reserves. Globally, transport and construction sectors consume about half of aluminium, but in India, it is quite different. About half of aluminium is consumed in the electrical sector, as Indian power companies prefer aluminium over copper due its cost. Naturally, growth of the power sector has played a major role in the growth of aluminium industry in India.

India is estimated to have about 2 per cent of global copper reserves. However, Indian copper production is just about 0.2 per cent of global production (IBM 2020). Nevertheless, Indian refined copper production is about 4 per cent of global production, and it had been a net exporter of refined copper and copper products – though it imports copper ores and concentrates in substantial quantity.[4] Industrial copper production in India started in 1967 with the establishment of government-owned Hindustan Copper Limited (HCL). A few private companies have come up, but HCL remains a dominant player in mining, production, and export of refined copper. Private companies depend entirely on imported ores and concentrates or secondary material. Globally, about half of copper is used in construction, but in India, about one-third of consumption of copper occurs in the electrical goods industry, while the construction industry depends more on steel.

Zinc production and consumption have been increasing, primarily because galvanizing consumes about 70 per cent of zinc in India. This industry also owes its origin to the public sector as the Hindustan Zinc Limited, a government-established company, has been the major producer. The company went into private hands in 2002, but it is still the major producer. Another company, Binani Zinc, produces small quantities of zinc. The current production capacity in India is about 1.5 million tonnes, and about one-third of it is exported (IBM 2020).

India also produces about 100,000 tonnes of lead in a year, mostly by Hindustan Zinc. Lead is consumed mostly in batteries, and a substantial part of that is used in the automotive sector. The recent thrust on solar energy has been boosting the demand for batteries, and hence, lead as well.

An important factor that catalyzed the growth of the basic metals industry in India has been the availability of ores, in particular for steel and aluminium. Until recently, the government allotted coal and iron ore on first-come, first-served basis at negligible costs. The Indian basic metal industry is largely steel-making, and India having substantial deposits of iron ore of good quality has been a boon to this industry. To facilitate more, the government also from time to time imposed different forms of restrictions on the export of iron ore. Export duty was imposed in 2007, which was relaxed later for low grade iron ore. Earlier, iron ore could be exported only through State Trading Corporation (STC) and Minerals and Metals Trading Corporation (MMTC), and hence, there was restriction on exports (Lok Sabha Secretariat 2013).

Demand for basic metals in India grew in the wake of growing activities in infrastructure, construction, automobiles, and power. The government played a direct or indirect role in all of these sectors. Until recently, before China developed a huge excess capacity in steel, Indian consumers rarely imported it, as Indian steel was competitive. Though there was no official policy of preference for domestic steel, as has been announced by the government recently, the government usually bought Indian steel for its projects.

Preference in public procurement to domestically produced goods also helped the industry. According to the General Financial Rules (GFR), 1963, which guided public procurement in India, "The policy of Government is to make purchases of stores for public service in such a way as to encourage development of indigenous production of stores to the utmost possible extent and to make the country self-sufficient in the matter of its own

108   *India's industrial performance*

requirements" (cited in Hoda and Bansal 2004). Apart from government departments, GFR applies to various government agencies, as well as government-owned companies. According to GFR, the goods wholly produced in India get the first preference, while goods that are manufactured in India from imported materials and the goods produced by foreign manufactures but held in stock in India get the second and third preferences, respectively. Then come the turn of Indian agents or India-based establishments that offer to supply by importing from abroad. Two other types of preferences are also admissible. While domestically produced goods are preferred over imported goods, goods produced by cottage and small-scale industry are also preferred over the goods made by large producers. Since steel has been among the major items that government departments, agencies and government-owned companies procured, particularly in infrastructure development like roads, railways, ports and power plants, the steel industry benefitted greatly from the policy of preference for domestic products in public procurement.

Favourable policy in consuming sectors has also been important in promoting this industry. Apart from the different infrastructure sectors that the government promoted, the automobile industry that the government actively promoted is also an important industry that consumes steel and copper. Despite not having enough deposits of copper, India is a major producer of copper products. This is largely due to favourable policy for the copper consuming sector. Development of capability in steel has also been a catalyst for developing other sectors like aluminium, copper and zinc.

Development finance could also have been an important stimulator for the growth of this sector in India. According to Nayyar (2015), this sector attracted about 8.5 per cent of total development finance during the 1980s, which went up to more than 12 per cent in the 1990s. While India received technologies for the development of this industry from countries like the UK, Germany, and Russia (previously, the Soviet Union), the technology required to produce steel is relatively simple and largely embedded in plants and machineries that are available from market (Lall 1987).

4.6.3   *Petroleum products*

The petroleum products industry is among the very few industries where India is considered to be a global player. It is the fourth largest petroleum refiner in the world only after the US, China, and Russia. Even Brazil, despite having substantial petroleum reserves, is an importer of refined petroleum products. In 2015–16, India produced 36.95 million tonnes of crude petroleum but it produced 231.92 million tonnes of petroleum products (MOPNG 2016).

Although India imports more than 75 per cent of its crude oil requirements and a small part of the refined petroleum product requirements, India's processing capacity for different petroleum products is far in excess of its domestic requirements, and hence, it exports the same in substantial quantity. In

2015–16, India exported 60.53 million tonnes of petroleum products, almost double of its export of 33.62 million tonnes in 2006–07 (MOPNG 2016). Indian petroleum companies have also acquired substantial assets (oil and gas fields) in different parts of the world, particularly over the last decade or so.

The petroleum and petroleum products industry took off in India in 1901 as the Assam Oil Company (AOC) set up an oil refining plant in Digboi in the state of Assam. AOC was bought by Burmah Oil Company, which later came to be known as Burmah Shell, and then Shell. The refinery is still functional after several rounds of expansion and modernization. Yet, the industry overall did not see much progress until the early 1950s, and India met its demand largely through imports from Iran by three companies: Burmah Shell, Standard Vacuum, and Caltex.

After Independence, India became keen to explore crude and to enhance its refining capacity. India approached these companies for setting up refineries in India in 1951, but it was difficult to finalize the terms under which such refineries could be set up, as these companies bargained very hard. In 1951, Iran nationalized its Abdan refinery, which was the main source of refined oil for India. After this, these companies considered India to be safer and an attractive place for investment. All three companies signed agreements with the government to set up refineries in India.

Meanwhile, AOC found oil in Naharkotia in 1953, but the negotiations on the terms under which the oil would be exploited became difficult. After six years of negotiations, AOC and the government decided to set up a 67:33 joint venture to exploit the Naharkotia oilfield and Oil India Limited came into being. In 1961, Oil India became a 50:50 joint venture. Meanwhile, in 1953, the Indian government and Standard Vacuum formed a 25:75 joint venture for conducting a survey in the state of West Bengal. Though some prospecting was done and some gas was found, it was unviable for commercial exploitation, and no oil was found. However, many believed that Standard Vacuum did not put enough effort as it had easy access to cheap crude from the Gulf (Kaul 1991).

The Indian government, therefore, established the Oil and Natural Gas Commission in 1956 with the objective of exploring oil and gas in India. ONGC started its operations with the help of Soviet and Romanian technology, machinery, and personnel, and soon discovered oil in Gujarat. As a result, the government decided to set up Indian Refineries in 1958. The Indian Oil Company set up in 1959 was given the responsibility of distribution. Soon the two were merged to form Indian Oil Corporation, which was given the exclusive right to import refined petroleum products into India. Very soon, the company established a lead over the three foreign companies in distribution business. Thus, the petroleum industry got well established in India with government leadership. By 1979, the subsidiaries of foreign oil companies also came into government fold. What was earlier Burmah Shell is now Bharat Petroleum, and the combined entity of Standard Vacuum and Caltex is now Hindustan Petroleum.

110 *India's industrial performance*

To take advantage of the growing petroleum refining capacity, and hence, the easy availability of raw materials, the Indian Petrochemical Corporation Limited (IPCL) was established by the government of India in 1969. In the 1980s, Reliance also entered the field. After the government of India decided to dilute its stake, Reliance acquired a 26 per cent stake in the IPCL in 2002. Eventually, IPCL was merged with Reliance in 2007. Meanwhile, Reliance also entered the petroleum refining business after the sector was liberalized. It commissioned its Jamnagar refinery plant in 1999. The Jamnagar refinery complex, with an aggregate refining capacity of 1.24 million barrels (197,000 m^3) of oil per day, has now become the world's largest refining complex. The complex was accorded a Special Economic Zone status in December 2008 due to its export orientation, and thus India went on to become a major exporter of refined petroleum in the world.

It is doubtful if Indian petroleum refining and petrochemical industry could have reached where it is today without huge government investment and regulation. It is quite clear that foreign companies were quite reluctant to make substantial investments in this sector. For the private sector, finance and technology are serious constraints. The fact that oil-rich countries like Brazil and Nigeria have not been able to create a processing capacity in their countries amply shows how difficult it is to develop this industry in a developing country. The Indian government could access the required technologies that were needed through diplomatic channels, which would have been difficult otherwise. Later on, when the private sector made a foray into this sector, it had the advantage of having easy access to the technology available within the country. It also benefitted from access to skilled human resources trained by government-owned companies.

The Indian market has been protected from foreign competition, not just through import tariffs, but the domestic market for petroleum retail trading was virtually reserved for state-owned companies. While petroleum products attracted a substantial tax, for a long period, the government also reduced the burden by giving some subsidies only to state-owned companies. Contrary to the popular perception that petroleum prices were subsidized, India kept prices of petroleum product on the higher side, giving domestic petroleum companies a substantial advantage. Since government most often linked the regulated price of petroleum products to international prices, domestic companies benefitted from the crude that they produced within India, the costs of which were much lower from the international prices. This sector also attracted substantial development finance, particularly in the 1990s (Nayyar 2015).

4.6.4 *Pharmaceuticals*

The pharmaceutical industry has become one of the major industries in India. Currently, it contributes about 1.72 per cent to Indian GDP and accounts for about 11 per cent of manufacturing value added in India (DOP 2020). The industry has shown a steady growth in recent years. From a modest turnover of about $1 billion in 1990, it reached a turnover of about $39 billion in 2019. In 2019–20, its exports crossed $16 billion, with about one-third of it going to the US, the most complex and regulated market in the world (IBEF 2020). India now occupies the third position in the world in terms of volume with a 10 per cent share in global production, and 14th position in value terms, holding a 1.5 per cent share in the world (IBEF 2020).

India's modern pharmaceutical industry dates back to the early twentieth century, when the noted scientist Acharya Prafulla Chandra Roy, driven by his nationalistic urge, established Bengal Chemical and Pharmaceutical Work (BCPW) Ltd in Calcutta (now Kolkata) in 1901. A few years later, Alembic Chemical Works Co. Ltd. was set up in Baroda (now Vadodara) in 1907 by T. K. Grajjar, Rajmitra and B. D. Amin. Nevertheless, the Indian pharmaceutical industry could not show any remarkable performance until 1970. With a more than 75 per cent share of the domestic market, foreign suppliers dominated the market and the consumers were forced to pay relatively high prices (Nanda and Khan 2006).

Given this situation, during 1950–70, the government relied on government-owned companies to ensure supply of essential medicines at affordable prices. These government companies, along with government research organizations led by the Council of Scientific and Industrial Research, played a key role in developing local capabilities in India. These government entities can be credited with building the foundation of the India pharmaceutical industry, even though they have now virtually faded out from the pharmaceutical industry scene in the country. Public sector pharmaceutical companies as well as domestic private companies still get preference in government procurement of medicines (CUTS 2012). This can be considered the first phase of the Indian pharmaceutical industry.

The second phase of the Indian pharmaceutical industry started with a major shift in its patent regime that denied product patents in medicines and allowed process patents only through a 1970 amendment to the Patents Act, 1911. It is now considered to be the key factor that helped establish a healthy and vibrant pharmaceutical industry in India. While product patent offers exclusive monopoly right to the inventor of a new drug or molecule, a "process only" patent regime allows other firms to produce the same drug or molecule, provided that they are able to devise a new process or method of production.

The new regime provided substantial leeway to Indian drug makers to produce a range of medicines by developing new methods to produce the existing drugs through reverse engineering, which they were simply not allowed to engage in earlier. The industry was also given substantial protection through import duty, except for life-saving drugs. Price regulation also came as an opportunity for many domestic companies, as foreign companies were reluctant to manufacture those medicines, leaving the space for domestic companies (Nanda and Khan 2006). This attracted many Indian

112 *India's industrial performance*

companies to enter the industry. The liberalization of 1991 gave further boost to the industry.

Since the R&D costs for developing new methods or process were substantially lower compared to the development of the product itself, Indian companies could offer them at substantially lower prices. Moreover, these medicines – often referred to as generic drugs – brought competition in the market, forcing the original inventors also to price them moderately to remain in business. The new patent policy played an important role in bringing medicine prices within the reach of common people, but it also enabled several domestic entrepreneurs jump into the industry and grow their businesses therein. As a result, a domestic drug manufacturing industry that could compete globally and produce a wide range of medicines developed (Chaudhuri 2005).

Indian IPR policy was essentially to promote affordable medicines for the people of India, but it ended up promoting the pharmaceutical industry, as well. The ability of Indian pharmaceutical producers to manufacture a wide range of medicines at cheaper cost eventually made medicines affordable to the entire developing world and beyond, making it an important global player. As a result, India is often described as the pharmacy of the developing world.

The establishment of the WTO and liberalization of trade regimes across the globe in 1995 gave a further boost to the industry as Indian companies took to exports in a big way. The period 1995–2005 can be considered the third stage when the industry consolidated its position, not only in India but also globally. India now exports medicines to almost all countries in the world, with the US, Western Europe, Japan, and Australia – which are known for having highly regulated markets – emerging as major destinations. Today, India is also among the very few countries in the world, including the developed countries, where the domestic market is dominated by indigenous producers with TNC drug makers playing a secondary role. Considering where India was in 1970, this is a spectacular achievement with few parallels in the history of industrial development.

The Indian government also regulates prices of a large number of medicines. Apprehensions are often expressed that price regulation can lead to disappearing of medicines from the market, as companies will be reluctant to produce them, but in India, it worked in a different way. Big TNCs often show reluctance to produce medicines in developing countries, and if there is demand, they supply from their bases in developed countries. However, in the face of price regulation, they had to set up bases in India, as supplying to Indian market with regulated prices from developed country production was difficult. They could produce at cheaper costs only if they produced in India. And if they decided not to produce in India, the local companies could fill up the vacated space, taking advantage of India's relaxed patent regime.

In most countries, procurement of medicines by the government forms a substantial share of the domestic market. Although the Indian healthcare sector is dominated by private service providers, government facilities where medicines are available free of cost or at subsidized rates are quite substantial. According to an estimate (Planning Commission 2011), the combined procurement of drugs by governments at centre and the states accounted for about 13 per cent of the domestic sale of drug in 2010–11. Obviously, owing to its procurement policy, these medicines were procured from within India, giving a boost to the domestic pharmaceutical industry.

Along with state support like the relaxed patent regime and regulation, the Indian pharmaceutical industry also attracted a substantial amount of development finance. While it is difficult to get an estimate for the amount of development finance going to the pharmaceutical industry, according to Nayyar (2015), chemicals, fertilizers, and pharmaceuticals together accounted for 13 per cent of DF during 1980–85, which went up to 20.4 per cent during 1990–95 and remained at 16.1 per cent during 1995–2000.

Despite overwhelming success and promising indicators, the Indian pharmaceutical industry is faced with enormous challenges today. The re-introduction of product patents in 2005 brought new challenges to Indian companies. In the increasingly de-regulated and a new patent environment, many Indian companies are finding it difficult to remain in business, as many generic medicines are becoming obsolete. Even if they are able to develop new medicines, they are finding it difficult to introduce them into Western markets, due to difficulties in wading through complex regulations. The global TNC drug makers are now eying Indian pharmaceutical producers that are giving them tough competition with the objective of eliminating competition not only in the Indian market, but also in the global market (Saraswathy 2016).

4.6.5 Electrical machinery

In 2017–18, India produced about $27 billion worth of electrical machines and exported about $6.5 billion worth, down by almost 50 per cent from its 2011 level when it exported about $11.5 billion worth of electrical machines (IEEMA 2021). The industry contributes about 8 per cent to manufacturing value added and about 1.3 per cent to GDP. China and India are the only two countries in the developing world that have developed the capabilities to make the entire range of power generation and transmission equipment. The Indian electrical equipment market, however, is dominated by transmission and distribution (T&D) equipment representing about 85 per cent of the industrial production, and the generation equipment segment occupies the rest. Indian technological capability in this industry is also at par with the global standards in most segments. Consequently, Indian electrical equipment makers have been able to make forays into all major markets not only in developing countries like Brazil, Nigeria, the UAE, Egypt, Malaysia, and Saudi Arabia, but also in developed country markets like the US, the UK, Germany, France, Canada, and Australia.

114 *India's industrial performance*

For a long time, Indian electrical machinery industry was synonymous with the government-owned electrical equipment maker, Bharat Heavy Electricals Limited (BHEL), established in 1964. Not only it is the largest power plant equipment manufacturer of India, but it is also among the very few electrical equipment makers in the world with the capability to produce the entire range of generation equipment. With 17 production units, and about 20,000 MW of annual capacity for generation equipment making, it executes more than 150 projects at a time.

BHEL supplied generation equipment to about 57 per cent of all the conventional installed power generation capacities (excluding segments like solar and wind power), and the share is much higher at 65 per cent in the case of coal-based thermal capacity – which dominates the power sector in India – with about 60 per cent of installed capacity. BHEL has been constructing power plants and supplying equipment to 76 countries throughout the world. Its technological capability can be gauged from the fact that it has developed the IGCC-based model, as well as advanced ultra-supercritical technologies which are considered to be the latest technologies in this field.

While several new companies have entered the industry since the 1970s, and there is a large number of small and medium enterprises, BHEL is the mainstay of the electrical machinery industry in India. Other important players are Siemens, ABB, Crompton Greaves, Larsen & Toubro, Thermax, etc. The industry was reasonably protected from imports until at least 2001–02, but what really helped the industry grow is the massive expansion of the power sector in India over the last few decades in which government-owned power generators and utilities, both at the centre and in the states, played a major role.

Government procurement, including procurement by different departments and public sector enterprises, give preference to public sector enterprises (CUTS 2012). Moreover, the officials responsible for government procurement decision-making often find it easier to buy from public sector enterprises, as this does not bring any allegation of corruption in procurement decision. Since the power sector has largely been with the government, this has helped BHEL immensely.

4.6.6 *Textiles and apparel*

As the textile industry responds to the demand for one of the basic needs, and the fact that its technology has diffused widely, it has played a central role in the overall industrialization of many countries (Rose 2006). In a sense, from the UK to the US, Japan to South Korea and China, success in textile industry has been a precursor of overall industrialization success. This has also meant that this industry has seen many new entrants, and as a result has been among the most competitive industries. While the textile industry has been central to early industrialization in most countries, its importance fell in relative terms as a country developed. This is because even though its

India's industrial performance 115

Table 4.1 Changing Tariff Profile of India (tariffs in per cent)

Product group	1997–98		2001–02		2006		2010		2015	
	Avg. tariff	*Peak tariff*	*Avg. tariff*	*Peak tariff*	*Avg. tariff*	*Peak tariff*	*Avg. tariff*	*Peak tariff*	*Avg. tariff*	*Peak tariff*
Sugar Confections					34.4	60	34.4	60	35.9	60
Beverages and spirits	114.8	260	96.9	210	70.8	150	70.8	150	68.6	150
Fish products	20.3	60	35	35	29.6	30	29.6	30	29.9	30
Minerals	37.5	45	30.6	55	7.4	10	7.4	10	7.9	15
Metals	32.5	45	32	35						
Chemicals	34.6	192	33.8	170	7.9	100	7.8	10	7.9	10
Leather, footwear	39.8	45	32.1	35	10.1	70	10.1	70	10.1	70
Paper/furniture	30.1	45	29.3	35	9.1	10	9.1	10	9	10
Textiles	43.7	55	31.3	35	14.1	122	13.3	106	11.8	147
Apparel					19.9	97	15.1	315	12.3	53
Transport equipment	41.7	45	40.5	105	14.8	100	15.5	60	19.4	100
Non-electric machinery	27.1	45	25.9	35	7.1	10	7.2	10	7.1	10
Electric Machinery	34.7	45	26.8	35	6.9	10	6.9	10	7.2	10
Petroleum	31.0	35	25	35	9	10	8.2	10	4.9	10
Other Non-agricultural	37.1	55	30	35	8.8	10	8.7	10	8.8	10

Sources: WTO (2002), Trade Policy Review – India, Geneva: World Trade Organization; and WTO, World Tariff Profiles, Various Issues, Geneva: World Trade Organization.

demand does not fall, it does not grow as fast as the income grows. Rates of growth of textile industry, therefore, are much faster in developing countries than in developed countries.

The textile and apparel industry is one of the oldest industries in India, even though its rich traditional textile industry was virtually destroyed during the colonial period. The modern textile industry in India started in the early nineteenth century when the first textile mill in the country was established by the British in the Fort Gloster area of Howrah near Calcutta (now Kolkata) in 1818. This was not a success, and the mill was closed down after a few years. The real beginning of the industry, however, had to wait until 1854, when a Parsi cotton merchant, C. N. Davar, engaged in trading, established a cotton textile mill in Bombay (now Mumbai). Several other Parsi merchants who were engaged in trading of yarn and cloth in India, China, and Africa soon followed suit and established more textile mills, and Bombay became a centre of textile production. Less than a decade, a textile mill was established in Ahmedabad in 1861 by a Gujarati trader. Similar to

116 *India's industrial performance*

Bombay, many other Gujrati traders followed suit, and Ahmedabad soon became a rival centre.

Even though British entrepreneurs were the first to establish cotton textile mills in India, they somehow did not continue, and the Indian cotton textile industry was developed entirely by indigenous entrepreneurs. Interestingly, British entrepreneurs continued with their interest in jute textiles, and virtually controlled this segment of the industry until the time they left India after Independence. Today, the textile and apparel industry has become a vital contributor to the Indian economy, accounting for 2 per cent of GDP, 7 per cent of industrial output, and 15 per cent of export earnings in 2018–19. It is also the second largest employer in the country after agriculture, and the largest industrial employer with about 45 million of direct employment, including more than three million handloom workers across the country (Invest India 2020).

Textile broadly refers to a range of products covering woven fabrics, yarns, and fibres made from jute, polyester, cotton, wool, etc.[5] However, in a broader sense, it also includes apparel or readymade garments. The Indian textile and apparel industry has strengths across the entire value chain from fibre (both natural and synthetic), yarn, and fabric to apparel. In terms of industrial structure, it is also highly diversified with a large number of handlooms, power looms, and large and modern spinning and weaving facilities and specialized apparel. India also has abundant availability of raw materials such as cotton, silk, wool, etc., and a petrochemical industry to provide basic materials for synthetic fibres. In 1918–19, India produced about 58.1 billion square metres of cloth. While the actual figure for apparel production is not available, India exports about $40 billion worth of textiles and nearly half of that belonged to apparel, and the domestic market is estimated to be about $100 billion.

However, these figures are neither too impressive, considering the long history of the industry, nor has the industry grown to its full potential. While the Indian textile industry took birth almost a century before the British left India, it is quite obvious that they were not too enthusiastic about the growth of this industry in India. Two industries that formed the basis of British industrial revolution – namely, cotton textiles and iron and steel – had to wait in India until Indian businessmen decided to try their luck. Until the 1870s, the growth was rather lacklustre, though several mills went up; however, it posted steady growth since then. Apart from serving internal markets, Indian made yarn also found markets in China and Japan. The British textile industry was alarmed, and persuaded the British-ruled Indian government to remove duties on textile products. Interestingly, the handloom industry – which was in bad shape by then – got a new lease of life as mill-made yarn improved their viability.

Meanwhile, Japan developed its own capability and gradually pushed Indian yarn out of China and Korea by the turn of the century. So far, Indian mills were, by and large, producing yarn only. But now losing its markets in China, Japan and Korea, Indian mills also started weaving. Thus, the Indian mills became composite with both spinning and weaving facilities, as against British mills which specialized either in spinning or in weaving.

World War I broke out in 1914, which also brought good times to the Indian cotton textiles industry, as it was difficult to bring products to India from the UK. It also brought some difficulty for the industry as supply of machineries and parts that would come from the UK were disrupted. The boom, however, continued beyond the war and sustained until the Great Depression. But the Indian cotton textile industry was having hard time even before the Depression due to fierce Japanese competition. The British Indian government re-imposed import duties to protect Indian markets from Japanese competition, but also introduced imperial preference, which meant products from the UK would not attract duties. This was hardly a relief for the Indian industry, which went out of gear and many mills had to close down. The fact that the Indian economy was virtually stagnant during the inter-war period did not help the industry.

World War II brought another period of boom for the industry, but also brought the problem of disruption in the supply of machinery and parts. As a result, at Independence, the Indian textile industry was in a run-down condition. To make it worse, due to partition, cotton-growing areas went to Pakistan, causing a shortage of raw materials for the industry. While there was shortage in the market during the war years due to war purchases, the shortage continued due to partition. As a result, the government imposed several restrictions on the industry, including controls on price, production, distribution, trade and supply, etc.

With the Industrial Policy of 1948, the industry was left for the private sector to invest in, but was brought under licensing. The textile industry was divided into five groups – cotton, man-made fibres, jute, wool, and silk – for licensing and other regulatory purposes. During the planning era, the focus was on making India self-reliant in textile machinery, which started with manufacturing of spare parts. Priority was given to enhance domestic cotton production rather than its import. However, the industry also benefitted due to import restriction. The Cotton Textiles Export Promotion Council (TEX-PROCIL) was established in 1954 to promote exports of textile products, but overall, this industry got less importance compared to steel, cement, and fertilizers. Within textiles, handlooms and power looms were given preference. Eight items were reserved exclusively for production by handlooms. The National Textile Policy 1956 was adopted essentially as a follow-up to the recommendations of the Khadi and Village Industries Committee, and hence, it focused more on promoting handlooms for expanding employment and livelihood. The Khadi and Village Industries Commission was established in 1957. As a result, while the spinning segment of the mill production showed substantial growth, weaving was done more by the decentralized producers, rather than by composite or weaving mills.

118 *India's industrial performance*

During the Second Five Year Plan (1956–1961), two committees were formed: Kanungo Committee and Carve Committee. These committees came with two important recommendations: a conversion scheme for handlooms to power looms, as the productivity of handlooms was considered low and it was thought to be difficult to increase; and preference to handlooms or power looms over mill production for supplying additional requirement of cloth. Price control was relaxed, but the mill sector was subjected to excise duty, from which handlooms and power looms were exempted. A large number of power looms came up in the process, grabbing the benefits that were meant for handlooms. Due to a shortage of cotton, the government relaxed imports, but prices of cloth could not be checked. As a result, the government negotiated with the industry in which it would supply at a regulated price schedule. The decline of the mill sector continued.

In the 1960s, with the Third Five Year Plan, the government decided to encourage exports of textile products to ease foreign exchange shortages. The restriction on capacity addition on the mill sector was relaxed, and they were allowed to import modern looms. However, these did not enthuse the mill sector, especially the composite mills with weaving facilities. The spinning segment of mill sector, however, expanded a bit. Production fell far short of the government target, and the prices started increasing due to cost escalation. To cope with this, the government introduced further control and the industry was forced to devote 45 per cent of production capacity to certain varieties of cloth to be sold at government-regulated prices.

Meanwhile, the whole world – including India – witnessed a shift towards synthetic textiles which were more durable compared to cotton cloth. Initially, only the richer people favoured them due to higher price, but gradually, even poorer people started using them, as they offered value for money due to durability and certain other qualities. Realizing the need for getting into this segment, the government allowed production of synthetic fibres. Production of nylon started in 1961 and production of polyester in 1965. These were, however, seen as luxury goods, and hence, they attracted substantial excise and custom duties. But the government mandated only power looms to use such yarn. The government, however, made efforts to expand cotton cultivation area, as well as productivity enhancement through minimum price support and promotion of high-yielding varieties through research and extension services. To provide institutional support for implementing these measures, the Cotton Corporation of India was established in 1970.

This period also saw massive increases in food prices, along with increases in the price of cotton, which in turn increased the price of cloth. This meant people were left with less purchasing power, which – coupled with higher cloth prices – depressed the demand for cloth in India. These, coupled with an unfavourable policy environment, brought severe recession to the industry, and many textile firms went bankrupt. The government, faced with a spectre of massive job losses and shortfalls in cloth production, decided to take over struggling mills through the Cotton Textiles Companies (Management of Undertaking and Liquidations or Reconstructions) Act, 1967. In all, 103 mills were taken over by the government. To manage these mills, the government established the National Textile Corporation (NTC) in 1968. The power loom sector, however, continued to grow. One important policy decision that could have affected the sector was the abolition of the managing agency system – in the mid-1960s, almost one-fourth of the textile mills were under the managing agency system – but the abolition did not make much of impact on the performance of the sector.

Several policy measures were adopted in the 1970s, as well. In 1973, the Hank Yarn Obligations were imposed on the spinning mills. Hank is a form of packing yarn which handlooms can use easily. This was done to encourage the use of handlooms. In 1975, the government imposed some credit restrictions to this sector to make credit easily available to other emerging sectors. However, this measure disadvantaged the textile mills. In a big relief to the mills, the obligation of supplying controlled cloth was shifted largely to the mills operated by the NTC.

Alarmed by the growing sickness in the industry, the government set up a task force in 1974 which recommended modernization of the industry by providing subsidized capital to the textile machinery sector. The task force also recognized the need for soft loan–based modernization of the mills. This policy also encouraged flow of development finance to the sector from institutions like IDBI, IFCI, and ICICI. In the process, dependency on imported machineries was reduced substantially. In 1974, the government established the Sivaraman Committee to study the problems of the handlooms and suggest appropriate strategies. On a recommendation of the committee, the government delicensed the spinning industry up to a capacity of 50,000 spindles to stabilize the yarn supply for handlooms and to encourage co-operatives to get into spinning.

As a result of shortage of cotton in 1975–76, the government decided to step up imports of viscose and also mandated the mills to use synthetic fibres for at least 10 per cent of their raw materials. This came to be known as the Multi-Fibre Policy. Meanwhile, the government was facing a foreign exchange crisis due to the oil price shock. Hence, it stepped up efforts to manufacture synthetic fibres domestically and allocated several licenses to produce different varieties of synthetic fibres. The government also decided to give the responsibility of producing controlled cloth to NTC and handlooms, giving a big relief to the private mills.

In 1978, the National Textile Policy was announced for the first time as an integrated policy. The policy emphasized adequate production and availability of cloth, improved arrangements for distribution of cloth, rapid development of handlooms, khadi and sericulture for generations of employment, and maintaining a harmonious balance between the use of cotton and synthetic fibres. The government also took a bold decision to give legitimacy to the power looms by adopting a policy to regularize the unauthorized power looms. But all these efforts did not make much of difference in terms of

120 *India's industrial performance*

accelerating production in the sector. Cloth production witnessed marginal increase with the effect that per capita production of cloth witnessed a marginal decline. The government, therefore, adopted another National Textile Policy in 1981. The objectives of the new policy were roughly similar to the earlier policy, with the addition of emphasis on quality of cloth produced, increased availability of natural and man-made fibres and yarn, and to produce surplus yarn for the world market at competitive prices.

Despite all these policy changes in the late 1970s and the new policy of 1981, the textile industry failed to pick up even during the first half of the 1980s which roughly coincided with the Sixth Five Year Plan, the target of which with respect to cloth production was missed by a wide margin. Apart from the slow growth of market demand, a shortfall in crop production and an unprecedented strike in a large number of textile mills during 1982–83 could have been responsible for such outcomes. Industrial sickness worsened, and the NTC had to take over quite a few more struggling mills.

As the government was about to launch the Seventh Five Year Plan, it formed a high-powered expert committee in 1984 to look into the problems of the industry and suggest appropriate measures. Pursuant to the committee's recommendations, the government announced a new National Textile Policy, 1985. The same year, a separate Ministry of Textiles was also created to give special attention to this sector. The new policy retained the objectives of the earlier policy, but emphasized the modernization of the industry, and closure of unviable mills. Accordingly, in 1986, a Textile Modernisation Fund of Rs 7,500 million was created. A Textile Workers' Rehabilitation Fund was also created to provide interim relief to workers losing jobs due to closure of the unviable textile units. However, it also kept the option of revival of struggling units wherever possible. The policy also proposed withdrawal of restriction on capacity of synthetic fibre plants, and spinning and weaving mills. Keeping its focus on development of handlooms, the government enacted a new law, the Handlooms (Reservation of Articles for Production) Act, 1985 to reserve 22 items for exclusive production by handlooms. The earlier provision of reservation for handlooms was essentially being usurped by the power looms due to some loopholes which the new law tried to close.

Very soon, the government constituted another high-powered committee in 1988 to review the implementation of the Textile Policy of 1985 under the chairmanship of Abid Hussain. The committee focused on restructuring and modernization of the organized mill sector and recommended institutional arrangement like area-based Textile Restructuring Assets Trusts (TRATs) for improving efficiency. It also suggested measures for upgradation of cotton processing facilities and increasing exports of textile products.

The second half of the 1980s witnessed substantial growth as the cloth production went up by 9.52 per cent between 1984–85 and 1991–92, taking the decadal CAGR to 7.48 per cent between 1981–82 and 1991–1992. Compared to the annual growth rates of 4.3 per cent between 1950–51, 1.2 per cent between 1960–61 and 1970–71, and 3.2 per cent between 1970–71 and

1981–82, this was a huge success. Broadly, this sector followed a pattern that was seen for the overall growth of the industry in India – namely, reasonably good growth to start with since the beginning of the planning era, a period of poor performance between the mid-1960s and early 1980s, and recovery during the 1980s. Until 1970, exports from this sector were negligible, but now it emerged as an important exporting sector of India. There was, however, significant structural change in the process. In 1950–51, 79 per cent of cloth production came from the mills sector, which came down to 36 per cent in 1981–82 and just 11 per cent in 1990–91.

During this period, the apparel industry also emerged as a vibrant industry. As a matter of fact, the apparel industry in India started growing in the 1970s as a response to demand in the Western markets that India could ensure due to the quota system under the MFA. Prior to this, Indian consumers relied more on local tailors for stitching their garments. Knitted underwear and children's clothes were an exception. Seeing the prospects of exports of readymade garments, the Apparel Export Promotion Council (AEPC) was established in 1978 to provide assistance to Indian apparel exporters, as well as foreign importers interested in buying from India. The National Institute of Fashion Technology (NIFT) was established in 1985 to create skilled personnel for designing of apparel. In the early 1970s, total textile exports were in the order of about $500 million, and readymade garments constituted just about 5 per cent of it.

However, during 1970–85, readymade garments exports went up by about 24.5 per cent per year, but growth of exports of fabric and yarn stagnated at 5.6 per cent per year. During 1985–90, exports of fabrics and yarn witnessed a growth of 16.4 per cent. Along with a growth of 23.2 per cent for the apparel segment, the overall export growth of textiles and clothing for the period was 19.8 per cent per year, highest ever quinquennial growth of exports achieved by the industry. As a result, the share of readymade garments in total exports surpassed 50 per cent by 1990 (Abraham and Sasikumar 2010).

This success of the late 1980s, however, could not be maintained for long as the average annual growth rate of cloth production fell down to 6.46 per cent between 1991–92 and 2000–01 and further down to 4.61 per cent between 2000–01 and 2009–10. The share of the mills sector in total cloth production came down from about 11 per cent in 1990–91 to about 4 per cent in 2000–01, and about 3 per cent in 2009–10. The absolute production of the mills sector, however, increased between 2000–01 and 2009–10, after a long time, from 1,670 million metres to 2,016 million metres (OTC 2010). The growth rate of textiles exports also fell drastically, and the dream run of apparel exports growth was also over.

Reforms, however, continued in the 1990s and beyond. The textile industry was completely deregulated through the Textiles (Development and Regulation) Order 1993. Following this, no licenses were required for setting up of power looms, knitting units, ring frames, or rotor spinning units, or

122 India's industrial performance

for production of synthetic fibres and their intermediates. The import duty on capital goods was brought down to 25 per cent, and under the Export Promotion of Capital Goods scheme, machineries could be imported duty free, as well. Import duties were gradually brought down on textile fibres, yarns, fibre intermediates, and raw materials. In 1994, the Export Entitlement Distribution Policy was adopted to make allocation of export quota more transparent and simpler, and to export more goods of high value and encourage non-quota export of garments. The Handloom Reservation Act, 1995 reduced the number of handloom items from 22 to 11. The Technology Upgradation Fund Scheme (TUFS) was launched in 1999 to facilitate soft loans for modernization of textile units.

The new millennium started with a new National Textile Policy, 2000, as a follow-up to an expert committee known as Sathyam Committee. While it retained most of the objectives of the earlier policy, it also emphasized on enhancement of productivity and quality. It declared the government's intention to promote adoption of IT in the textile industry, and proposed to restructure export promotion councils, silk boards, and other such organizations to make them more effective. In a major departure from the earlier policy, reservation of apparel production for small-scale industries was done away with in 2000. Tariffs were reduced substantially, then raised again in 2002 when quantitative restrictions were removed, but they were brought down once again gradually, though substantial protection continued for some of the products. In 2005, the Scheme for Integrated Textile Parks (SITP) was launched to provide world-class infrastructure for common facilities, such as roads, water supply, power generation and distribution, design centres, warehouses, effluent treatment, etc. A total of 59 such parks were sanctioned, but as of July 2019, only 22 parks were completed.

Meanwhile, NTC closed down 78 unviable mills during 2002–11, and transferred two mills in the state of Pondicherry to the state government. For the rest (18), it launched a modernization, expansion, and product diversification programme, and ventured into technical textiles. It also set up three greenfield composite textile units, in Ahmedabad (Gujarat), Achalpur (Maharashtra), and Hassan (Karnataka). More recently, The Directorate General of Foreign Trade (DGFT) enhanced incentives for exports of ready-made garments and textiles made up under the Merchandise Exports from India Scheme (MEIS), from 2 per cent to 4 per cent. The government also enhanced the basic custom duty to encourage domestic production under its "Make in India" programme.

The 2000 New Textile Policy set a target of $50 billion by 2010 for exports of textile and apparel, with the share of garments and other textile products each at $25 billion. Similarly, the Planning Commission, during its 12th Five Year Plan (2012–17), set up a target of $64.41 billion by March 2017 for exports of textiles and apparel. Needless to say, none of these targets could be achieved. In fact, the 2010 target could not be achieved even by 2020.

In the 1950s, textiles were the most developed industry that the free India inherited from its colonial regime. However, it also had its share of problems even in those days. Restrictive policies of the first three decades undoubtedly obstructed its growth. However, it was a matter of difficult choice. India had its capital scarcity and it decided to regulate its capital flows and channelized them to industries that government thought important. It is certainly a difficult question to address if it would have been better to let this industry grow and not to bother about other industries like iron and steel.

However, such policies started changing from the 1970s and more so in the 1980s, and since then have been changing all along. But the golden period for this was the period between the mid-1980s and the early 1990s. This can lead us to the idea of optimum liberalization or optimum policy framework or an optimum path of policy dynamics. It is quite obvious that liberalization or reforms in one direction and uniform speed might not be the ideal path. There is an indication that internal liberalization has been good for the industry, but liberalization on the external front did not benefit much. Tariff reduction started from the mid-1990s, but that did not provide any boost to the industry.

While there was great expectation that post-MFA India will benefit in terms of higher exports, the MFA started to be dismantled by 1995 and the process was completed by 2015. But exports did not show any sign of pick up during or after this period. There were, of course, studies that indicated that India was doing rather well in the quota regime, and dismantling of the quota regime would not necessarily help (Anubhai 1988; Verma 2002).

A distinguishing feature of the Indian textile industry is that it is almost entirely homegrown compared all other late-developing countries that found success in this industry. Even China received substantial Japanese and Korean investments in this industry. Tewari (2006) argued for taking note of this unique feature of the Indian textile industry in managing policy reforms. Nevertheless, India expected FDI to play a major role in making the textile industry competitive and boosting exports, and accordingly, allowed 100 per cent FDI through automatic route. In reality, not much FDI came to India. Moreover, whatever little was received came from Mauritius, and it is likely that a substantial part of it was not real FDI but round-tripping of Indian capital. In most developing countries, inflow of FDI follows a sequence like textile, chemicals, steel, automobiles, electronics, and so on. FDI is also known for not coming to an industry which is already quite developed in the destination country unless it is through mergers and acquisition. Hence, it is unlikely that India will get substantial FDI in the textiles industry.

Another aspect of the industry that received substantial attention in policy debate is the issue of cost competitiveness. In this context, the issue of labour costs has been discussed at length, though studies have found that labour costs in India are actually lower than most competing countries except Bangladesh. Rather, power and capital costs are relatively higher compared to competing countries, China in particular. Of course, it has also been argued

124 *India's industrial performance*

that costs in India are lower mainly because of the fact that the Indian industry is dominated by power looms, which have cost advantages (Goswami 1990).

However, it has also been observed that success in the global market does not come only because of cost advantage (Mass and Lazonick 2006). Marketing efforts and other aspects are also important. For example, many Indian exporters were found to be reluctant to take long-term delivery commitments beyond six months (Anubhai 1988). Even though the government launched a scheme to promote modernization of the industry, many textile units took advantage to import 30-year-old second-hand machines rather than importing state-of-the-art machinery. Such attitudinal issues might also have been responsible for not-so-good performance of the industry. This also reinforces the argument in favour of better regulation of government schemes.

4.6.7 *Electronics and information technology*

Electronics is probably the most important industry today, not only because of the importance of its own, but also because of the increasing role it has been playing in all other industries. Thus, in the prevailing techno-economic space, success in the electronics industry is crucial for overall industrialization effort in the context of a large economy like that of India. Global electronics production was estimated to be about $2 trillion in 2017–18, in which India's share was just about $60 billion (MEITY 2019). During the period between 2008–09 and 2017–18, the demand for electronic products in India has grown from about $45 billion to about $106 billion. While domestic production has increased from $23 billion to $60 billion over the same period, India's imports have grown from $22 billion to $46 billion. Thus, India witnessed a massive increase in import volume, even though import dependence has declined a bit, from 49 per cent to roughly about 43 per cent (MEITY 2019).

The Indian electronics industry is of relatively recent origin, beginning when some private firms started producing radio receivers in the 1950s with imported components. By the end of the decade, some radio-manufacturers were also making some of the components for themselves. However, it is also noteworthy that P. C. Mahalanobis – who played a pivotal role in the Second Five Year Plan – also got India's first general purpose computer at the Indian Statistical Institute in Calcutta (now Kolkata) in 1956, which was a UK-made Hollerith Electronic Computer (HEC). This was followed by the acquisition of an IBM computer at the Tata Institute of Fundamental Research, Bombay (now Mumbai), at that time headed by Dr Homi Bhabha (Sharma 2009).

As these were made possible through approvals at high levels, it can be said that the importance of the electronics industry in general and computers in particular was recognized at the highest levels. The government turned to Dr Bhabha to develop a roadmap for the electronics industry in India, and the Electronics Committee was set up in 1963 under his chairmanship. The committee submitted its report in 1966 that emphasized on the importance of the electronics industry, along with a strong component base for both techno-economic and strategic reasons, and also gave a ten-year roadmap for the industry. It also emphasized on producing in large quantities and providing adequate R&D support to keep the industry technologically advanced.

The Electronics Corporation of India Limited (ECIL) was established in 1967 under the Department of Atomic Energy (DAE), which itself was established with Dr Homi Bhabha as its first secretary, with the objective of commercializing electronic systems developed at the Atomic Research Centre under the Department.[6] Very soon, the government constituted another Electronics Committee, under the chairmanship of Vikram Sarabhai, to identify urgent needs of the industry and the sectors where indigenous production capability could be built up, and make appropriate recommendations. Both the Bhabha Committee and the Sarabhai Committee emphasized on the development of an indigenous computer industry, and accordingly, computer production facilities in the public sector, ECIL was established. ECIL was primarily responsible for commercializing the electronic systems developed at the Atomic Research Centre, but by 1971, it became a computer manufacturing enterprise.

During the 1960s, a modest base for the manufacture of electronics components was developed, and the Indian electronics industry was dominated by consumer goods. In that context, the Bhabha Committee also emphasized the need for development of the electronics industry – both for its success in industrialization efforts as well for strategic reasons – and the government made efforts to create basic infrastructure and created a separate Department of Electronics in 1970. The following year, the Sarabhai Committee created earlier was converted into the Electronics Commission with the objective of rolling out a well-directed and well-coordinated programme for the rapid development of the electronics industry. The Commission was given the task of coordination among different ministries and departments of the government including communication, railways, atomic energy, information and broadcasting, etc., and preparing plans for creating capacities in different sectors.

These measures were followed by modest performance of the sector, even though the overall industrial scenario was not doing so well in the 1970s. The electronics industry showed better performance in terms of production, exports, diversification of products, areas of applications, geographical spread, and growth of small industries. During 1970–80, the industry experienced a compounded average growth rate of 16.2 per cent, but the next decade was considered the golden era for the industry. During 1980–91, the industry experienced a growth rate of 26.8 per cent. The sector did quite well in terms of exports, as well, as it grew by 19.4 per cent during the period 1981–92.

In the mid-1980s, the sector was dominated by consumer electronics, which accounted for about 39 per cent of production in the sector. While

126 *India's industrial performance*

in the 1970s, the industry made mostly radio receivers, PA systems, amplifiers, and record players, in the 1980s it was making TV sets, tape recorders, calculators, car radios, electronic watches and clocks, gas lighters, etc. In 1982, the Asian Games were held in Delhi, which also motivated the only broadcaster, the government-owned Doordarshan, to start telecasting colour TV programmes. The government allowed import of 50,000 colour TV sets for the Games, but this also influenced the Indian electronics industry to start making colour TV sets in India. About 90 per cent of these products were made in the private sector.

In the 1970s, the basic direction of the government policy in this sector was to develop the industry with the involvement of governments both at the central and state levels. In the 1980s, the policy direction shifted in favour of private players taking the lead role. There was a reason for the kind of strategy that was followed in the 1970s, as the same was suggested by a study group set up by the Electronics Commission. The study group suggested that ECIL would satisfy the requirements of computers in India, though those were expected to be designed and assembled in India with imported components and peripherals.

However, by the end of the decade, it was quite apparent that it was not able to rise to the occasion, as it was neither able to satisfy the demand nor able to supply expected quality at competitive prices. Hence, in 1978, the government relaxed the licensing norms for the computer industry, inviting the entry of private enterprises. The broad banding of licenses was extended to the electronics sector also, which allowed the firms to change their product mix in keeping with fluctuating demand patterns or high profit areas, leading to optimal utilization of their investments. The government also removed excise duty on a large number of electronic components, computers, and computer peripherals. Meanwhile, in 1975, Computer Management Corporation (CMC) was established as a government-owned company.

The year 1978 also saw an important event in the history of information technology of India as the famous multinational IBM decided to leave India. There were allegations that the company was selling obsolete technologies, as it was selling second-hand computers and charging higher rates for maintenance of computers in India. Even the Electronics Committee, headed by Vikram Sarabhai, noted that IBM was selling old and refurbished computers in India at higher prices. It wanted an end to this practice, as well as end to monopoly of IBM in the Indian market. But the company left India due to disputes over FERA violations. Interestingly, IBM came to India in the 1950s, at the invitation of Jawaharlal Nehru (Sharma 2013). When IBM left India, CMC took over the maintenance of IBM installations at over 800 locations around India.

The 1980s also saw some important policy changes pertaining to the electronics sector. In 1983, the government adopted the Electronics Industry Policy, through which it reduced custom duties on several raw materials used in the industry. Realizing the importance of bringing the latest technologies, multinational companies were encouraged for computer manufacturing and collaboration arrangements for transfer of technology, along with progressive indigenization. Industries were encouraged to develop their in-house technology base so as to minimize repeated import of technologies.

The New Computer Policy, 1984 simplified the existing procedures for obtaining computers, as well as to promote applications of computers that were expected to promote development and efficiency. In line with this, various measures, such as investment allowance; permission to install viable capacity without upper limits; protection of domestic computers; liberal import of know-how, designs and drawings, and software; simplification of the procedure for imports of raw materials and components, etc., were also adopted. Both MRTP and FERA norms were relaxed for the industry. The Department of Electronics was entrusted with the job of setting up an extensive research, design, and development facility to develop technologies and make them available to users. It was also asked to set up a Software Development Promotion Agency to encourage intensive software development for domestic requirements, as well as exports. Very soon, New Electronics Policy, 1985 was adopted to make acquisition of sophisticated technologies even easier. It also made import of computers for government easier. To develop domestic capabilities, Centre for Development of Telematics (C-DoT) was established in 1984, while Centre for Development of Advanced Computing (C-DAC) was established in 1988. In December 1986, the government declared Software Policy which emphasized on development of software and its exports (Rajaraman 2012).

There is enough evidence to suggest that the measures adopted during the late 1970s and early 1980s did yield positive outcomes. The period between 1984 and 1990 has been described as the golden period for the electronics industry (ELCINA 2012). However, in reality, the period between 1981 and 1985 experienced much better performance, with the sector showing an annual growth rate of almost 33 per cent, while the growth rate during the 1985–1991 was 26.7 per cent, which was also quite impressive.[7]

With the adoption of New Economic Policy in 1991, sweeping changes were introduced that affected the electronics sector as well. Apart from delicensing, entry barriers for FDI were reduced and the telecom sector was fully opened up to foreign investors. Even though the major multinational companies entered India, there was not much of genuine investment (Rao and Dhar 2018). India signed the Information Technology Agreement of 1997 (ITA) and removed tariffs on IT products, but it did not help bring foreign investment in the electronics industry, as much of the FDI was meant for assembling only, which require very little investment (Francis 2018).

The software sector, however, attracted substantial FDI (Dhar and Joseph 2019). This was also because the government, through its Software Policy 1986, consciously preferred software over hardware for a thrust in exports, and initiated measures to facilitate entry of foreign firms and technology. However, the policy changes since 1991 and the ITA made it worse. ITA,

128 *India's industrial performance*

under which the duties on 217 ICT products and their components were removed, was implemented in 2005.

The New Economic Policy 1991 emphasized sunrise industries like computers and electronics, but in reality, the growth rate of the electronics industry started declining. During 1991–2002, the industry grew at a CAGR of 11.6 per cent, compared to a CAGR of 26.8 per cent during 1980–91. It was 15 per cent during 1992–97, but fell down to 10.3 per cent during 1997–2002. During 2002–09, the growth rate recovered a bit, as it achieved a CAGR of 16.4 per cent. The growth rate fell down to about 12 per cent during 2009–14, making a growth rate of 14.5 per cent for the period 2002–2014 (MEITY 2014).

In recent years, the electronics industry has shown signs of revival. Electronics production has grown at CAGR of about 24.5 per cent between 2014–15 and 2018–19 (MEITY 2019). The "Make in India" programme, launched in 2014 and introducing measures like increasing the Basic Customs Duty (BCD) on several consumer electronic goods, allowing 100 per cent FDI in the consumer electronics through the automatic route, and providing capital expenditure subsidy under the Modified Special Incentive Package Scheme (M-SIPS), could have helped make this possible. However, much of this growth has come largely from the success in the mobile phone manufacturing. The Phased Manufacturing Programme (PMP) for cellular mobile handsets and related sub-assemblies/parts manufacturing has increased domestic value addition, but it merely moved from semi-knocked down (SKD) to completely knocked down (CKD) level of manufacturing (MEITY 2019).

The global electronics industry has a structure (Table 4.2) wherein an international division of production and labour operates under the control of multinational electronic companies. In this structure, traditionally, electronic goods are designed and the capital-intensive production is carried out in the high technology countries of Japan, the US and Europe, while labour-intensive semi-skilled assembly production occurs in developing countries. Over the years, South Korea and Taiwan have moved up the value chain. In recent years, China and Thailand have also made some progress, but India continues to be engaged in low-skilled assembly operations.

Ernst (2014) observed that India's production base for components has been declining. In particular, lack of a vibrant domestic component industry, disconnect between domestic manufacturing and technical capabilities, and an absence of integrated innovation system are the key challenges identified by him. Interestingly, he also observed that though India had acquired capabilities in some areas, much of the designing activities done in India are by MNCs, which are transferred to their manufacturing location in other countries, especially in China. Hence, technical capabilities in India were not linked to domestic manufacturing in India. While R&D investment in India is already quite low, whatever technologies are developed are used in production in other countries. In India, the foreign original equipment manufacturers do not look beyond final assembly.

Table 4.2 Structure and Growth in the Electronics Industry

	1985 structure	Growth 1981–85	2018 structure	Growth 2014–18
Consumer electronics	38.7	43.1	16.8	8.38
Communication equipment	14.3	25.3		
Strategic electronics	7.4	29.8	6.2	15.8
Industrial and computers	21.0	31.1	22.3	15.4
Industrial electronics			17.7	19.7
Computer hardware			4.6	3.2
Electronic components	15.4	24.1	14.8	14.3
Mobile phones			37.1	75
LED products			2.8	56
Total	100	33	100	24.5

Source: Agarwal (1985), MEITY (2019).

The experience of the electronics industry clearly shows that the period of the highest growth started with internal liberalization measures of the late 1970s and early 1980s. However, such high growth was moderated with the introduction of the moderate external liberalization measures since the mid-1980s. Since the sector was largely liberalized internally in the 1980s, the delicensing measures of 1991 did not affect the sector much. However, the growth performance of the sector collapsed after 1991, which must have been largely due to liberalization on the external front. The ITA and the preference of software over hardware, along with technical changes, made the situation worse. Ironically, the preference for software over hardware was not even necessary for the growth of the software that the country witnessed over the years, as hardware constituted a very small share of the software costs in India.

In 1985, the communication and broadcasting sector contributed about 14.3 per cent to the total output in electronics industry, and the entire production happened in the public sector. The same was the case with aerospace and defence sector that produced 7.4 per cent of the total output. In 1985, consumer electronics had the highest share with 38.7 per cent, but all other sub-sectors had good presence and healthy growth, including the electronic components. Since 2014, the growth has been rather skewed, with only mobile phone showing high growth and high share, followed by LED products, but most other sub-sectors are virtually languishing. For example, domestic production of LCD/LED TVs went up from 0.87 crore units in 2014–15 to 1.6 crore units in 2017–18, registering a growth of about 16.5 per cent, but the consumer electronics sector grew only by 8.38 per cent.[8] Earlier, the principal component of a TV set was the picture tube, which would not be considered an IT product, but now components that replaced picture tube are IT products and are imported free of duty.

130 *India's industrial performance*

One important factor that has been responsible for India's inability to make a mark in this sector is its inability to move up the technology ladder. Comparing five strategic industries including electronics, Abraham (2017) concludes that technological success depends on a host of factors including government policy, the structure and maturity of the industry, and the technology policy and strategy adopted. An important feature of policy making in India in the earlier years until the 1970s was the involvement of several scientists like P. C. Mahalanobis, Homi J. Bhabha, and Vikram Sarabhai in policy making. Since 1980s, policy making was more or less taken over by the economists. This could have created a disconnect between technology and policy.

4.7   Conclusion

In view of some limitations of the widely used methods of measuring industrial performance – namely, price-cost margin, total factor productivity, technical efficiency, and revealed comparative advantage – some new indicators were tried here. These are based on India's share in the global value added, as well as India's exports and imports. One is called the global competitiveness ratio, which is simply India's share of total global production. Competitiveness performance index, which is the ratio of the share of an individual sector in global production of that sector and the share of total Indian industrial production in total global industrial production, was also considered.

RCA is one indicator that has been used widely to understand comparative advantages that a country can have. This is relative performance of one sector vis-à-vis total exports of a country compared to the relative export performance of that sector globally. However, since the formula does not include imports, there is a chance that the results are misleading. Hence, the relative performance of one sector in exports is compared with the relative dependence of that sector on imports, which called the absolute competitive advantage.

Based on these estimates, whatever indicator one chooses, performance of different industrial sectors was not quite encouraging in the post-WTO period. Only a few sectors showed performance that can be termed good or above average. These are automobiles, basic metals, petroleum products, pharmaceuticals, and electrical machinery.

In all these cases, the public sector played an important role in the growth of the industry. In some sectors, such growth would probably have been impossible without the public sector taking the lead in the formative years of the 1950s and 1960s. In some sectors, the public sector plays an important role even now. Not only just public enterprises, but even domestic private enterprises also benefitted from the preference they received in public procurement. The sectors that might have benefitted the most in this regard are basic metals, electrical machinery, and pharmaceuticals. Government regulations also played some role in the growth of some of these sectors.

As far as development finance is concerned, it might have played a role in the growth of the pharmaceutical and basic metals industries in the 1980s and 1990s, as it saw a greater share of development finance going into these sectors. The machinery, automobiles, and petroleum products industries might have benefitted from increased shares of the flow of development finance. Since 2000, however, development finance has mostly been going into the infrastructure and services sector, along with an overall decline of development finance itself (Nayyar 2015).

While many studies have identified the pre- and post-1991 years with import-substituting and export-led industrialization strategies, in reality, Indian tariff rates were quite high until about 2002, and it is very high in the case of automobiles even today. Moreover, in most of the sectors those have shown better performance, the growth has been led by domestic demand rather than exports, except possibly the pharmaceuticals sector. While trade liberalization in India might have played only a minor role in some sectors, trade liberalization in the rest of the world might have played a role in some of the sectors. But for several sectors that could not perform well, the question about the importance of trade liberalization cries for answers. The experience of textiles and electronics and IT hardware shows that while internal liberalization played a positive role in the 1980s, the external liberalization in later period might have had adverse impacts.

Among the better-performing sectors, foreign investment played a major role only in the automobiles sector. Yet, it cannot be confidently claimed that it was because foreign investors were granted unfettered access to domestic markets that led to the success; rather, it was strict performance requirements imposed by the government on the foreign manufacturers that did the trick. FDI simply bypassed the textiles and apparel sector, while the electronics sector received substantial FDI without creating substantive production capacity.

It is also noteworthy that most of the better-performing industries in India use technologies that are relatively mature and have not seen major innovations for decades. Automobile and pharmaceutical industries are exceptions in this regard. However, as noted before, in the automobile sector, foreign companies who were attracted to India due to its market size were forced to bring their technologies. In the pharmaceuticals industry, it was the reverse engineering facilitated by a relatively relaxed IPR regime that helped build technological capabilities. Nevertheless, India's technological capabilities are not cutting edge. India simply lost out in industries like electronics and IT hardware where technology is changing quickly. Manufacturing sub-sectors are classified into early, middle, and late industries (Haraguchi 2015). One puzzle about the Indian industrialization experience is that its successful sub-sectors belong to either middle (basic metals, petroleum products) or late (automobiles, electrical machinery, pharmaceuticals) categories, though going by the global experience, India's per capita income is not high enough to make success in such industries, yet India could not show enough success in the so-called early industries like food and beverages or textiles and clothing.

132 *India's industrial performance*

While foreign direct investment has acted as a source of technology in the automobiles sector, it was the strategy of weaker intellectual property rights that helped the pharmaceuticals sector. In the basic metals and petroleum products, access to technology was ensured through foreign collaboration where diplomacy played an important role. There is now a concern that unregulated acquisition of successful domestic companies by foreign giants, particularly in the pharmaceuticals sector, can have adverse impacts. Such acquisitions could be part of the strategy to thwart competition. In the IT hardware sector, a foreign IT giant had a dominant role in India but it brought only obsolete technologies.

Over the last few years, the phenomenon of development of a global value chain has received huge attention, and it has often been argued that getting integrated into the global production network is important for industrial development in developing countries (Taglioni and Winkler 2014; OECD 2015; IMF 2015). While the subject can be a matter of other research, it may be useful to note that the Indian experience is quite different, though there has not been much research in the Indian context. For example, Indian automobile makers source their components largely from Indian producers. Tata Motors sources almost 95 per cent of its components domestically (Nag et al. 2007). While Indian auto components manufacturers are integrated with the global production network, Indian car makers are not. Clothing, footwear, and consumer electronics are some of the sectors where the global value chain matters. Though these sectors are beyond the scope of discussion here, *prima facie*, the inability to integrate into the global value chain could have been one of the factors for their limited success in early industries in India.

While it might be difficult in small countries to develop a comprehensive component manufacturing industry, in India's case, it is quite possible. In developed countries, it might be important to source a significant proportion of components at low-cost from developing countries. For India, therefore, development of the local value chain produced better results. This seems to be consistent with the Ocampo (2017) hypothesis that diffusion of learning is important for sustained industrialization, which might be difficult if a small part of the global value chain is located in a country. Hence, integrating with global production networks could be useful, but not unambiguously. In particular, engaging in FTAs to promote value chains without properly understanding their implications can prove disastrous (Francis 2019)

Finally, it is quite clear that industrial policy played an important role in the better-performing industries. However, different elements of industrial policy played different kinds of role in different industrial sub-sectors (Table 4.3). While state involvement was more important in basic metals and electrical machinery, performance requirements and trade protection played the major roles in the automobile industry. The pharmaceuticals industry had a very different context, whereby relaxed IPR regime played the decisive role. Public procurement made some contribution to almost all industries.

Table 4.3 Policy Factors Influencing Performance in Select Industries in India

Industries	Policy factors
Basic metals	State involvement Preferential access to raw materials Public procurement Development finance Favourable policy for consuming sectors
Petroleum products	State involvement Price regulation Development finance
Pharmaceuticals/chemicals	State involvement Price regulation Relaxed IPR protection Public procurement Development finance
Electrical goods	State involvement Public procurement State involvement in consuming sectors
Automobiles	State involvement Foreign investment along with performance requirements Tariff protection Development finance

Source: Author's compilation.

Industrial policy, therefore, needs to be sector specific and also keep in mind the current context and the emerging scenario.

However, it is important to note that there is no "one size fits all" optimal policy mix for all industrial sub-sectors. Nevertheless, it is also important to have a balanced policy mix, and following just one or two might not work. For example, a high degree of tariff protection might not produce the desired results in the absence of other relevant policy measures. At the same time, too much protection can also be counterproductive. In view of the difficulty in following many of the alternative measures, preferential public procurement can be an option that could be used with relative ease.

Notes

1 Industrial sector is broader in concept, as it includes manufacturing sector, as well. The classification also varies from country to country. The industrial sector usually includes, apart from manufacturing, construction, electricity, gas, and water. In the previous chapter, the industrial sector also included mining and quarrying, though often it is considered to be part of the "primary sector". In the empirical industrial performance literature, industry is generally equated with the manufacturing sector.

2 Technical progress indicates that technology or the technical capability to convert inputs into output has improved, whereas technical efficiency indicates that more

134 *India's industrial performance*

output is obtained from the same inputs – even with the same technology – due to the removal of managerial slackness.

3 In the real world, world export is different from world import, as export is estimated at free on board price while the import price also includes insurance and freight charges. Moreover, as there is a time lag between an export consignment exiting a country and when it reaches the other country when it becomes import, export and import are often accounted for in different years.

4 The situation has changed drastically due to closure of a copper plant in 2018 in the state of Tamil Nadu due to protests over environmental impacts.

5 Jute textiles or jute products are not considered here, as they followed a very different trajectory compared to cotton or synthetic textiles and their products. While jute was more important than cotton in terms of exports at the time of Independence, the importance of jute has declined over years. In jute, India has no competitor other than Bangladesh.

6 Dr Bhabha died in 1966, even before ECIL was established.

7 The growth rates mentioned here are nominal growth rates.

8 Assuming an average inflation rate of about 4 per cent, the difference between volume growth and value growth is about 12 per cent. This could be, to a significant extent, due to low domestic value addition.

5 Intensity of competition in Indian industry

5.1 Introduction

It is widely believed that a competitive market makes firms in an industry efficient, and hence, a competitive market can improve the performance of firms in a liberalized economy. Thus, it becomes crucial to understand the nature and degree of competition prevailing in an economy. One of the basic theoretical propositions in economics is that, in a market economy, the competitive process will work towards equalizing rates of return within and across industries.

While market concentration very often is not policy-driven in a free market economy, in the Indian context, it could be considered to be influenced by policy to a large extent. This is due to the policy of industrial licensing that India had until 1991. While licensing was abolished in most industries post-1991, its impact could linger, as it is not easy to challenge well-entrenched existing players.

There has been a significant amount of work in applied industrial economics literature that looked at the rate of return or profitability as a measure of performance of industries. Performance in this context means that the market is competitive, firms do not command any market power, and, of course, price is equated to marginal cost. Based on this understanding, Abba Lerner (1934) formulated his index of market power that captures the extent to which price deviated from marginal cost, which is given as, $L = (P - MC)/P$. However, given that it is almost impossible to measure the marginal costs in practice, there was a search for alternative measures for market power.

The structure-conduct-performance (SCP) paradigm was considered to be of some help in this context. In this paradigm, market structure dictates the conduct of the firms operating in an industry, which in turn impacts the performance of the entire industry, as well as the firms within the industry. The structure of a body means the pattern or form in which the components of the body are organized. So market structure would mean the manner in which its different constituent entities – namely, buyers and sellers – are linked together. To put in the words of Bain, "this means those characteristics of the organization of a market that seems to exercise a strategic influence on the nature of competition and pricing within the market" (Bain 1959, p. 7).

DOI: 10.4324/9781003047490-5

136 *Competition in Indian industry*

Market structure is a multi-dimensional concept, and hence, it is not possible to measure it using a single variable. A set of variables related to different aspects of it may be used simultaneously to measure market structure. There are market share, concentration, diversification, product differentiation, and barriers to entry. Of these, concentration (with respect to sellers) has received, by far, the greatest attention. Market share and barriers to entry (or a proxy) have also been used in some studies. The market share of a firm is the primary basis of its market position and power, and it is also considered to be one of the company motivations. Like any other element of market structure, market share can play a crucial role in determining the level of profit it can earn. In the SCP paradigm, the general hypothesis is that there is a positive relationship between market share and profitability.

Market concentration is often considered to be the most important element of market structure. While the concept of market share relates to an individual firm, concentration is an industry-based concept. Although it is not possible to derive a universal and unbiased summary index of market structure, concentration tells us how far an industry or market is controlled by a small number of leading sellers.

Two variables that are of importance for market concentration are the number of firms in the market and their size distribution. Concentration is sometimes presented as the combined market share of the leading firms. This is called concentration ratio. Generally, this group of firms is not less than two or more than eight. A four-firm concentration ratio or the eight-firm concentration ratio is most often used in the literature. Apart from the concentration ratio, several other quantitative indices have been suggested to measure the market concentration but the one that has been used most is the Hirschman-Herfindahl Index, measured as:

$$HHI = \Sigma_{i=1}^{n}P_i^2 \tag{5.1}$$

Where P_i is the market share of the ith firm (i = 1, 2, . . . n) and n is the number of firms operating in the market. The value of HHI would range between (1/n) and one.

Many studies were conducted that tried to understand market structure. However, it gradually became quite apparent that structural characteristics are not good enough to reveal the intensity of competition in a market. In a globalized world, markets are highly likely to be contestable, as there is always a possibility of a short-term supply surge from foreign competitors (Baumol et al. 1982). Then there is also the question of defining the relevant market. For example, in pharmaceutical products, each therapeutic category is a different relevant market. In aviation, for example, each pair of cities could be a different relevant market.

Then there is also the issue of conduct. A particular type of market structure does not guarantee any specific theoretically defined firm behaviour. At the theoretical level, under certain conditions, if firms behave as Cournot

Competition in Indian industry 137

(1838) assumed, the outcome will be highly monopolistic, but if they behaved as Bertrand assumed, the outcome would be competitive. At the practical level, concentration might be high in an industry, yet there might be intense competition over market share where firms may compete through differentiated or new products, aggressive advertising, etc.

Hence, the focus was shifted back to measuring performance by looking at a variant of the Lerner's index, where marginal cost is estimated by using average variable cost as a proxy. In most studies, price-cost margin is approximated as:

$$PCM = (\text{Value added} - \text{cost of labour} + \Delta\text{Inventories})/$$
$$(\text{Sales} + \Delta\text{Inventories}) \tag{5.2}$$

PCM may be considered to be a good choice in cases where the barriers-to-entry theory of the relationship of structure and performance is being examined. The theory is about price exceeding cost – it is only indirectly a theory of return on capital. The attraction to a new entrant is not the size of the margin, but rather the return on capital. A high margin in a sector that requires a high capital output ratio can give low return, and hence, cannot attract a new entrant. On the other hand, even with a low margin, a sector associated with low capital output ratio can give high return on capital. Hence, it was necessary to look at the rate of return, as well. Profits are usually shown by net income after tax. The rate of profit is then, given as:

$$\text{Rate of return} = (\text{Profit after tax})/(\text{capital stock}) \tag{5.3}$$

There is no satisfactory measure for capital stock, however, since there are no well-functioning second-hand markets in which their opportunity costs can be evaluated as assets. The valuation of the firm may, of course, be provided by the stock market, but if the firm is earning monopoly profits, then that will tend to overestimate the market valuation of the firm. So, we get a valuation of the firm including its market position – not of the assets themselves – so, a firm earning monopoly profits is likely to have overvalued assets, and hence, the rate of return may be underestimated. Moreover, speculative expectation may also overvalue or undervalue the assets of a company. Due to the absence of an alternative, researchers have been using such measures of capital in different studies.

The limitation of using profitability to measure performance or the intensity of competition became apparent as it was recognized that competition evolves due to the presence of abnormal profit in an industry. Hence, treating profitability as a measure of competition is problematic. Though abnormal profits cannot persist in an industry for a long time, such abnormal profits arise and persist temporarily due to presence of short-run barriers to entry and exit.

Above-normal profits, even in a competitive environment, can arise due to innovation efforts. Using R&D, business agents develop new products or

138 *Competition in Indian industry*

efficient production processes which attract profits. If the incumbent firms make profits beyond the normal rate of return, other businesses will be attracted to enter the industry, but in the long run, if there are no entry or exit barriers, development of competitive products or processes also take place. This results in more and more businesses competing for customers, and thus, such a process of competition results in erosion of abnormal profits over time.

There are broadly two views – static and dynamic – regarding persistence of profits in a competitive environment. Cournot (1838) and Bain (1956) are the proponents of the static view, which explains persistence of above-normal profit through industry characteristics like industry concentration and elasticity of demand. On the other hand, Joseph Schumpeter (1934, 1950) is the proponent of the dynamic view, which explains the persistence of abnormal profits using the characteristics of firms like size/growth/share and effectiveness of R&D.

In a competitive environment, firms compete with each other through innovation and/or copying the innovation of their competitors. Innovation provides a "first mover advantage" to a firm and provides the opportunity to earn above-normal profit in the short run. Over time, when such innovation is adopted by the competitors, the "monopoly power" of the innovator converges to "competition" and results in erosion of above-normal profit.

Hence, one way of measuring the intensity of competition is to examine the dynamics of the competitive process by considering the persistence of profits. Since competition is a dynamic process that works over time, rather than an event that happens at a point in time, it is not appropriate to take a static view of profits. One way of capturing such competitive dynamics is to examine the persistence of profits in different firms and the industry.

With intense competition, it is unlikely that differences in profit will persist for long. On the other hand, with low intensity of competition, differences in profitability will persist. This is consistent with the rise and persistence of above-normal profit for some point of time. Thus, it is important to identify and measure different firm and industry characteristics/behaviour to explain persistence and erosion of abnormal profit.

This chapter is divided into five sections. The second section provides a review of literature with regard to competition and profitability, with special reference to empirical studies in India. The third section discusses the key objective of the chapter and also elaborates on the methodology and the data used. The fourth section provides an analysis of the empirical findings, while the fifth section concludes the chapter.

5.2 Existing studies on competition and persistence of profit

Interestingly, the interest in industrial concentration in India has its origin in a government initiative, when the government of India established in 1964 the Monopolies Inquiry Commission headed by Justice K. C. Dasgupta. The major objective of the Commission was to understand the extent of concentration of economic power in private hands and its impact on market outcomes, including possible existence of monopolistic practices. The Commission was also asked to suggest necessary measures, including the legal framework, in view of their findings. The public sector and agriculture were excluded from the purview of inquiry.

The Commission investigated "product-wise concentration" and inter-industry concentration, and came to the conclusion that, indeed, there was concentration of economic power in a few hands. The Commission also noted that big businesses had advantages over smaller businesses in securing financial accommodation and that "Big business by its very bigness sometimes succeeds in keeping out competition" (MCA 1965, p. 137) as monopolistic and restrictive trade practices were quite rampant. It also observed that controls and licenses had a major part in the creation and growth of monopolies. As recommended by the Commission, the Monopolies and Restrictive Trade Practices Act was adopted in 1969.

The findings of the Commission also triggered several studies on industrial concentration and profitability in Indian industries. The earliest studies among these indicated that market concentration in India had been quite high due to several factors. While some could be linked to economic situation, policy-driven factors also had substantial impacts (Saluja 1968; Gupta 1968; Ghosh 1974, 1975; Panchamukhi 1974; Sandesara 1979).

Earlier studies, by and large, indicated that higher market concentrations were linked with higher price-cost margins (Sawhney and Sawhney 1973). They also found that industries with lower import penetration but higher export orientation, as well as higher levels of protection, tended to have higher PCM (Katrak 1980). It is quite possible that Indian firms were quite competitive compared to their foreign counterparts, and hence, higher exports meant higher PCM. Interestingly, he also found that PCM increases, along with concentration, only up to a point but starts decreasing from there. While earlier studies found a link between concentration and policy factors like industrial licensing, Apte and Vaidyanathan (1982) observed that licensing did not have any significant impacts on performance.

Siddharthan and Dasgupta (1983) observed that profitability in Indian industry was largely determined by human skill and advertisement expenditure, but R&D expenditure and market concentration did not have any significant impact. Low R&D expenditure across the board might have been responsible for this. Based on an analysis of 43 industries at three-digit level, Kumar (1990) observed that market concentration, import protections, or advertisement expenditures did not have any significant impact on profitability, but intra-industry structure (in terms of strategic heterogeneity) was a key determinant of profitability. Skill and technology, however, were used effectively by the MNCs as entry barriers. In a study of the automobile industry over the period between 1966–67 and 1986–87, Agarwal (1991)

140 *Competition in Indian industry*

could not find much evidence for the working of either the SCP paradigm or the relative efficiency hypothesis in the industry.[1]

The 1991 economic reforms, once again, triggered several studies, most of which were to understand if the adoption of liberalized economic policies impacted market concentration, degree of competition, or competitiveness of Indian industries. Several of these studies indicated declining market concentration in the wake of economic liberalization (Athreye and Kapur 2006; Kambhampati and Kattuman 2005; Barua et al. 2010). However, though PCMs started showing a declining trend in many industries in the aftermath of the 1991 reforms (Krishna and Mitra 1998), some later studies indicate an opposite trend.

Goldar and Aggarwal (2004) estimated an econometric model with panel data for 137 industries for the years 1980–81 to 1997–98 to understand the impacts of trade liberalization on PCMs. The results of their analysis indicate that the reduction of tariffs and substantial elimination of quantitative restrictions in the 1990s could not reduce the PCMs in the manufacturing industry. On the contrary, PCMs showed an increasing trend in most sub-sectors, as well as at the aggregate level. The authors argued that though there was a tendency for trade liberalization to depress price-cost margins, it was probably offset by a significant decline in the real wage growth rates, and a substantial fall in the share of labour/wages in manufacturing value added.

Pant and Pattanayak (2005) studied the "Imports As Market Discipline Hypothesis", which states that increased imports can raise the level of competition and reduce profit mark-ups. They used firm level data for 1989–2001 and calculated mark-ups of different industries by using PCM and regressed it on the data on CR4 (four-firm concentration ratio), wage share, openness, and a time specific dummy variable for the post-1991 years. Their analysis suggests that trade openness did not in itself reduce the profit mark-ups. They also observed that the estimated margins were in general high over the 1990s, and in most of the industries these margins increased over 1995–2000.

Ramaswamy (2006) assessed the intensity of competition in the Indian market by measuring the Hirschman-Herfindahl Index for 40 different industries. He captured the effect of FDI and tariff barriers by calculating import penetration ratios for different industries. He found that there was high market concentration among various industrial sectors, which could be an indication of anti-competitive conduct. By exploring the "Imports As Market Discipline Hypothesis", the study also found that allowing foreign firms in the domestic market does not guarantee lowering of concentration or an increase in competition.

Athreye and Kapur (2006) studied industrial concentration in Indian manufacturing sectors over the period 1970–99, and found that, post-1991 reforms, industry characteristics showed stronger linkage with concentration. However, factors that were not related to industry characteristics continued

Competition in Indian industry 141

to impact industry concentration, signifying the continuing role of policy variables in determining market concentration.

Bhandari (2010) examined the validity of the conventional SCP paradigm with panel data econometric analysis. The results suggest that PCMs in Indian industries are determined by market concentration, R&D expenditure, advertising intensity considered to reflect entry barriers and product differentiation, and the extent of vertical integration. The study, therefore, implied that the SCP paradigm was quite valid for explaining the nature of competition and its outcomes in the Indian manufacturing industry.

Barua et al. (2010) evaluated the effects of economic reforms on competitiveness of select Indian manufacturing industries using firm level data for the period 1990–2008. The analysis suggests that there has been a declining trend in the level of concentration over the period, probably indicating easing of entry barriers due to reforms. However, a commensurate general trend could not be observed for PCMs, as they behaved differently across sub-sectors, probably due to impacts of technical changes. Interestingly, the size of the firms were found to be significantly linked with export performance.

Mehta et al. (2016) studied the Indian pharmaceutical industry at the aggregate level, as well as five therapeutic segments within the industry. Using the HHI as the indicator of market concentration, the study found that even though there was relatively low concentration (HHI = 0.0226) for the pharmaceutical industry as a whole, when looking at the individual therapeutic segments, more than two-thirds of the market in terms of value were of at least moderate concentration (HHI between 0.3 and 0.5).

While there have been several studies on industrial concentration, the rate of return, and PCM, relatively few studies have been conducted to understand the intensity of competition using the persistence of profits method that analyzes the static and dynamic long-run equilibrium profit. Hence, it would be useful to look at a few studies that have been conducted in the context of other countries. While the seminal work in this approach was done by Mueller (1977, 1986, 1990), there have been several other important studies including Connolly and Schwartz (1985), Geroski and Jacquemin (1988), Jacobsen (1988), Kambhampati (1995), Waring (1996) and Cable and Jackson (2008).

These studies have analyzed persistence of abnormal profits for different economies in different time periods. Using a sample of about 600 firms with data for the years 1950–72, Mueller (1990) found that firms show a tendency to converge to the average rate of profit rate in the industry, but the process of convergence is incomplete, meaning that do not really converge. Geroski and Jacquemin (1988) analyzed the data of large firms from the UK, France, and Germany to find that that the UK firms displayed lower variation in profits, but the profits tended to persist over time. In contrast, larger variations in profits were observed in France and Germany, but interestingly, they showed lower persistence and tended to converge quickly to the average

142 *Competition in Indian industry*

rate of profit for the industry. Schwalbach et al. (1989) found similar results for German firms.

Jacobsen (1988) studied a sample of 241 US firms with data over 20 years, and found that market concentration did not have any significant impact on profitability, and that abnormal profits vanished rather quickly. Connolly and Schwartz (1985) came out with interesting findings as an asymmetry was found in the way different types of firms converged to the average rate of profit in the industry. While firms with lower than average profit tend to converge to the average level quickly, the firms with higher than average profit tend to persist with higher profits. They also found that the persistence of profits also tended to vary across industries and factors like R&D impacted the speed of convergence significantly.

On the basis of analysis of US firm level data for a period of 20 years, Waring (1996) observed that in the US automobile industry, the three major firms had persistent profitability differences throughout the 1970s. Cable and Jackson (2008) used a trend-based analysis instead of a standard first-order auto-regression model to study the persistence of profits for a sample of UK companies. They found the non-eroding profit persistence to be present in around 60 per cent of the companies.

Gschwandtner (2010) analyzed the data for US firms, allowing the assumption that firms can enter or exit the industry. He observed a constant increase in competition in the US economy, after the opening of the economy to international competition in the 1960s–80s. He highlighted that the key determinants of persistence of profit were the firm and industry size, industry growth, and more recently risk, advertising, and exports.

Among the very few studies on persistence of profit that were conducted in the Indian context, one important one is by Kambhampati (1995) which focused on the pre-liberalization period. The study considered 16 years of data (1970–85) and 42 firms to understand the persistence of profit in the Indian manufacturing industry. It observed that in several industrial sub-sectors, above average profit persisted over time and the level of persistence was higher in industries with higher growth rates which also tended to have lower competitive pressure. As expected, industrial sub-sectors that had higher strategic barriers like higher advertising intensity also showed higher profit persistence.

In the study by Glenn et al. (1999), though India was not the focus, it was one of the nine developing countries (Argentina, India, Jordan, South Korea, Malaysia, Mexico, Peru, Thailand, and Zimbabwe) for which intensity of competition was measured for the period 1980–92. It also tried to separate the results for pre- and post-liberalization periods. In the post-liberalization period, they observed improvements in capital efficiency and reduction in profit margins in the emerging markets. They also concluded that intensity of competition in developing countries is at least as high as that in developed countries. While in another study, Glenn et al. (2001) found similar results when they considered seven emerging markets and dropped three

Competition in Indian industry   143

countries – Argentina, Peru and Thailand – they found that emerging economies showed lower persistence of profit compared to developed economies.

There is a possibility of bias, given the choice of period of analysis due to the limited availability of post-liberalization data in Glenn et al. (1999) and Glenn et al. (2001). In India, post-1991 economic liberalization and economic changes (like abolition of licensing and allowance of FDI in different sectors) might have changed the industrial structure. Because of domestic protection and prevalence of the licensing system before 1988 or 1991, firms might have enjoyed abnormal profits. Also, identification of long-run profits – which is a crucial factor affecting convergence of profit – was not addressed in those studies. Thus, it is important to analyze their impact, and how the firms and the overall industry behave in a liberalizing economic environment. However, it is also important to note that even for a period that was largely before liberalization, the study found that persistence of profit in India was lower than advanced countries.

Very few studies have measured the competitive rate of profit in the Indian manufacturing industry. Pushpangadan and Shanta (2008) studied the dynamics of competition in select manufacturing industries. They estimated that the long-run competitive rate of profit was 9.2 per cent, and the persistence of profit (percentage of short-run profit carried over to the next year) was at 46.5 per cent, much higher than that estimated by Glenn et al. (1999). Interestingly, a similar trend was observed in PCM estimates, although conceptually, the two are very different. However, the period analyzed by them was until 2001, while major reduction in tariffs took place in India since 1995 when the WTO and the Uruguay Round agreements came into effect. Moreover, it was only in 2002 that the quantitative restrictions on imports were removed. Hence, a study that includes data until the year 2001 is unlikely to bring the impacts of economic liberalization. Thus, an attempt is made here to analyze the presence and nature of competition and persistence of profit (for selected manufacturing industries) for more recent years (2002–15).

5.3   Measuring competition through persistence of profit[2]

Though ease of estimation makes PCM a widely used measure of competition, its theoretical foundations as a competition measure are not robust (Boone 2008). This chapter explores the presence and nature of competition in select manufacturing industries (based on their relevance in the Indian economy) and measures the level of competition in those industries. With the most recent available data (from 2002 onwards), this chapter assesses the dynamics of competition through persistence of profit using Mueller's methodology. It also measures competitive rate of profit for the selected manufacturing industries, which helps to decompose the profit rate into short-term and long-term components. Finally, the chapter also evaluates the strength of competition using Cubbin and Geroski's (1990) half-life measure.

144 *Competition in Indian industry*

To explore the persistence of profits, decomposition of profits is necessary. Observed total profit (P_{it}) enjoyed by a firm can broadly be decomposed into normal competitive return (C), firm-specific permanent rent (R_i), and a short-term transitory rent (S_{it}), which is also firm specific and converges to zero over time.

$$P_{it} = C + R_i + S_{it} \qquad (5.4)$$

In a competitive environment, in the long run, above-normal profits cannot exist. Thus, equilibrium profit will converge to the competitive return. In that case, $R_i = 0$ and $E(S_{it}) = 0$ as t approaches infinity.

The short-run component of profit in Equation 5.4 is assumed to be inversely related to time (t) so that the limiting value of the profit function as t tends to infinity can be taken as the estimate of the long-term component ($C + R_i$).

More specifically,

$$S_{it} = \alpha_{1i}(1/t) + \varepsilon_{it} \qquad (5.5)$$

Substituting (5.5) in (5.4) gives the profit equation:

$$P_{it} = C + R_i + \alpha_{1i}(1/t) + \varepsilon_{it} = \alpha_{0i} + \alpha_{1i}(1/t) + \varepsilon_{it} \qquad (5.6)$$

where $\alpha_{0i} = C + R_i$

The limit of $E(P_{it})$ as $t \to \infty$ is α_{0i}, which is taken as the long-term component of profit.

One limitation of the model is that it exhibits an inherent bias towards convergence. Moreover, the speed of adjustment of the short-run rent cannot be assessed in this model. To overcome these limitations, it is postulated that the short-run rents are inter-temporally related but converge to zero over time. Under this specification,

$$S_{it} = \lambda_i S_{it-1} + \mu_i \qquad (5.7)$$

Where λ_i is the speed of convergence/adjustment coefficient, the persistence with which profits differ from period to period from their long-term level. $|\lambda_i| < 1$ for stability and convergence over time, and μ_i is the error term with the mean value of zero and constant variance.

Multiplying Equation 5.4 for period t–1 by λ_i gives:

$$\lambda_i P_{it-1} = \lambda_i(C + R_i) + \lambda_i S_{it-1} \qquad (5.8)$$

Subtracting Equation 5.8 from Equation 5.4 gives:

$$P_{it} - \lambda_i P_{it-1} = C + R_i + S_{it} - \lambda_i(C + R_i) - \lambda_i S_{it-1}$$

Rearranging the terms gives:

$$P_{it} = (1 - \lambda_i)(C + R_i) + \lambda_1 P_{it-1} + S_{it} - \lambda_1 S_{it-1} \qquad (5.9)$$

Substituting Equation 5.7 in Equation 5.9 generates:

$$P_{it} = \alpha_i + \lambda_i P_{it-1} + \mu_i \qquad (5.10)$$

Where $\alpha_i = (1 - \lambda_i)(C + R_i)$.

This final Equation 5.10 represents the dynamic process (autoregressive time series of order 1 (AR1) which is estimated here.

Taking expectation of Equation 5.10 gives:

$$E(P_{it}) = \alpha_i + \lambda_i E(P_{it-1})$$

Since $E(P_{it}) = E(P_{it-1}) = \hat{P}_i$, it also means:

$$\hat{P}_i = \frac{\hat{\alpha}_i}{1 - \hat{\lambda}_i}$$

$\hat{P}_i$ also represents normal competitive return which cannot be eroded by competition, while $\hat{\lambda}_i$ is a measure of competition. If it is close to zero, competition is strong and adjustment process is fast. Now, $\hat{\lambda}_i$ and $\hat{\alpha}_i$ represent the firm and industry characteristics. Industry size, industry growth, firm size, firm growth, growth of competing firms, share of the firm in the industry, and R&D in the firm and in its competitors are some of the important factors (other than industrial policy) which lead to generation of abnormal profits or convergence to normal competitive return.

The model is estimated with firm-level data obtained from the Capitaline database.[3] The database is an unbalanced panel. The nature of the dataset is such that the sample changes every year as some firms are dropped and some are added. The most probable reason for dropping some firms is non-availability of data and, therefore, they cannot be taken as entry or exit of firms from an industry. A panel of 257 firms for the period 2002/03–2015/16 is considered for the analysis. Apart from all-industry analysis, the analysis also evaluates nature and strength of competition in eight major manufacturing industries:[4] While the selection of manufacturing industries was largely driven by the availability of data, the findings of the previous chapter also played a role. The petroleum industry was not included, although it was found to be among the better-performing industries, as it was until recently highly regulated in India. Automobiles (cars), automobiles (HCV/LCVs), cement (major north), cement (major south), cotton textiles, drugs and pharmaceuticals, electronics, electrical machinery, food products, and iron and steel (large) are industries taken up for the analysis.

146 *Competition in Indian industry*

5.4 Estimates of competition parameters and possible implications

In this study, the profit rate has been defined as the profit after tax plus interest payment as a share of total asset (excluding revaluation and depreciation). This is the most common and widely used definition of profit rate in the literature. Moreover, a potential entrant in an industry will look at profit after tax rather than profit before tax for making an entry decision. The study has checked for the presence of auto-correlation (auto-correlation of order one was present) and data were adjusted accordingly for further analysis.

In the current study, firm level data from Indian manufacturing industries for the period 2002–15 have been used. The data have been collected from Capitaline database. Few data points (data for a particular year) are missing for a number of firms. Thus, the firms for which most continuous data is available within the select time span have been considered. Finally, 257 firms qualified for this analysis which are distributed across eight manufacturing industries as follows: automobiles (cars) (16), automobiles (HCV/LCVs) (16), cement (major north) (11), cement (major south) (4), cotton textiles (38), drugs and pharmaceuticals (88), electronics (20), electric machinery (33), food products (18), and iron and steel (large) (13).

The auto-profit equations (Equation 5.10) are estimated for 257 firms to identify and measure the long-term profit (i.e., normal competitive return and long-term firm-specific rent) and the short-term profit, which is carried over from one year to the next year. Table 5.1 shows the average value of λ_i (adjustment coefficient for short-term profit) and P_{ip} (long-term profit). Table 5.1 shows that while on average the adjustment coefficient for short-term profit (transitory rent) is about 0.29, indicating that 29 per cent of short-term profit is carried over to the next year, which also gives the measure for persistence of profit, the long-term profit rate is only 5.7 per cent for the selected industries taken together.

One previous study (Glenn et al. 2001) found that the persistence of short-term profit was 22 per cent during 1982–92. Another study by Pushpangadan and Shanta (2008) found that the adjustment coefficient was 0.47. Thus, over time, both long-term profit and the persistence of short-term profit – and hence, competition – might have changed in the Indian industry.

Table 5.1 Summary of λ_i (adjustment coefficient for short-run profit) and P_{ip} (long-term profit)

Variable	Observations	Mean	Min.	Max.	Standard error
P_{ip}	257	.0567	−2.5309	.6150	0.1218
λ_i	257	.2908	−5.6269	8.0982	0.2912

Competition in Indian industry   147

To explore the nature and trend of short-term temporary profit and long-term profit, which includes normal competitive return and long-term firm-specific permanent rent, an evaluation of the frequency distribution of λ_i and P_{ip} ($P_{ip} = C + R_i)^5$ is important (Tables 5.2 and 5.3). Out of 257 firms, 89 (7 + 12 + 52 + 18) firms lie beyond the range specified in the profit function (0–1), i.e., outside range (Table 5.2). Only 65 per cent of the sample firms (168 of 257 firms) are valid, i.e., had λ_i positive and significantly different from zero (at 5 per cent level of confidence).

As indicated in Table 5.3, 46 firms have negative long-term profit and most firms lie in the ranges (0.0–0.1) or (0.1–0.5). This indicates that the competitive profit rate will belong in the range (0–0.5). The exact value of the competitive normal return is calculated based on Mueller's search procedure.

According to Mueller (1990), competitive return is the level of profit at which number of firms is the minimum. If profit increases beyond that level, more firms are attracted towards the industry, and this competition will lead to erosion of profit to the permanent rent level. Based on Mueller's search procedure, this study estimates the competitive return for the Indian manufacturing industry. Repeating the process for each profit interval, this study finds that 0.035 is the normal competitive rate of profit for the Indian manufacturing industry. This also helps to estimate the long-term firm-specific rent which is measured by long-term profit less the normal competitive return.

Table 5.2 Distribution of Adjustment Coefficient of Short-run Profit (λ_i)

Interval	Frequency
Less than –1	7
Between –1 and –0.5	12
Between –0.5 and 0	52
Between 0 and 0.5	95
Between 0.5 and 1	73
Greater than 1	18

Table 5.3 Distribution of Long-term Profit Rates (P_{ip})

Interval	Frequency
Less than –0.5	5
Between –0.5 and –0.1	9
Between –0.1 and 0	32
Between 0 and 0.1	115
Between 0.1 and 0.5	95
Greater than 0.5	1

148 *Competition in Indian industry*

As per the sample, the average firm-specific long-term rent is about 2.2 per cent (5.7–3.5 per cent) for the Indian industry. One previous study by Push-pangadan and Shanta (2008) using Indian industry data until 2001 found that competitive profit rate was 5 per cent but long-term firm-specific rent was 4.2 per cent. It seems that both competitive normal return and long-run firm-specific rent have declined over time.

The inter-industry variation of observed profit and its components are also estimated. Table 5.4 shows the average profit rate and its decomposition across various industries. All the selected industries enjoy presence of positive level of observed profit. Among the selected industries, cement (major north) (11.38 per cent), drugs and pharmaceuticals (11.23 per cent), and food products (10.51 per cent) enjoy relatively high level of observed profit. Long-term rent (R_i) is also high for these three industries. On the other hand, short-term profit (S_{it}) is the highest for cotton textiles (14.1 per cent), followed by automobiles (cars) at 6.45 per cent.

After industry-wise decomposition of profit, the intra-industry or inter-firm (within same industry) variation of long-term profit is explored. Since normal competitive return is the same across all industries and firms, exploring the intra-industry variation in the long-term rent serves the purpose. To explore the equality of long-term profit across firms and number of firms having equal profit, we need to check the equality (of long-term rent) between two firms for all possible combinations of firms within a particular industry.

The results generated through this technique are shown in Table 5.5. For example, in case of iron and steel (large) industry, there are 13 firms, and hence, there are 78 combinations of firms to check the equality of long-term profit between two firms. In 32 of the 78 cases, equality of long-term profit was rejected by t-test. As indicated in Table 5.5, equality of long-term profit is highest

Table 5.4 Decomposition of Profit Rates by Industry

Industry	Average observed profit rate	Average long-term profit rate	Average short-run profit rate
Cotton textiles	0.031	–0.11	0.141
Automobiles (cars)	0.014	–0.05	0.064
Automobiles (HCV/LCVs)	0.072	0.038	0.034
Cement (major south)	0.089	0.048	0.041
Cement (major north)	0.114	0.061	0.054
Iron and steel (large)	0.071	0.038	0.033
Pharmaceuticals	0.112	0.064	0.048
Electric machinery	0.076	0.038	0.038
Food products	0.105	0.08	0.025
Electronics	0.038	0.012	0.026

Competition in Indian industry 149

Table 5.5 Test of Equality of Long-term Profit by Industry

Industry	No. of firms	No. of tests	No. of tests statistically significant*
Cotton textiles	38	703	525 (75%)
Automobiles (cars)	16	120	87 (73%)
Automobiles (HCV/LCVs)	16	120	83 (69%)
Cement (major south)	4	6	4 (67%)
Cement (major north)	11	55	28 (51%)
Iron and steel (large)	13	78	32 (41%)
Drugs and pharmaceuticals	88	3,828	1,083 (28%)
Electric machinery	33	528	142 (27%)
Food products	18	153	31 (21%)
Electronics	20	190	38 (20%)

* 5% level of significance (two-tailed t-test).

for electronics sector and lowest in cotton textiles. In 75 per cent of the cotton textile industry cases, equality of long-term profit rate across firms is rejected.

Next, the strength of competition at industry level is assessed. Strength of competition depends on the adjustment coefficient of short-term profit or the transitional part (λ_i) of the profit which is carried over from one year to the next year. The higher the value of λ_i, the higher is the persistence of profit and lower is the level of competition. The strength of competition can also be measured in terms of the time required to wipe out the transitional (short-term) component of profit. However, as suggested by Cubbin and Geroski (1990), the strength of competition is measured as the time required for the transitional rent to be halved (half-life). Half-life time is calculated as: T = log (1/2)/log λ_i.

As per model specification, λ_i should vary within the range 0–1. This study calculates the strength of competition for the firms which satisfies this criterion. Table 5.6 portrays the strength of dynamic competition in each of the selected manufacturing industries in terms of average λ_i value (transitional rent carried over from one period to next period) and half-life (time required to wipe out the transitional rent to be halved).

As shown in Table 5.6, persistence of profit (transitional) is the highest for the cotton textile sector, while it is the lowest in the electronics and food products sectors. The λ_i itself indicates variation of strength of competition across selected industries. It is found that the cotton textile sector has the highest half-life time (1.48 years). Pushpangadan and Shanta (2008), using Indian industry data until 2001, also found that cotton textiles (1.12 years) had the second highest half-life time. A minute comparison indicates that while half-life time has increased for cotton textile and iron and steel, for other comparable sectors, it has declined over time.

150 *Competition in Indian industry*

Table 5.6 Strength of Dynamic Competition in Indian Manufacturing Industries

Industry	No. of firms	Mean λ_i	Half-life (years)
Electronics	11	0.33	0.63
Food products	11	0.33	0.63
Drugs and pharmaceuticals	58	0.38	0.71
Electric machinery	22	0.40	0.76
Automobiles (cars)	10	0.42	0.81
Cement (major south)	3	0.47	0.91
Iron and steel (large)	10	0.48	0.95
Cement (major north)	7	0.49	0.99
Automobiles (HCV/LCVs)	8	0.54	1.12
Cotton textiles	28	0.63	1.48
All industries	168	0.44	0.84

Table 5.7 Composite Index for Intensity of Competition in Indian Manufacturing

Industry	Equality of profit rejected		Half-life (years)		Long-term profit		Short-run profit		Composite index	
	%	R	Time	R	Rate	R	Rate	R	Index	R
Cotton textiles	75	1	1.48	1	−0.11	10	0.136	1	13	1
Automobiles (cars)	73	2	0.81	6	−0.05	9	0.064	2	19	5
Automobiles (HCV/LCVs)	69	3	1.12	2	0.038	5	0.034	7	17	3
Cement (south)	67	4	0.91	5	0.048	4	0.041	5	18	4
Cement (north)	51	5	0.99	3	0.061	3	0.054	3	14	2
Iron and steel	41	6	0.95	4	0.038	6	0.033	8	24	7
Pharmaceuticals	28	7	0.71	8	0.064	2	0.048	4	21	6
Electric machinery	27	8	0.76	7	0.038	7	0.038	6	28	8
Food products	21	9	0.63	9	0.08	1	0.025	10	29	9
Electronics	20	10	0.63	10	0.012	8	0.026	9	37	10

We have also formulated a composite index for intensity of competition in different industries. The index captures the extent to which the equality of profit hypothesis is rejected in an industry, half-life for short-run profit to become zero,[6] and long-term profit and short-run profit. First, industries are ranked based on these criteria. A rank of 1 means low competition, while a rank of 10 means high competition. Rank values for each of these criteria are added to get the composite index. The industries are ranked for overall intensity of competition based on the ranks of the composite indices. The results of the exercise are shown in Table 5.7. The cotton textiles industry

Competition in Indian industry   151

seems to have the lowest level of competition, which is quite surprising. The cement and LCV/HCVs industries are also subject to low levels of competition. Electronics seems to have the highest level of competition, which is quite expected.

5.5   Conclusion

This chapter assessed the degree of competition prevailing in different sub-sectors of Indian industry. Price-cost margin has been used widely to understand the presence or intensity of competition in an industry. However, as the theoretical foundation of price-cost margin is not robust enough, a measure of persistence of profit was used to assess the dynamic nature of competition by calculating long-term and short-run profits in select manufacturing sub-sectors.

To do this, profit was decomposed into three components: normal competitive return, firm-specific permanent rent, and transitory rent. In a competitive environment, in the long run, above-normal profit cannot exist, and hence, equilibrium profit will be at the level of normal competitive return. It is postulated that the short-run rents are inter-temporally related, but converge to zero over time. Estimation of the appropriate equation by econometric technique gives the estimates of long-term profit as well as adjustment coefficient, the speed at which the transitory rent erodes over time.

An analysis of the estimates indicates that there might have been a decline in long-term profit in Indian industry in recent years. This could be due to the fact that, following the 2007–08 crisis, industries are doing poorly all over the world. While the competitive normal return is about 3.5 per cent, the average long-term firm-specific rent is about 2.2 per cent in recent years. Moreover, immediately after the liberalization exercise, short-run profit might have increased, though in recent years, it might have declined. However, it needs to be noted that short-run (transitory) profit is quite significant in cotton textiles, automobiles (cars), cement (south) and pharmaceuticals industries.

While competition intensity is reasonably strong in the automobile industry, the LCV/HCVs segment appears to have rather weak competition intensity. It is not difficult to explain this by pointing out that the automobile industry in India has almost all global car manufacturers, but there are just a few players in the LCV/HCVs segment. It is also to be noted that this industry still enjoys a high degree of import protection, which could also be responsible for long-term and short-run profit behaving so differently.

As with the observed profits, long-term permanent rent is also high in cement (major north), pharmaceuticals, and food products, while short-term profit is relatively high in the cotton textiles industry. Persistence of profit is the highest in the cotton textiles industry and the lowest in the electronics industry. Cement (major north) companies enjoy higher long-term profits, as well as persistence of profit. This could be due to the fact that the regional markets are not integrated well, as it is a bulky product, and hence, difficult

152   *Competition in Indian industry*

to serve long distance markets. It may also be noted that time and again, concerns have been expressed that there might have been cartelization in the industry. It shows that there are reasons to raise such suspicions.

Long-term profits of pharmaceuticals are high globally, and hence, it is quite expected, particularly in the post-TRIPS scenario. The pharmaceutical industry is also characterized by a situation whereby consumers do not make buying decisions and the doctors might not decide the cheapest available alternatives for the patients. This might have led to higher profitability in the industry. Although persistence of profit is not very high in this industry, the long-term profit is quite high. This could be due to the fact that firm-specific permanent rent captures the impacts of patents.

Equality of profit across firms within an industry is the highest for electronics industry, while it is the lowest in the cotton textiles industry. The existing firms in the electronics industry might have equal competitive strength, which can be reflected in equality of their profits. Even the persistence of profits is quite low in this industry. Hence, the intensity of competition is very high. Apart from electronic goods, food products and electrical goods also appear to have high intensity of competition. Competition intensity is also fairly strong in the iron and steel industry.

However, the lower level of equality of profit in the textile industry *prima facie* appears to be surprising, given that with the dismantling of not only the domestic protection but also the global Multi-Fibre Arrangement, the intensity of competition should have been high in this industry. However, it could be due to the fact that a developing country market for textiles and clothing industry has one group of firms that compete on price, while there are firms that compete on their brand value. Hence, it could be due to the existence of highly heterogeneous firms in the industry. This could also be due to the fact that some items in this industry enjoy a very high degree of import protection (Table 4.1). But overall, competition intensity does not seem to be strong in the industry.

Notes

1 According to this hypothesis, managerial capability or X-efficiency is responsible for higher profits in firms, rather than market structure.
2 Sections 5.3 and 5.4 are partly drawn from a paper titled "Presence of Profit and Competition in Indian Industry", presented by the author (Nitya Nanda) at the National Conference on Economics of Competition Law, held on March 2, 2017 at New Delhi.
3 Available at www.capitaline.com
4 Two of the industries are divided into two sub-groups each, taking the total number of industries to ten.
5 $\hat{P}_i = \hat{P}_{ip} = C$
6 Adjustment coefficient for short-run profit is similar to half-life, and hence, is not included in the composite index.

6   Concluding observations

The industrial performance literature very often looked at the performance of individual firms within an industry, as the subject has been dominated by the SCP paradigm. It focused on characteristics of markets and how such characteristics influence the performance of individual firms or even an industry. However, such an approach cannot understand the macro performance of an industry, particularly in a developing country where the level of industrialization is low and economic development is often considered to be synonymous with industrialization.

Another difficulty with this approach is that though it might be useful to understand producers' surplus issues and consumers' surplus issues that might offer important insights from a competition policy perspective, it does not cast light on industrial policy or macroeconomic policy implications. Hence, if industrial performance also includes industrial growth from a national or global perspective, a different approach might be required so that one can offer some perspectives on industrial policy and its possible impacts on it.

India has been adopting "industrial policy" from time to time since Independence, and the objective has always been to promote industrialization. However, the notion of industrial policy that is being considered here is broader in scope and includes several other policies that might have any bearing on macro and micro industrial performance. Industrial policy is more about strategic efforts made to promote industrialization in a country. This study made an endeavour to understand industrial performance that can combine both macro and micro performance issues, and can be linked to industrial policy of the country. Characterization of the macroeconomic framework, as well as the industrial policy, is also important to understand the linkage.

6.1   Policies influencing performance

For long, trade policy has been receiving substantial attention as the one policy domain that influences industrialization, as well as the industrial productivity and efficiency of a country. However, it is difficult to find any clear

DOI: 10.4324/9781003047490-6

154 *Concluding observations*

theoretical as well as empirical basis to establish a clear causal relationship between trade policy and industrialization. While trade – exports in particular – played an important role, by no means does it indicate that a liberalized trade policy automatically ensures industrialization, economic growth, or efficiency. Most countries that have achieved economic development followed a strategic interventionist trade policy at least during some period of their development experience.

Since developed countries have generally been major capital exporting countries in terms of investing abroad, early developers did not receive any foreign investment in their development process. The current situation, however, is quite different. While early developers had colonies that helped them in mobilizing and accessing resources, late developers did not have such options. Hence, FDI can complement domestic capital formation. Moreover, the global IPR regime under TRIPS has made it much more difficult to access technologies from developed countries or to develop their own technologies. Given this context, foreign investment can be a conduit of technology transfer to developing countries.

However, free flow of foreign investment to developing countries does not guarantee that it will lead to industrialization in developing countries. Global experience shows that FDI can also be harmful in some cases involving acquisition of existing business by foreign firms, as much of such FDI flows to consolidate regional or global market power by the TNCs. With some generalization, it can be said that while greenfield foreign investments are likely to bring benefits, acquisition-type FDI brings very little – if any – benefit. Hence, countries that can channelize FDI according to their development needs do better in drawing development benefits from FDI.

The prevailing global economic situation and how a particular country is positioned therein influence industrial development. While it is difficult to imagine that a country will industrialize quickly when the global economy is not growing fast enough, the development experience of Asian economies also shows that the global position of a country is also important. This region has often been referred to as benefitting from a flying geese pattern of development diffusion. When a country achieves a particular level of development, the resulting wage increase facilitates industrialization in another country, particularly in labour-intensive sectors. This is how countries like Japan, South Korea, Taiwan, Malaysia, and Thailand took turns in industrialization. The entry of China in the chain changed the scenario, since its huge army of reserve labour is refusing to permit a wage increase.

Broadly speaking, while the state was observed to play an important role in almost all economies in their early stages of development, the late industrializers generally followed even more interventionist economic policies. In general, state-led economic development or interventionist economic policies are often considered to be associated with the East Asian growth experience. However, the so-called Asian model is not purely Asian, as one can also argue that Germany is the actual birthplace of such an economic model. The visionary ideas that informed the post-war coordinated model of development in Germany were suggested by a group of economists who are now collectively known as the Freiburg School. East Asian countries embraced the model – with their own modifications to suit local conditions, of course.

6.2 Macro policy context and performance

6.2.1 Characterizing the Indian economy and industrialization strategy

Characterizing a state based on the importance of government expenditure in the economy can be misleading. The share of government in the gross national expenditure of the US expanded after 1929 and reached the level of 27 per cent in 1952, and this did not decline afterward. Similarly, in 1960, the government of West Germany had its share in the gross national product even higher than that of the US. Nobody ever claimed West Germany to be a socialist country; rather, it was considered to be among the most important free-enterprise economies of the world. India, with much less share of the government in the national economy, was considered a Soviet-type planned economy!

West Germany also followed a universal banking system, and the government coordinated the activities of major producer groups. In South Korea also, several state-owned companies were established, companies were given export targets, and export performance was linked with import licenses and tax exemptions for imports – and since the government envisaged a major role for the banks, it nationalized the banking sector and established full control over all forms of institutional credit. In contrast, in India, banks were largely in the private sector during the 1950s and 1960s: India nationalized the Imperial Bank to establish the State Bank of India in 1955, and other major banks were nationalized only in 1969.

Though India has often been characterized as a "mixed economy", the term has not been used elsewhere so widely, and it could easily give in to misinterpretation. It is quite odd to associate India's development planning with a "centrally planned economy". The facts that India became politically quite close to the communist bloc; used technologies from the Soviet bloc, particularly in state-owned enterprise in steel and the oil and gas sector; and also developed close trade linkages with the bloc; could have been responsible for such a perception.

These were, to a large extent, a political necessity for India and also due to the fact that these are the countries that could give India their technologies easily at cheaper costs. In the Western world, the technologies are generally held by companies and not the government, and hence, it is quite

156 Concluding observations

difficult to access them at cheaper costs from there – even if the governments were willing. Hence, it would be more appropriate to characterize India's development planning with coordinated market economies like Germany, South Korea, or Taiwan, rather than as a Soviet-type centrally planned economy

While the alleged fascination of India's first prime minister, Jawaharlal Nehru, towards "Fabian socialism" is often cited as a proof for describing the Indian system as a "Soviet-type socialist planned economy", what is simply ignored is the fact that the first industrial policy of the country was introduced by the then-industries minister Dr Shyama Prasad Mukherjee, who was known for his anti-communist credentials. The main opposition party of that time was the Communist Party of India, which never believed that India was anywhere near socialism.

Similarly, it is also difficult to characterize Indian economic policy in terms of a pre- and post-1991 binary. Major course changes took place even in the Second and Third Five Year Plans in terms of putting emphasis on heavy industry in the former and export promotion in the latter. A major policy intervention took place in 1969, when all major commercial banks were nationalized. Similarly, major policy changes continued to occur even after 1991.

While India became more open to foreign direct investment in 1991, by no means was it a one-time event: the gradual liberalization of the FDI regime continued well after 2014 when the new government made substantial liberalization. It is possibly in case of public sector enterprises that one can claim the existence of pre- and post-1991 differences, as the number of public sector enterprises stopped growing after 1991; it remained almost the same for more than 15 years and increased again afterwards.

While exports were not a priority in the 1950s, since the Third Five Year Plan, export promotion became an important part of planning. India was a pioneer in conceptualizing and establishing an export processing zone in 1965, ahead of South Korea, Taiwan, and China. The next year, India devalued its currency substantially to boost its exports. Despite this, the pre-1991 economic policy regime in India is assumed to follow an import-substituting industrialization strategy as against the export-led industrialization strategy, even though the country tried its best to promote exports for a full three decades before 1991.

On the other hand, there is a clear example of growth of the automobile industry in India after 1991 that has been driven by domestic demand under import-substituting trade regime, as the import tariff is still high in this sector. Clearly, it is quite problematic to term industrialization strategy before 1991 to be import substituting and that of post-1991 to be export led. Rather, as many economists have pointed out in the case of South Korea, India also followed a combination of export-led and import-substituting industrialization strategies all along.

6.2.2 *A macro perspective on economic and industrial performance*

While there were several studies that claimed that economic growth of India experienced a structural break around the year 1991, it is now well established that the overall economic growth in India accelerated in the early 1980s rather than in the early 1990s. Nayyar (2006) points out that if one has to accept the 1980 structural break in economic growth rate in India, one has to also accept that there was another structural break around 1950 which was, in fact, more drastic than the one that took place around 1980.

This study established that if there was a structural break around the 1980s, then there was a structural break around 1965, as well. The Indian economy, as well as Indian industry, indeed took off around 1950, but could not retain the momentum beyond the mid-1960s. This could have been due to factors mostly outside the domain of economic or industrial policy. The poor performance continued until about 1980, when the economy recovered once again.

Moreover, the lower GDP growth rates of the 1950s and 1960s are more a reflection of relative shares of different sectors in GDP – namely, agriculture, industry, and services. When India started its development planning exercise, the share of agriculture was high compared to industry and services. An important characteristic of the growth process is that agriculture always showed a lower growth rate. This led to a drastic fall in the share of agriculture and a sharp rise in the share of the services. Hence, even if the growth rate of agriculture was low in the 1980s and 1990s, it could not have much impact on the overall GDP growth, and on the other hand, the higher growth rate of the services sector showed much higher positive impact on the overall GDP growth due to its higher share. Such simple issues have not been adequately highlighted in the literature on the Indian economic growth experience, largely due to the fact that recent studies always centred on the pre- and post-1991 binary.

When India adopted its development planning exercise around 1950, its initial conditions were much worse compared to where it was in the 1980s and 1990s. In particular, the share of savings in GDP was much lower, and poorer agricultural performance meant that it was a net food importing country, which meant that a substantial part of its investible fund had to be diverted to meet food imports. Hence, one can also argue that the growth performance shown during the period 1950–65 was the best in the recent history of India.

6.3 Industrial performance in India

Despite substantial methodological innovations for measuring industrial performance over the last few decades, it remains a challenge. While there are some sophisticated techniques to measure industrial performance, the black

158   *Concluding observations*

box–type nature of such tools makes it difficult to relate the estimates using such tools to different aspects of industrial policy.

A measure like technical efficiency gives average efficiency of firms within a country and does not permit a comparison to the international benchmark – a serious limitation of this and other similar techniques. While theoretically it is possible to measure technical efficiency using a global benchmark, in practice, it is almost impossible.

Moreover, if there is an inefficient firm operating in an economy, the efficiency of the economy can be improved by two means. One is to close it down, which is technically quite easy but enormously painful. The other is to turn the inefficient firm into an efficient one, which could be extremely difficult but highly rewarding at the end. The moot question in a situation where estimation of performance or efficiency shows that there has been an improvement over a time period is what has been the underlying process of such improvement: the first, or the second.

In this study, the first alternative was not accepted as an improvement in performance. Moreover, while it is important to measure performance in terms of a global benchmark, it might not be appropriate to see industrial performance in terms of export performance only. It is important to see performance in the global market, including both domestic and foreign markets. Another objective was to ensure that the measure of performance is simple and easy to understand intuitively, so that it can be linked easily with policy trends.

Given such objectives, this study zeroed in on three different performance indicators that were used to measure industrial performance in India: (i) the global competitiveness ratio, which is defined as the share of a country in the global value addition in any particular industrial sector; (ii) The competitive performance index, or the relative share of a particular industry in global value addition measured as the ratio of the share of a country in the global value addition in a particular sector, and its share in the global value addition in the manufacturing sector as a whole; (iii) the absolute competitive advantage, or the ratio of exports to imports of a particular item in a country. All these indicators have been suggested and used for the first time in this study. The first two indicators were estimated with data from UNIDO industrial statistics, while the third indicator was estimated using COMTRADE data on exports and imports.

The performance of most industries remained rather stagnant until about 1995, and started showing improvement since then. However, it must also be noted that this was the time when most developed countries were shedding their share in global production, and hence vacated their space to be occupied by developing countries. Nevertheless, only a few industries could improve or retain their performance level beyond 2002. Sectors like textiles, apparel, and leather goods are some that could not continue with good performance. Ultimately, a few sectors that could maintain their good performance were automobiles, basic metals, electrical machinery, petroleum products, and pharmaceuticals. Electronic goods and information technology products are some areas where India lost opportunities.

From the experience of different industries in terms of their performance, especially those that showed relatively better performance, it appears that industrial policy played an important role. However, it is not the case that there exists a "one-size-fits-all" industrial policy that can bring success. Different industries might require different kinds of industrial policy.

6.4 Intensity of competition

How is this performance profile related to the intensity of competition that might have prevailed in the Indian manufacturing industries? The intensity of competition was assessed through the persistence of profits in various manufacturing industries, which gives a measure of dynamic competition. A composite index for intensity of competition was developed and estimated. From both counts, electronic goods and textiles and clothing were found to be at the opposite ends of the spectrum: the intensity was the highest in electronics and the lowest in textiles and clothing – but both of these industries lost out in terms of performance as measured in this study. The difference is that textiles and clothing showed some promise in the 1990s; in the case of electronics, no such improvement was observed.

Among the better-performing industries, the intensity of competition was high in the electrical machinery industry. In the case of the iron and steel industry, which is the major component of basic metals in India, the intensity of dynamic competition is not so high, though it appears that it had reasonably high competition intensity as per the composite index. The case of the pharmaceuticals industry, which has performed well, is quite peculiar. The industry shows high profitability from a long-term perspective, but it also showed a relatively higher level of short-term competition. Globally, the pharmaceuticals industry is known to maintain high levels of profit, and hence, this seems to be the case also in India, but pharmaceutical companies might be engaging in non-price competition quite aggressively.

The automobile industry that was among the better-performing industries comes in the middle in terms of intensity of competition both from the perspective of dynamic competition and the composite index. Hence, it is quite difficult to establish a clear relationship between market structure or market dynamics and performance of Indian manufacturing industries.

A comprehensive analysis linking competition with the measures of performance is, of course, made difficult due to the fact that industrial categories are slightly different. Time periods are also different, with just about eight years of overlap. Table 6.1 has included only those sectors that are common or highly overlapping. Different sectors have been ranked on the basis of intensity of competition as well as different measures of performance (rank of 1 indicates high competition or performance).

160　*Concluding observations*

Table 6.1 Competition and Measures of Performance

Industry	Composite index of competition	GCR	CPI	ACA
Cotton textiles	7	5	7	7
Automobiles (cars)	6	2	2	1
Iron and steel	4	1	3	4
Pharmaceuticals	5	3	6	2
Electric machinery	3	4	1	3
Food products	2	6	4	5
Electronics	1	7	5	6
Rank correlation		−0.54	0.25	−0.21

It is observed that intensity of competition does not necessarily lead to better performance. While in case of CPI, there is a weak positive relationship, in the cases of GCR and ACA, competition tends to have a negative relationship. However, the relationship is not quite straightforward. While cotton textiles has low competition, it also has low performance. On the other hand, electronics has high competition, yet it has shown low performance. Intensity of competition is not very high in automobiles, but this sector has shown high performance. Surely, all industries are not similar in nature in terms of technology orientation and the global market structure. It is likely that competition can have varying impacts, depending on the nature of the industry. This might require deeper analysis, which is out of scope of this study. But this pattern (poor linkage between competition and performance) also indicates that "industrial policy" might have played the determining role.

6.5　Linking policy and performance

India has not abandoned its industrial policy fully, but it has been diluted substantially over the last two decades, impacting its industrial performance and leading to premature deindustrialization. While structuralist economics and the concept of "industrial policy" developed in the context of a core-periphery model, wherein countries in the periphery faced challenges from countries at the core, in the current context, this has changed. This has been primarily due to the fact that while most countries have diluted or abandoned their industrial policy, China is still following it quite vigorously. In the process, China has made substantial progress in the last three decades, and most developing countries would find it difficult to compete with it without a strategic industrial policy. Even though labour is cheaper in India, transport, energy, and finance all are relatively expensive in India (Box 6.1).

This has been mainly due to the retreat of the state, but also due to inadequate response of the private sector and the failure of the regulatory

Concluding observations 161

framework to ensure quality services at competitive rates. China's progress brought substantial challenges for India. Not only has it made India's export-led growth strategy ineffective, as it found it difficult to compete with China in the global market, but India has also been challenged in its domestic market. When countries like South Korea and Taiwan made similar achievements, they did not impact the global economy so much, but the sheer size of the Chinese economy disrupted the global economy.

Most countries are aware of it, and that is the reason many WTO members, including India, refused to recognize China as a market economy and targeted it with anti-dumping actions (Nanda 2020). But this is hardly enough to deal with a country that follows "industrial policy" quite vigorously. Anti-dumping actions are initiated at the request of affected domestic companies, but when domestic companies decide to stop production and shift their production to the dumping country, or simply start importing from there, it becomes ineffective.

Box 6.1   India and China: diverging industrial policy and performance

It may sound unbelievable, but according to World Bank estimates, in 1987, India's GDP (in US$) was slightly higher than that of China, and since China had a higher population, India's per capita GDP was substantially higher than that of China, which was maintained until 1990. By 2018, China's GDP as well as per capita GDP both become almost five times those of India. However, the structure of the Chinese GDP contained its seeds for higher growth rates for the future. In 1990, the share of agriculture in China was 26.8 per cent as against 30.7 per cent in India. The share of industry in China was 41.2 per cent as against 32.2 per cent in India, while the shares of service sector were 32.2 per cent and 47.2 per cent, respectively (Nayyar 2019). Since agriculture has a tendency to post a lower growth rate, India was at a disadvantage with a higher share of agriculture. India also had a much higher share of services. But estimates of service sector income are always problematic, as a part of it might contain income from rent-seeking activities, which cannot only be unproductive but may also have adverse implications (Nanda 2019). Moreover, with higher service sectors, it was quite difficult to embark on an export-led growth path, which China, with a much higher industrial sector, could take advantage of.

The higher share of industrial sector was also because of its massive push for construction of infrastructure, wherein it was building railways, roads, ports, power plants, etc. But in 1991, India thought it was better to give such responsibility to the private players. While the government in India almost stopped investing in such activities, the private sector was not yet ready, due to inherent risks, an absence of proper financing mechanism, and the regulatory environment. Private investment was too little and too late. When the government realized it, it was too late. Finally, the government decided to make an investment in infrastructure, but a decade was lost, and the country was struggling with poor infrastructure (Nagraj 2003).

So China built huge railway networks and new roads; in India there was hardly any addition to the existing railway network, and construction of roads started picking up after a gap of a decade. The only two major railway projects that were approved in 2006 were the western and eastern dedicated freight corridors. But 15 years down the line, they are not likely to be operational in the near future. Similarly, construction of power plants picked up only around 2010 – but the price of electricity, especially for industrial use, remains much higher in India compared to China. It has often been argued that privatization of power generation is also partly responsible for higher electricity prices in India. As with electricity, China also maintained a much lower diesel price. Until 1993, China was self-sufficient in oil, and hence did not find it difficult to maintain a low price (Nanda 2008a). India is not only dependent on imports for much of its oil supply, but government (both at the centre and in the states) treated it as a major source of revenue.

In China, the finance and banking system is heavily controlled by the government, and most important banks are under government ownership. More importantly, China has been able to ensure credit facilities for its bourgeoning industry at low interest rates. Not just real interest rates were low, but even interest spreads were quite low in China. In India, even though the government still owns major banks, the interest rates are higher, and so are the interest spreads, and as a result, interest on deposit is also quite low. This often influences people to invest their savings on unproductive assets like gold and land rather than putting their money in the banks that industry could access.

Before it entered the WTO in 2002, China's intellectual property regime was quite weak, making it easier to access foreign technologies for industrial development (Barpujari and Nanda 2013). What also made China's job easier is the adult literacy level as well as the mean years of schooling, which are much higher than those in India. Sen (2015) argued that much of the difference in development achievements between India and China can be explained by the difference in educational achievements.

Even with a large number of private firms and foreign companies and a much reduced role of public sector enterprises, China has retained a major role for the National Development and Reform Commission (NDRC) – the government planning agency that formulate strategies for industrialization, and it played a major role in China emerging as the leader in solar photovoltaic manufactures, even though the actual production is being led by private companies.

6.5.1 Role of state and industrial performance

While the state is expected to provide an appropriate policy and regulatory environment, historically, it helped industrial development of a country by three other important channels: by directly engaging in business or production, by public procurement, and by helping firms in developing markets outside, as well as accessing finance, raw materials, and technology.

As India envisaged an important role for the public sector, it helped its public sector enterprises through all such channels. Its regulatory and industrial policies favoured public sector enterprises, and they were also helped particularly in accessing technologies through diplomatic channels from friendly countries, and to some extent also in acquiring raw materials.

Public sector enterprises also benefitted from public procurement through direct and indirect means. R&D activities carried out in government laboratories also benefitted public sector enterprises. However, such close linkages of government institutions could not be established with private sector enterprises, as was observed in case of countries like Germany, South Korea, and Taiwan. Private companies in some sectors, of course, benefitted from public procurement. Industrial performance also seems to be somehow linked with growth of development finance, not only in terms of performance over time, but there also seems to be some evidence that the sectors that did relatively better saw higher shares of development finance, particularly in the 1980s and 1990s.

However, it needs to be recognized that in almost all industries in which India has been showing better performance, the state played a major role through all the channels previously described. State-owned enterprises played a key role in all the better-performing sub-sectors, at least during the initial years, and in some, they are still important. If in basic metals, state-owned enterprises played a dominant role, in pharmaceuticals, India's unique IPR policy made the difference. In automobiles, it was both state ownership and imposition of performance requirements on the foreign companies that were crucial for development. Public procurement was important in all these sectors.

While the role of the state – including state ownership – was an important factor in countries like South Korea and Taiwan, as well, there are two ways in which India differed from them. As was also warned by J. K. Galbraith when he was the US Ambassador to India, Indian public sector enterprises

164   *Concluding observations*

became bureaucratized from the very beginning. This, Galbraith thought, could jeopardize even the basic objective of creating them in the first place. Later experience has shown that state-owned enterprises that were managed professionally showed better performance compared to the ones that were bureaucratized (Sengupta 2007). Taiwan and South Korea managed them professionally, and as a result, could give birth to companies like POSCO that is considered to be among the most efficient steel makers in the world.

Another way that India differed was that India never had an exit plan for state-owned enterprises. While South Korea realized that the private sector was unlikely to establish a steel plant in the country, it established POSCO in the public sector against all possible advice that came from different quarters, but when it was up and running, the government privatized such enterprises (Box 2.2). In India, by and large, once established by the government, it always remained a state-owned company and as a result the number of such companies kept on growing even after the 1991 economic reforms (Table 3.4). While the number of enterprises fell only between 1990 and 2002 (from 244 in 1990 to 240 in 2002), the amount of cumulative investment in real terms fell only between 2002 and 2007.

India also could think of privatizing its state-owned enterprises in industries in which the presence of the public sector was not needed anymore, and could invest the money in sectors that private investors would perceive to be high risk, but can have good future and important for its sustainable industrialization. However, it is to be noted that privatization does not necessarily mean selling a publicly owned firm to a private company. Most successful privatization (including POSCO) involved divesting in favour of public holding rather than a private party.

6.5.2 *Trade policy and industrial performance*

Most studies that tried to understand the impact of trade liberalization on industrial performance in India examined if the performance has improved or deteriorated after the 1991 economic reforms. However, as it has already been observed, trade liberalization started in 1988 and continued until at least 2010. In other words, trade liberalization has been a process rather than an event, and of course the process included some bouts.

As noted earlier, many Indian industries, after remaining stagnant for several years, started showing improved performance around the year 1995. It may be noted that while there was a bout of trade liberalization around that time, there were also bouts of such liberalization around 1988 and 1991. The question arises: why is it that among such three bouts, only the 1995 one could make a positive impact on industrial performance of India, particularly when the earlier two were accompanied by several other measures of internal liberalization in the economy? The answer may lie in the fact that one more thing also happened in 1995. In 1995, the Uruguay Round of trade agreements came into effect and the WTO was established.

Hence, while the earlier two episodes of trade liberalization happened only in India, in 1995, the entire world went for drastic liberalization of trade regimes. One can thus argue that the trade liberalization of 1988 and 1991 done by India unilaterally, as well as by WTO mandate in 1995, did not impact India adversely. But it was only the 1995 one that brought benefits to India, as it was part of a multilateral trade liberalization initiative – though the extent of trade liberalization commitment made by India was far greater than the commitment made by the rest of the world. It has also been argued that trade liberalization did not worsen India's trade balance, largely due to successful growth of industries such as pharmaceuticals which developed due to earlier policies and strategies followed by India (Chaudhuri 2013).

However, India could not continue with its improvement in performance in several industries beyond the year 2002. Three things happened around this time. In 2002, India had to remove its quantitative restrictions on trade without getting any commensurate trade liberalization in the rest of world, particularly in countries that were India's major export markets. India also had to remove indigenization and performance requirements after it lost a dispute at the WTO. However, what was possibly more important – and had far-reaching consequences – is that, in December 2001, China became a member of the WTO. Moreover, during this period, India also signed FTAs with a large number of countries wherein tariff cuts made by partner countries were far lower than the tariff cuts made by India (Dhar 2018). Such FTAs might have adversely impacted India's industrial performance (Francis 2019).

In 2005, the Multi-Fibre Arrangement that meant a quota system for textile exporters was dismantled. India always expected better performance in this sector after the dismantling of the MFA regime. However, the experience of post-2005 showed that India's assessment was not correct, as India's performance in textiles and wearing apparel had declined. It might have erred in its assessment in this regard largely due to its inability to anticipate the disruptive impact of the arrival of China onto the scene.

Since 2002, it was not just India but several other countries – particularly in the developed world – which started showing poorer industrial performance. For India, the sectors that were badly hit by this phenomenon were textiles, wearing apparel, and electronic goods. These sectors suffered premature deindustrialization. The information technology (hardware) industry did not even take off in India. This might have been due to the impact of the Information Technology Agreement (ITA) signed at the WTO in 1996 which came into force the next year. This had an adverse impact on electronics industry, as well.

It is quite possible that India was ready to withstand trade liberalization that was mandated by the WTO in 1995. However, it went on its trade liberalization path much beyond what was required by its WTO commitments, in particular, even after China arrived at the scene. Not only did India fail to anticipate the impacts of China's entry into the WTO on its industrial performance, and that of most other countries, it continued with its trade

166 *Concluding observations*

liberalization all along. While India could stop reducing its trade barriers, particularly after the arrival of China into the scene as it already fulfilled its WTO commitments, it will be quite difficult to erect higher trade barriers once again.

It could also be the case that the performance gain achieved by India during 1995–2002 could be due to internal liberalization measures like delicensing and deregulation of capital markets. The trade liberalization made until this time was modest, and hence, it could not make much of impact on performance. However, when drastic liberalization was put in place since 2002, India started losing on industrial performance.

6.5.3 *FDI policy and industrial performance*

While it is true that India's FDI policy was quite restrictive in the 1970s and 1980s, by no means is it the case that it was equally restrictive in the 1950s and 1960s, as well. In fact, in the 1950s, there were efforts to involve foreign companies in the Indian development process, but without much success. In the early 1950s, India tried to promote its petroleum refining industry with the help of foreign companies that were present in India rather than public sector investment. However, the experience was quite frustrating, forcing the government to take the public sector route.

Similarly, as India tried to nudge the foreign automobile companies which were simply assembling cars with imported components, the foreign companies decided to leave India rather than engage in production of components. The Indian pharmaceuticals industry was dominated by foreign companies until 1970, and almost all major pharmaceutical companies had their presence in India, but none of them took the pains of taking any major initiative in India.

While there were a few instances of nationalization of foreign companies, they were limited to sectors like and oil and gas. Companies that were operating in several other sectors, like consumer goods, continued their operations without any such threats. In fact, many such companies and their brands became, and still are, household names in India.[1] While some regulations in the 1970s put some restrictions on foreign companies, most of them continued with their activities, with the exception of Coca-Cola and IBM. While the political leadership perceived Coca-Cola's technologies to be not important for the country, IBM was allegedly dumping obsolete technologies without taking the industry forward in India.

After 1991, however, the situation changed gradually but substantially. Keeping with this trend, several companies came to India and expanded their activities. However, when it comes to industrial performance, it is indeed difficult to find instances where they contributed to industrial growth and performance substantially with their finances and technology, except in the automobiles sector. Even in this sector, foreign companies brought technologies and sourced components from India largely because they were forced to do so through indigenization and performance requirements.

Overall, however, India did not receive much FDI in manufacturing, and much of what was received was market seeking rather than efficiency seeking. Moreover, while foreign investment in the automobiles sector was largely through the greenfield route, in most other sectors, it came through the mergers and acquisitions route. As has been pointed out in several studies, this route of entry for foreign investors is unlikely to bring much benefit to the host country. India also now faces the spectre of its successful companies being taken over by foreign companies primarily to thwart competition both inside and outside India – particularly in the pharmaceuticals sector. India thus needs to explore how it can maintain a liberal FDI regime and at the same time ensure that it contributes to industrial performance.

India might also face pressure to strengthen its IPR regime, particularly from foreign firms operating in India which might use the relatively flexible yet WTO-compatible IPR regime as an alibi for not scaling up their activities in India, though the same might be guided by their own strategic concerns. It will be important to remember that before 1970, India followed an IPR regime similar to most other developed countries, yet the foreign pharmaceutical companies that dominated the Indian market did precious little for the growth of the industry in India. India still faces issues with accessing technologies. Neither is it the case that Indian companies have become hugely capable of path-breaking innovations ready to reap IPR benefits of their own. Not only can a stronger IPR regime hinder access to technologies; it can also stifle innovation activities in India by hindering the flow of knowledge.

6.6   Some final remarks

Despite the rhetoric of India being among the fastest growing and the major emerging economies of the world, the fact remains that the economic foundations of its industrial sector remain quite weak. Hence, it would be quite impossible for the Indian industry to show superior performance purely on the basis of market-driven growth strategies. No country actually started its growth experiment with any particular pre-decided model of economic growth. Rather, countries started with multiple strategies and trial-and-error processes, and when someone succeeded, that became a "model". It may be argued that India might not have had a perfect model, but incorrect characterization of its "model" and condemning it to be a failure could bring the risk of throwing out the baby with the bathwater.

If India had five-year plans, several other countries had such planning too, including South Korea and Taiwan. Yet India is considered to have followed a centrally planned model. India, just like Germany, South Korea, and Taiwan, followed a coordinated market economy. If the results were different, then the answer lies not in economic or industrial policy, but in factors like achievements in health and education or socio-cultural factors like entrepreneurial traits of the people, as well as the quality of governance which are beyond the scope of this study.

168 *Concluding observations*

Much of the recent literature pertaining to India's economic reforms, as well as economic and industrial performance, has followed a pre- and post-1991 binary approach. However, as we have seen, economic reforms are not an event but a process. Moreover, the economic reforms process is also not a homogenous entity. In common parlance, economic reforms have been defined to be a package of liberalization, privatization, and globalization. These three components might not have similar impacts on outcomes. While trade liberalization cannot be linked to superior performance of an industrial sub-sector, high intensity of competition does not necessarily lead to superior performance. Moreover, once an economy is globalized, what happens in the rest of the world becomes more important for its own performance. Hence, treating economic reforms as a homogenous entity can lead to misleading conclusions. Further studies may focus more on separating the impacts of different elements of economic reforms on economic or industrial performance.

It is also important to recognize that not all countries have to follow similar policies related to all areas of LPG. There are a very few examples where a country did not use a strategic trade or industrialization policy, at least in initial years of its development experience. On the other hand, there are examples of countries like Singapore which might have followed a free trade approach, but maintained a highly regulated economy and a dominant public sector which represented about 60 per cent of its GDP in 1993 (Chang 2007).

While India did make mistakes, it has also done several things right, considering the prevailing domestic and global scenario. India needs an industrial policy with an appropriate role for the state. The "Make in India" initiative and the recent measure to make procurement of Indian steel mandatory for government projects are indeed the recognition of the need for such an industrial policy. It has also to be recognized that several tools that other countries or even India used in the past may not be used in today's context. Thus, it is unlikely that India will achieve its goal of a higher level of manufacturing activity simply by following liberalized policies, and there is a need for innovations and experiments with industrialization policy and strategy – even if they involve some mistakes in the process.

While protection from unequal competition is an essential component of industrial policy, it is not about protection only. Nevertheless, it is not just about high tariff walls, and the level of protection must be commensurate with the level of unequal competition that the domestic industry faces. Excessive protection can defeat the purpose. It is also essential to accept the role of the state in providing an enabling environment through correction of market failures, including externalities; provisioning of support through intra- and inter-sectoral coordination; ensuring quality infrastructural services and finance at competitive rates; and supporting technology acquisition and development. Appropriately designed regulatory and dispute settlement mechanisms, and mass education are not generally treated as part of industrial policy, but absent them, industrial policy cannot work. What is needed is a comprehensive industrial policy, along with a strategic framework that can address the needs of different sub-sectors.

One important issue that might have impacted industrialization in India, especially in the post-1991 period, is the narrative of service-led growth, as there is now evidence that such a growth strategy can have serious limitations (Nanda 2019). This has not been discussed in detail in this book, but deserves critical analysis, even though it might not be considered an industrial policy issue in traditional sense. While the fact that entrepreneurs preferred IT software over hardware could be partly policy-influenced, it might also be true in a broader sense whereby entrepreneurs might have preferred the service sector over the manufacturing sector. Telecom equipment manufacturers turning into telecom service providers, pharmaceuticals producers turning into healthcare service providers, and other manufacturers trying their luck in retail trade, are some examples of perceived relative ease of making profits in services sector in India. The service sector is also protected from foreign competition, and hence, enjoys natural protection. This, along with substantial deregulation of services in the post-1991 period, might have made service sector more attractive. But whether this might have had an adverse impact on manufacturing investment is an issue for further studies.

Note

1 Hindustan Lever, Colgate, Britannia, and Bata, to name a few. Brands like Surf, Dalda, and Colgate became synonymous with detergent powder, hydrogenated vegetable oil, and toothpaste, respectively.

References

Abraham, Itty (2017). "From the Commission to the Mission Model: Technology Czars and the Indian Middle Class", *The Journal of Asian Studies*, 76(3): 675–696.

Abraham, V., and S. K. Sasikumar (2010). "Labour Cost and Export Behaviour of Firms in Indian Textile and Clothing Industry", *Munich Personal RePEc Archive Paper No: 22784, Munich: Munich University Library*.

Acemoglu, Daron, and James Robinson (2012). *Why Nations Fail: The Origins of Power, Prosperity, and Poverty*, New York: Crown.

Agarwal, R. N. (1991). "Market Structure and Profitability Relationship in a Regulated Industry", *Indian Economic Journal*, 39(2): 120–135.

Agarwal, S. M. (1985). "Electronics in India: Strategies and Future Possibilities", *World Development*, 13(3): 273–292.

Aggarwal, A. K., and Ganesh Kumar (1991). "Indian Manufacturing Industry: Verdoorn's Law Revisited", *Indian Economic Journal*, 39(2): 61–81.

Agrawal, P., S. Gokarn, V. Mishra, K. Parikh, and K. Sen (2000). *Policy Regimes and Industrial Competitiveness: A Comparative Study of East Asia and India*, London: Palgrave-Macmillan.

Ahluwalia, I. J. (1991). *Productivity and Growth in Indian Manufacturing*, Delhi: Oxford University Press.

Ahluwalia, I. J. (1993). "Industrial Reforms of Public Sector Enterprises and Privatisation in India", paper presented at the conference on *India – The Future of Reforms*, Merton College, Oxford, June 1993.

Ahluwalia, Montek S. (2002). "Economic Reforms in India since 1991: Has Gradualism Worked?", *Journal of Economic Perspectives*, 16(7): 67–88.

Ahluwalia, Montek S. (2016). "The 1991 Reforms: How Home-grown Were They?", *Economic and Political Weekly*, 51(29): 39–46.

Aiginger, Karl, and Dani Rodrik (2020). "Rebirth of Industrial Policy and an Agenda for the Twenty-First Century", *Journal of Industry, Competition and Trade*, 20(2): 189–207.

Amable, Bruno (2000). "Institutional Complementarity and Diversity of Social Systems of Innovation and Production", *Review of International Political Economy*, 7: 645–687.

Amsden, Alice H. (1989). *Asia's Next Giant: South Korea and Late Industrialization*, New York: Oxford University Press.

Amsden, Alice H. (2001). *The Rise of "The Rest": Challenges to the West from Late-Industrializing Economies*. New York: Oxford University Press.

References   171

Anand, Rahul, Kalpana Kochhar, and Saurabh Mishra (2015). "Make in India: Which Exports Can Drive the Next Wave of Growth?", *IMF Working Paper 15/119*, Asia and Pacific Department, Washington, DC: International Monetary Fund.

Andreoni, Antonio (2017). "Varieties of Industrial Policy: Models, Packages and Transformation Cycles", in Akbar Noman and Joseph E. Stiglitz (Eds.), *Efficiency, Finance and Varieties of Industrial Policy: Guiding Resources, Learning, and Technology for Sustained Growth*, New York: Columbia University Press, 245–305.

Antonelli, Cristiano (1995). "Dynamic Structuralism and Path-dependence: Industrial Economics in Italy", *Revue d'économie industrielle*, 73(1): 65–89.

Anubhai, Prafull (1988). "Sickness in Indian Textile Industry: Causes and Remedies", *Economic and Political Weekly*, 23(48): M147–M157.

Apte, P. G., and R. Vaidyanathan (1982). "Concentration, Controls and Performance in Twenty Nine Manufacturing Industries in India", *Indian Economic Review*, XVII(2–4): 241–262.

Arndt, H.W. (1985). "The Origins of Structuralism", *World Development*, 13(2): 151–159.

Asheghian, P. (2011). "Economic Growth Determinants and Foreign Direct Investment Causality in Canada", *International Journal of Business and Social Science*, 2(11): 1–9.

Athreye, Suma, and Sandeep Kapur (2006). "Industrial Concentration in a Liberalising Economy: A Study of Indian Manufacturing", *The Journal of Development Studies*, 42(6): 981–999.

Bagchi, A. K. (1987). *Public Intervention and Industrial Restructuring in China, India and Republic of Korea*, New Delhi: ILO-ARTEP (International Labour Organization – Asian Employment Programme).

Bagchi, A. K. (2002). "The Other Side of Foreign Investment by Imperial Powers: Transfer of Surplus from Colonies", *Economic and Political Weekly*, 27(3): 2229–2238.

Baghirathan, Ravi, Codrina Rada and Lance Taylor (2004). "Structuralist Economics: Worldly Philosophers, Models, and Methodology", *Social Research*, 71(2): 305–326.

Bain, J. S. (1956). *Barriers to New Competition*, Cambridge, MA: Harvard University Press.

Bain, J. S. (1959). *Industrial Organization: A Treatise*, New York: John Wiley (2nd edition 1968).

Balakrishnan, P., and K. Pushpangadan (1994). "Total Factor Productivity Growth in Manufacturing Industry: A Fresh Look", *Economic and Political Weekly*, 29(31): 2028–2035.

Balassa, B. (1965). "Trade Liberalization and Revealed Comparative Advantage", *The Manchester School of Economic and Social Studies*, 33: 99–123.

Balasubramanyam, V. N., and V. Mhambere (2003). "FDI in India. Transnational Corporations", *Indian Journal of Economics*, 12(2): 45–72.

Baldwin, Richard E. (2000). "Regulatory Protectionism, Developing Nations, and a Two-Tier World Trade System", *Brookings Trade Forum*, 3(1): 237–280.

Bardhan, Pranab, and Kenneth Kletzer (1984). "Dynamic Effects of Protection on Productivity", *Journal of International Economics*, 16(1–2): 45–57.

Barpujari, Indrani, and Nitya Nanda (2013) "Weak IPRs as Impediments to Technology Transfer: Findings from Select Asian Countries", *Journal of Intellectual Property Rights*, 18(5): 399–409.

172 References

Barua, Alokesh, Debashis Chakraborty, and C. G. Hariprasad (2010). "Entry, Competitiveness and Exports: Evidence from Firm Level Data of Indian Manufacturing", *MPRA Paper No. 22738*, Munich: University of Munich.

Basole, Amit, and Amay Narayan (2020). "Long-run Performance of the Organised Manufacturing Sector in India: An Analysis of Sub-periods and Industry-level Trends", *Economic & Political Weekly*, 55(10): 33–44.

Batra, Amita, and Zeba Khan (2005). "Revealed Comparative Advantage: An Analysis for India and China", *Working Paper No. 168*, New Delhi: ICRIER.

Baumol, William J., John C. Panzar, and Robert D. Willig (1982). *Contestable Markets and the Theory of Industry Structure*, New York: Harcourt Brace Jovanovich, Inc.

Behera, S. R., P. Dua, and B. Goldar (2012). "Foreign Direct Investment and Technology Spillover: Evidence Across Indian Manufacturing Industries", *The Singapore Economic Review*, 57(2): 1250011–1250023.

Bennett, J. T., and M. H. Johnson (1980). "Tax Reduction Without Sacrifice: xx Production of Public Services", *Public Finance Quarterly*, 8(4): 363–396.

Berger, F. (1979). "Korea's Experience with Export-led Industrial Development", in B. de Vries (Ed.), *Export Promotion Policies*, *Staff Working Paper No. 313*, Washington, DC: World Bank.

Bhagwati, J. (1988). "Export-Promoting Trade Strategy: Issues and Evidence", *World Bank Research Observer*, 3(1): 27–57.

Bhandari, Anup Kumar (2010). "Concentration, Entry Barriers and Profitability in the Indian Industries: An Empirical Analysis", *Journal of Quantitative Economics*, 8(2): 61–80.

Blankenburg, Stephanie; José Gabriel Palma and Fiona Tregenna (2008). "Structuralism", in Steven N. Durlauf and Lawrence E. Blume (Eds), *The New Palgrave Dictionary of Economics*, 6425–6430.

Block, F., and G. A. Burns (1986). "Productivity as a Social Problem: The Uses and Misuses of Social Indicators", *American Sociological Review*, 51(6): 767–780.

Blomström, M., and A. Kokko (2003). "The Economics of Foreign Direct Investment Incentives", *NBER Working Paper 9489, Cambridge (Mass.): National Bureau of Economic Research*.

Blomström, M., A. Kokko, and M. Zejan (2000). *Foreign Direct Investment – Firm and Host Country Strategies*, London: Macmillan.

Boardman, A. E., and A. R. Vining (1989). "Ownership and Performance in Competitive Environments: A Comparison of the Performance of Private, Mixed and State-owned Enterprises", *Journal of Law and Economics*, 32(19): 1–33.

Boone, J. (2008). "A New Way to Measure Competition", *Economic Journal*, 118(531): 1245–1261.

Borcherding, T. E., W. W. Pommerehne, and F. Schneider (1982). "Comparing the Efficiency of Private and Public Production: The Evidence from Five Countries", in D. Bos, R. A. Musgrave, and J. Wiseman (Eds.), *Public Production, Zeitschrift für Nationalokonomie/ Journal of Economics*, Supplement 2, 127–156.

Borensztein, E., J. De Gregorio, and J. W. Lee (1998). "How Does Foreign Investment Affect Growth?", *Journal of International Economics*, 45(1): 115–135.

Bos, D., and W. Peters. (1991). "Privatization of Public Enterprises: A Principal-Agent Approach Comparing Efficiency in Private and Public Sectors", *Empirica*, 18: 5–16.

Brandt, Karl (1963). "Growth of the 'Public Sector' as a By-Product of Price-Fixing and of Segregating Cost-Bearing from Benefit-Sharing", in Helmut Schoeck and

References 173

James W. Wiggins (Eds.), *The New Argument in Economics: The Public Versus the Private Sector*, New York: D. Van Nostrand Company, Inc.

Burange, L. G., and Sheetal J. Chaddha (2008). "India's Revealed Comparative Advantage in Merchandise Trade", *WP. No.: UDE28/6/2008*, Mumbai: University of Mumbai.

Bustelo, Pablo (1996). "Import Protection in Newly Industrializing Economies: Comparing Brazil and Mexico with South Korea and Taiwan, Comparative International Development: Trade Strategies and Foreign Investment", *The Association of American Geographers' 92nd Annual Meeting*, Charlotte, NC, 9–13 April 1996, www.ucm.es/info/eid/pb/charl.htm

Cable, J., and R. H. G. Jackson (2008). "The Persistence of Profits in the Long Run: A New Approach", *International Journal of the Economics of Business*, 15(2): 229–244.

Caves, R., and D. Barton (1990). *Efficiency in U.S. Marketing Industries*, Cambridge, MA: MIT Press.

CEMT (2004). "The Limits of (De-)Regulation of Transport Infrastructure Services", *European Conference of Ministers of Transport (CEMT), Committee of Deputies, Conclusions of Round Table 129 (CEMT/CS(2004)32)*.

Chadwick, Andrew, and Christopher May (2003). "Interaction between States and Citizens in the Age of the Internet: 'e-Government' in the United States, Britain, and the European Union", *Governance*, 16(2): 271–300.

Chang, Ha-Joon (2002). *Kicking Away the Ladder: Development Strategy in Historical Perspective*, London: Anthem Press.

Chang, Ha-Joon (2007). "State-Owned Enterprises Reform", *Policy Notes*, New York: United Nations Department of Economic and Social Affairs.

Chaudhary, Asiya (2016). "Revealed Comparative Advantage Index: An Analysis of Export Potential of Indian Textiles Industry in the Post MFA Period", *American Journal of Economics*, 6(6): 344–351.

Chaudhuri, Sudip (2005). *The WTO and India's Pharmaceuticals Industry- Patent Protection, TRIPS, and Developing Countries*, New Delhi: Oxford University Press.

Chaudhuri, Sudip (2013). "Manufacturing Trade Deficit and Industrial Policy in India", *Economic and Political Weekly*, 48(8): 41–50.

Chenery, Hollis B., Sherman Robinson, and Moshe Syrquin (1986). *Industrialization and Growth: A Comparative Study*, New York: Oxford University Press.

Chhibber, Ajay (2018). "The Surprising Genesis of Our State Albatross", in Sanjaya Baru and Meghnad Desai (Eds.), *The Bombay Plan: Blueprint for Economic Resurgence*, New Delhi: Rupa, 197–223.

Connolly, R. A., and S. Schwartz (1985). "The Intertemporal Behavior of Economic Profits", *International Journal of Industrial Organization*, 3(4): 379–400.

Cournot, A. A. (1838). Recherches sur les principes mathématiques de la théorie des richesses, Paris: Chez L. Hachette (English edition translated by Nathaniel T. Bacon published as: Cournot, A. A. (1897). *Researches into the Mathematical Principles of the Theory of Wealth*, London: Macmillan).

Cubbin, J. S., and P. A. Geroski (1990). "The Persistence of Profits in the United Kingdom", in D. C. Muller (Ed.), *The Dynamics of Company Profits: An International Comparison*, New York: Cambridge University Press.

CUTS (2012). *Government Procurement in India: Domestic Regulations & Trade Prospects*, Jaipur: CUTS.

174 References

Das, Deb Kusum (2016). "Trade Policy and Manufacturing Performance: Exploring the Level of Trade Openness in India's Organized Manufacturing in the Period 1990–2010", *Study No 41*, Development Research Group, Mumbai: Reserve Bank of India.

Das, Gurcharan (1998). "Strategic Response of Indian Companies to the Economic Reforms", in Ashok V. Desai and Tirthankar Roy (Eds.), *Economic Reforms: The Next Step*, New Delhi: Rajiv Gandhi Institute for Contemporary Studies & Frank Brothers and Company, 34–59.

Dasgupta, A. K. (1957). "Socialistic Pattern of Society and the Second Five Year Plan", *Economic Weekly*, 9(3–4–5): 91–92.

Deb, Arnab K., and Subhash C. Ray (2013). "Economic Reforms and Total Factor Productivity Growth of Indian Manufacturing: An Inter-State Analysis", *Working Paper 2013–04R*, Storrs: University of Connecticut.

De Fraja, G. (1993). "Productive Efficiency in Public and Private Firms", *Journal of Public Economics*, 50(1): 15–30.

De Long, J. Bradford (2003). "India since Independence: An Analytic Growth Narrative", in Dani Rodrik (Ed.), *In Search of Prosperity: Analytic Narratives on Economic Growth*, Princeton, NJ: Princeton University Press.

Demirhan, E., and M. Masca (2008). "Determinants of Foreign Direct Investment Flows", *Prague Economic Papers*, Prague: University of Economics.

Dhar, Biswajit (1988). "State Regulation of Foreign Private Capital in India", *Corporate Studies Group Working Paper*, New Delhi: ISID.

Dhar, Biswajit (2018). *India's Comprehensive Economic Partnership Agreements with ASEAN, Japan and Korea*, Penang: TWN.

Dhar, Biswajit, and Reji K. Joseph (2019). "India's Information Technology Industry: A Tale of Two Halves", in Kung-Chung Liu and Uday S. Racherla (Eds.), *Innovation, Economic Development, and Intellectual Property in India and China: Comparing Six Economic Sectors*, Basel: Springer.

di Filippo, A. (2009). "Latin American structuralism and economic theory", *CEPAL Review* (98):175–196.

Dollar, David, and Aart Kraay (2001). "Trade, Growth, and Poverty", *Working Paper No. 2615*, Washington, DC: World Bank.

DOP (2020), *Annual Report 2019-20*, Department of Pharmaceuticals, New Delhi: Government of India.

Dubey, M. (2020). "Towards a New Industrial Policy in India", in R. Saleth, S. Galab and E. Revathi (Eds), *Issues and Challenges of Inclusive Development*. Singapore: Springer, 151–172.

Dyson, Kenneth H. F. (1992). *The Politics of German Regulation*, London: Dartmouth Pub Co.

Eichengreen, Barry J. (2007), *The European Economy since 1945 – Coordinated Capitalism and Beyond*, Princeton, NJ: Princeton University Press.

ELCINA (2012). *Electronic Components, Hardware Market and Manufacturing Output Including Related Assemblies and Value Chain in India (ELCOMOS)*, New Delhi: Electronic Industries Association of India.

Ernst, D. (2014). *Upgrading India's Electronics Manufacturing Industry: Regulatory Reform and Industrial Policy*. Honolulu: East-West Centre.

Estrin, Saul, and Virginie Pérotin (1987). "Producer Cooperatives: The British Experience", *International Review of Applied Economics*, 1(2): 153–174.

References   175

Estrin, Saul, and Adeline Pelletier (2018). "Privatization in Developing Countries: What Are the Lessons of Recent Experience?", The World Bank Research Observer, 33(1): 65–102.

Ferraz, João Carlos (2017). "Development Finance: The Strategic Role of National Development Banks", in Akbar Noman and Joseph Stiglitz (Eds.), *Efficiency, Finance, and Varieties of Industrial Policy: Guiding Resources, Learning, and Technology for Sustained Growth*, New York: Columbia University Press, 105–130.

Foster, Karen R. (2016). *Productivity and Prosperity: A Historical Sociology of Productivist Thought*, Toronto: University of Toronto Press.

Foucault, Michel (1997). "On the Genealogy of Ethics: An Overview of Work in Progress", in Paul Rabinow (Ed.), *Ethics, Subjectivity and Truth*, New York: New Press, 253–280.

Francis, Smitha (2018). "India's Electronics Manufacturing Sector: Getting the Diagnosis Right", *Economic and Political Weekly*, 53(34): 112–117.

Francis, Smitha (2019). *Industrial Policy Challenges for India: Global Value Chains and Free Trade Agreements*, London: Routledge.

Ganesh-Kumar, A., Kunal Sen, and Rajendra R. Vaidya (2002). "International Competitiveness, Trade and Finance: India", in José María Fanelli and Rohinton Medhora (Eds.), *Finance and Competitiveness in Developing Countries*, Ottawa: IDRC.

Georgescu-Roegen, N. (1971). *The Entropy Law and the Economic Process*, Cambridge, MA: Harvard University Press.

Geroski, P. A. (1988). "In Pursuit of Monopoly Power: Recent Quantitative Work in Industrial Economics", *Journal of Applied Econometrics*, 3(2): 107–123.

Geroski, P. A., and A. Jacquemin (1988). "The Persistence of Profits: A European Comparison", *The Economic Journal*, 98(391): 375–389.

Gerschenkron, Alexander (1962). *Economic Backwardness in Historical Perspective*, Cambridge MA: Harvard University Press.

Ghosh, A. (1974). "Role of Large Business House in Indian Industries", *Indian Economic Journal*, 22(2): 316–345.

Ghosh, A. (1975). "Concentration and Growth of Indian Industries: 1948–68", *Journal of Industrial Economics*, 23(3): 203–222.

Giannakas, Konstantinos (2001). "The Economics of Intellectual Property Rights Under Imperfect Enforcement: Developing Countries, Biotechnology, and the TRIPS Agreement", *EPTD Discussion Paper No. 80*, Washington, DC: International Food Policy Research Institute.

Glenn, J., K. Lee, and A. Singh (2001). "Persistence of Profitability and Competition in Emerging Markets", *Economics Letters*, 72(2): 247–253.

Glenn, J., A. Singh, and R. Matthais (1999). "How Intensive Is Competition in the Emerging Markets: An Analysis of Corporate Rates of Return from Nine Emerging Markets", *IMF Working Paper 99/32*, Washington, DC: International Monetary Fund.

Goldar, Bishwanath (1986). *Productivity Growth in Indian Industry*, New Delhi: Allied Publishers.

Goldar, Bishwanath, and Suresh Chand Aggarwal (2004). "Trade Liberalization and Price-Cost Margin in Indian Industries", *Working Paper No. 130*, New Delhi: ICRIER.

Goldar, Bishwanath, Suresh Chand Aggarwal, Deb Kusum Das, Abdul A. Erumban, and Pilu Chandra Das (2016). "Productivity Growth and Levels – A Comparison

176   References

of Formal and Informal Manufacturing in India", Paper presented at the *Fourth World KLEMS Conference*, BBVA Foundation, Madrid, Spain, May 23–24.

Goldar, Biswanath (2004). "Indian Manufacturing: Productivity Trends in Pre- and Post-Reform Periods", *Economic and Political Weekly*, 39(46): 5033–5042.

Goldar, Biswanath, and Anita Kumari (2003). "Import Liberalisation and Productivity Growth in Indian Manufacturing Industries in the 1990s", *The Developing Economies*, 41(4): 436–460.

Goswami, Omkar (1990). "Sickness and Growth of India's Textile Industry: Analysis and Policy Options", *Economic and Political Weekly*, 25(44): 2429–2439.

Griffin, K. B. (1970). "Foreign Capital, Domestic Savings and Economic Development", *Bulletin of the Oxford Institute of Economics and Statistics*, 32(2): 99–112.

Griffith-Jones, Stephany, and Giovanni Cozzi (2017). "Development Finance: How They Can Promote Investment in Europe and Globally", in Akbar Noman and Joseph Stiglitz (Eds.), *Efficiency, Finance, and Varieties of Industrial Policy: Guiding Resources, Learning, and Technology for Sustained Growth*, New York: Columbia University Press, 131–155.

Gschwandtner, A. (2010). *Evolution of Profit Persistence in the US: Evidence from Three Periods*, Vienna: Department of Economics, University of Vienna.

Guadagno, Francesca (2016). "The role of industrial development banking in spurring structural change", *Working Paper 8/2016*, UNU-MERIT, Vienna: United Nations Industrial Development Organization.

Gupta, V. K. (1968). "Cost Functions, Concentrations and Barriers to Entry in Twenty-Nine Manufacturing Industries in India", *Journal of Industrial Economics*, 17(1): 57–72.

Haddad, M., and A. Harrison (1993). "Are There Positive Spillovers from Direct Foreign Investment? Evidence from Panel Data for Morocco", *Journal of Development Economics*, 42(1): 51–74.

Hall, Peter A., and David W. Soskice (2001). *Varieties of Capitalism: The Institutional Foundations of Comparative Advantage*, Oxford: Oxford University Press.

Haraguchi, Nobuya (2015). "Patterns of Structural Change and Manufacturing Development", in John Weiss and Michael Tribe (Eds.), *Routledge Handbook of Industry and Development*, London: Routledge.

Hatekar, N., and A. Dongre (2005). "Structural Breaks in India's Growth: Revisiting the Debate with a Longer Perspective", *Economic and Political Weekly*, 40(14): 1432–1435.

Herzer, D. (2012). "How Does Foreign Direct Investment Really Affect Developing Countries' Growth?", *Review of International Economics*, 20(2): 396–414.

Hoang, T. T., P. Wiboonchutikula, and B. Tubtimtong (2010). "Does Foreign Direct Investment Promote Economic Growth in Vietnam?", *ASEAN Economic Bulletin*, 27(3): 295–311.

Huo, Jingjing (2015). *How Nations Innovate: The Political Economy of Technological Innovation in Affluent Capitalist Economies*, New York: Oxford University Press.

Hoda, Anwarul, and Suchi Bansal (2004). "Transparency in Government Procurement", *ICRIER Working Paper No. 129*, New Delhi: Indian Council for Research on International Economic Relations.

Hopkins, Mathew, and Yin Li (2016). "The Rise of the Chinese Solar Photovoltaic Industry: Firms, Governments, and Global Competition", in Yu Zhou, William

References 177

Lazonick and Yifei Sun (Eds.) *China as an Innovation Nation*, Oxford: Oxford University Press, 306–332.

Huo, Jingjing (2015). *How Nations Innovate: The Political Economy of Technological Innovation in Affluent Capitalist Economies*, New York: Oxford University Press.

Hutchinson, G. (1991). "Efficiency Gains through Privatization of UK Industries", in K. Hartley and A. F. Ott (Eds.), *Privatization and Economic Efficiency: A Comparative Analysis of Developed and Developing Countries*, Aldershot: Edward Elgar.

IBEF (2020). Indian Pharmaceuticals Industry, India Brand Equity Foundation, (https://www.ibef.org/industry/pharmaceutical-india.aspx), (accessed on April 24, 2020).

IBM (2020). *Indian Minerals Yearbook 2019*, Nagpur: Indian Bureau of Mines.

IEEMA (2021). Industry Intelligence: Industry Update, New Delhi: Indian Electrical & Electronics Manufacturers' Association (https://ieema.org/industry-intelligence/industry-update/) (accessed on April 19, 2021).

IEGBIIP (International Expert Group on Biotechnology, Innovation and Intellectual Property) (2008). *Toward a New Era of Intellectual Property: From Confrontation to Negotiation*, Montreal, Canada: IEGBIIP.

IMF (2015). *Regional Economic Outlook – Asia and Pacific: Stabilizing and Outperforming Other Regions*, Washington, DC: International Monetary Fund.

Invest India (2020). *India - Knitting the Future*, https://www.investindia.gov.in/ (accessed on March 20, 2020).

Jacobsen, R. (1988). "The Persistence of Abnormal Returns", *Strategic Management Journal*, 9(5): 415–430.

Jaremski, Matthew S. (2013). "National Banking's Role in US Industrialization, 1850-1900", *NBER Working Paper No. 18789*, Cambridge, MA: National Bureau of Economic Research: NBER Program - Development of the American Economy.

Jorgenson, D. W., and Z. Griliches (1967). "The Explanation of Productivity Change", *Review of Economic Studies*, 34(3): 249–283.

Kambhampati, U. S. (1995). "The Persistence of Profit Differentials in Indian Industry", *Applied Economics*, 27(4): 353–361.

Kambhampati, U. S., and P. Kattuman (2005). "Has Liberalization Affected Profit Margins in Indian Industry?", *Bulletin of Economic Research*, 57(3): 273–304.

Kathuria, Vinish, Rajesh S. N. Raj, and Kunal Sen (2013). "Productivity Measurement in Indian Manufacturing: A Comparison of Alternative Methods", *Journal of Quantitative Economics*, 11(1&2): 148–179.

Katrak, H. (1980). "Industry Structure, Foreign Trade and Price-Cost Margins in Indian Manufacturing Industries", *Journal of Development Studies*, 17(1): 62–79.

Kaul, H. N. (1991). *K.D. Malaviya and the Evolution of India's Oil Policy*, New Delhi: Allied Publishers.

Kaushal, Neeraj (1995). "India's Defense Budget: Can It Be Reduced?", *ACDIS Occasional Paper* (ACDIS KAU:R1.1995), Urbana-Champaign: University of Illinois.

Khan, Mushtaq H. (2015). "Industrial Policy Design and Implementation Challenges", in Jesus Felipe (Ed.), *Development and Modern Industrial Policy in Practice: Issues and Country Experiences*, Cheltenham: Edward Elgar, 94–126.

178 References

Kirkpatrick, C., D. Parker, and Y. F. Zhang (2006). "An Empirical Analysis of State and Private-sector Provision of Water Services in Africa", *World Bank Economic Review*, 20(1): 143–163.

Klein, Lawrence R., and Thangavel Palanivel (2002). "Economic Reforms and Growth Prospects in India", in Montek S. Ahluwalia, Y. V. Reddy, and S. S. Tarapore (Eds.), *Macroeconomics and Monetary Policy: Issues for a Reforming Economy*, New Delhi: Oxford University Press.

Kohli, Atul (2006). "Politics of Economic Growth in India, 1980–2005", *Economic and Political Weekly*, 41(13 & 14): 1251–1260, 1361–1370.

Kojima, Kiyoshi (1973). "A Macroeconomic Approach to Foreign Direct Investment", *Hitotsubashi Journal of Economics*, 14(1): 1–21.

Kolster, Jacob (2015). "Does Foreign Direct Investment Improve Welfare in North African Countries?", *Working Paper, North Africa Policy Series 2162*, Abidjan: African Development Bank.

Kotrajaras, P., B. Tubtimtong, and P. Wiboonchutikula (2011). "Does FDI Enhance Economic Growth? New Evidence from East Asia", *ASEAN Economic Bulletin*, 28(2): 189–202.

Krishna, Pravin, and Devashish Mitra (1998). "Trade Liberalization, Market Discipline and Productivity Growth: New Evidence from India", *Journal of Development Economics*, 56(2): 447–462.

Krugman, Paul R. (1984). "Import Protection as Export Promotion: International Competition in the Presence of Oligopoly and Economies of Scale", in H. Kierskowski (Ed.), *Monopolistic Competition and International Trade*, Oxford: Clarendon Press, 180–193.

Krugman, Paul R. (1994). "Competitiveness: A Dangerous Obsession", *Foreign Affairs*, 73(2): 28–44.

Kuan, Leong Ming (2017). "Does Manufacturing Colocate with Intermediate Services", in Akbar Noman and Joseph E. Stiglitz (Eds.), *Efficiency, Finance and Varieties of Industrial Policy: Guiding Resources, Learning, and Technology for Sustained Growth*, New York: Columbia University Press, 447–481.

Kumar, N. (1990). "Mobility Barriers and Profitability of Multinational and Local Enterprises in Indian Manufacturing", *Journal of Industrial Economics*, 38(4): 449–463.

Kumar, N. (2018). "Reversing Premature Deindustrialisation for Job Creation: Lessons for Make-in-India from industrialised and East Asian countries", in Ananya Ghosh Dastidar, Rajeev Malhotra, and Vivek Suneja (Eds.), *Economic Theory and Policy amidst Global Discontent: Essays in Honour of Deepak Nayyar*, London: Routledge, 389–415.

Lall, Sanjaya (1987). *Learning to Industrialize: The Acquisition of Technological Capability by India*, Houndmills, Basingstoke, Hampshire/New York: Macmillan Press/St. Martin's Press.

Leibenstein, Harvey (1973). "Competition and X-Efficiency: Reply", *Journal of Political Economy*, 81(3): 765–777.

Lensink, Robert, and Gerard Kuper (2000). "Recent Advances in Economic Growth: A Policy Perspective", in Maaike S. Oosterbaan, Thijs de Ruyter van Steveninck, and Nico van der Windt (Eds.), *The Determinants of Economic Growth*, New York: Springer.

Lerner, A. P. (1934). "The Concept of Monopoly and the Measurement of Monopoly Power". *The Review of Economic Studies*. 1 (3): 157–175.

References   179

Lin, Justin Yifu (2011). "New Structural Economics: A Framework for Rethinking Development," *World Bank Research Observer*, 26(2): 193–221.

Lin, Justin Yifu (2017). "New Structural Economics and Industrial Policies for Catching-Up Economies", in Slavo Radosevic, Adrian Curaj, Radu Gheorghiu, Liviu Andreescu, and Imogen Wade (Eds), *Advances in the Theory and Practice of Smart Specialization*, London: Academic Press, 183–199.

Lin, Karen Jingrong, Xiaoyan Lu, Junsheng Zhang, and Ying Zheng (2020). "State-owned Enterprises in China: A Review of 40 Years of Research and Practice", *China Journal of Accounting Research*, 13(1): 31–55.

Lok Sabha Secretariat (2013). "Review of Export of Iron Ore Policy", *Standing Committee on Coal and Steel (2012–13)*, New Delhi: Lok Sabha Secretariat.

Loungani, Prakash, and Razin Assaf (2001). "How Beneficial Is Foreign Direct Investment for Developing Countries?", *Finance and Development*, 38(2): 6–10.

Lund, M. T. (2010). *Foreign Direct Investment: Catalyst of Economic Growth?* Department of Economics, Salt Lake City: The University of Utah.

Lyroudi, Katerina, John Papanastasiou, and Athanasios Vamvakidis (2004). "Foreign Direct Investment and Economic Growth in Transition Economies", *South-Eastern Europe Journal of Economics*, 2(1): 97–110.

Maddison, Angus (1991). *Dynamic Forces in Capitalist Development: A Long Run Comparative View*, London: Oxford University Press.

Maddison, Angus (1995). *Monitoring the World Economy: 1820–1992*, Paris: OECD Development Centre.

Madheswaran, S., Badri Narayan Rath, and Hailin Liao (2007). "Productivity Growth of Indian Manufacturing Sector: Panel Estimation of Stochastic Production Frontier and Technical Inefficiency", *The Journal of Developing Areas*, 40(2): 35–36.

Magdoff, Harry, and Paul Sweezy (1980). "The Uses and Abuses of Measuring Productivity", *Monthly Review*, 32(2): 1–9.

Mann, Preeti, Shibananda Nayak, and Vani Aggarwal (2015). "India's Manufacturing Exports: Technology Intensity Transition", *International Research Journal of Social Sciences*, 4(5): 67–75.

Maskus, Keith E. (2000). *Intellectual Property Rights in the Global Economy*, Washington, DC: Institute for International Economics.

Mass, William, and William Lazonick (2006). "The British Cotton Industry and International Competitive Advantage: The State of the Debates", in Mary B. Rose (Ed.), *International Competition and Strategic Response in the Textile Industries Since 1870*, London: Routledge, 9–65.

Mazumdar, Surajit (2008). "Investment and Growth in India under Liberalisation: Asymmetries and Instabilities", *Economic and Political Weekly*, 43(49): 68–77.

Mazumdar, Surajit (2010). "Industry and Services in Growth and Structural Change in India: Some Unexplored Features", *Working Papers 1002*, New Delhi: Institute for Studies in Industrial Development (ISID).

MCA (1965). *Report of the Monopolies Inquiry Commission*, Ministry of Corporate Affairs, New Delhi: Government of India.

Mehta, Aashna, Habib Hasan Farooqui, and Sakthivel Selvaraj (2016). "A Critical Analysis of Concentration and Competition in the Indian Pharmaceutical Market", *PLoS ONE*, 11(2): e0148951.

MEITY (2014). *Annual Report 2013–2014*, New Delhi: Ministry of Electronics and Information Technology, Government of India.

180 References

MEITY (2019). *Annual Report 2018–2019*, New Delhi: Ministry of Electronics and Information Technology, Government of India.

Miglani, Smita (2019). "The Growth of the Indian Automobile Industry: Analysis of the Roles of Government Policy and Other Enabling Factors", in Kung-Chung Liu and Uday S. Racherla (Eds.), *Innovation, Economic Development, and Intellectual Property in India and China: Comparing Six Economic Sectors*, Basel: Springer.

Millward, R., and D. Parker (1983). "Public and Private Enterprise, Comparative Behaviour and Relative Efficiency", in R. Millward, D. Parker, L. Rosenthal, M. T. Sumner, and N. Topham (Eds.), *Public Sector Economics*, London and New York: Longman, 199–274.

Ministry of Steel (2018). *Annual Report 2017-18*, New Delhi: Government of India.

Missio, Fabrício, Frederico G. Jayme Jr., and José Luís Oreiro (2015). "The structuralist tradition in economics: methodological and macroeconomics aspects", *Brazilian Journal of Political Economy (Revista de Economia Politica)*, 35(2): 247–266.

Mitra, A. (1999). "Total Factor Productivity Growth and Technical Efficiency in Indian Industries: A Study Based on Panel Data for Fifteen Major States", *Working Paper, No. E/ 203/ 99*, New Delhi: Institute of Economic Growth.

Mohan Rao, J. (1996). "Manufacturing Productivity Growth: Method and Measurement", *Economic and Political Weekly*, 31(44): 2927–2936.

MOPNG (2016). Indian Petroleum & Natural Gas Statistics 2015-16, Ministry of Petroleum and Natural Gas, New Delhi: Government of India.

Mueller, D. C. (1977). "The Persistence of Profits above the Norm", *Economica*, 44(176): 369–380.

Mueller, D. C. (1986). *Profits in the Long Run*, Cambridge: Cambridge University Press.

Mueller, D. C. (1990). "The Persistence of Profits in the United States", in Dennis C. Mueller (Ed.), *The Dynamics of Company Profits: An International Comparison*, Cambridge: Cambridge University Press.

Mukherjee, Shameek, and Shahana Mukherjee (2012). "Overview of India' Export Performance: Trends and Drivers", *Working Paper No: 363*, Bangalore: IIM.

Myint, H. (1958). "The 'Classical Theory' of International Trade and the Underdeveloped Countries", *Economic Journal*, 68(270): 317–337.

Nag, Biswajit, Saikat Banerjee, and Rittwik Chatterjee (2007). "Changing Features of the Automobile Industry in Asia: Comparison of Production, Trade and Market Structure in Selected Countries", *Asia-Pacific Research and Training Network on Trade Working Paper Series, No. 37*, Bangkok: UN-ESCAP.

Nagaraj, R. (2003). "Industrial Policy and Performance since 1980: Which Way Now?", *Economic and Political Weekly*, 38(35): 3707–3715.

Nagraj, R. (2017). "Economic Reforms and Manufacturing Sector Growth: Need for Reconfiguring the Industrialisation Model", *Economic and Political Weekly*, 52(2): 61–68.

Nanda, N. (2008). *Expanding Frontiers of Global Trade Rules: The Political Economy Dynamics of the International Trading System*, London: Routledge.

Nanda, Nitya (2008a), "Trading in World Energy Market" in Ligia Noronha and Anant Sudarshan (Eds.), *India's Energy Security*, London: Routledge, 51–63.

Nanda, Nitya (2009a). "The Indian Growth Story: Myths and Realities", *Journal of Asian and African Studies*, 44(6): 74–765.

References 181

Nanda, Nitya (2009b). "Growth Effects of FDI: Is Greenfield Greener?", *Perspectives on Global Development and Technology*, 8(1): 26–47.

Nanda, Nitya (2019). "Causes and Consequences of Service Sector Growth: Perceptions and Realities", in P. Biswas and P. Das (Eds.), *Indian Economy: Reforms and Development*, Singapore: Springer, 141–157.

Nanda, Nitya (2020). "Antidumping Measures: An Indian Perspective", in Ajitava Raychauduri, Prabir De, and Suranjan Gupta (Eds), *World Trade and India: Multilateralism, Progress and Policy Response*, New Delhi: Sage Publications, 263–286.

Nanda, Nitya, and Amirullah Khan (2006). "Competition Policy for the Pharmaceuticals Sector in India", in Pradeep Mehta (Ed.), *Towards a Functional Competition Policy for India*, New Delhi: Academic Foundation, 188–201.

Nanda, Nitya, and Nidhi Srivastava (2011). "Facilitating Technology Transfer for Climate Change Mitigation and Adaptation", *TERI COP 17 Discussion Paper*, New Delhi: TERI.

Narayana, D. (2000). "Banking Sector Reforms and the Emerging Inequalities in Commercial Credit Deployment in India", *Working Paper No. 300*, Thiruvananthapuram: Centre for Development Studies.

Nayyar, Deepak (2006). "Economic Growth in Independent India: Lumbering Elephant or Running Tiger?", *Economic and Political Weekly*, 41(15): 1451–1458.

Nayyar, Deepak (2013). *Catch Up: Developing Countries in the World Economy*, New York: Oxford University Press.

Nayyar, Deepak (2015). "Birth, Life and Death of Development Finance Institutions in India", *Economic and Political Weekly*, 50(33): 51–60.

Nayyar, Deepak (2017). "Economic Liberalisation in India: Then and Now", *Economic and Political Weekly*, 52(2): 41–48.

Nayyar, Deepak (2019). *Resurgent Asia: Diversity in Development*, New Delhi: Oxford University Press.

Nicolas, Françoise (2003). "FDI as a Factor of Economic Restructuring: The Case of South Korea", in A. Bende-Nabende (Ed.), *International Trade, Capital Flows and Economic Development in East Asia: The Challenge in the 21st Century*, London: Ashgate.

Nishimizu, Mieko, and Sherman Robinson (1984). "Trade Policies and Productivity Change in Semi-industrialized Countries", *Journal of Development Economics*, 16(1–2): 177–206.

Nunnenkamp, Peter, and Julius Spatz (2004). "FDI and Economic Growth in Developing Economies: How Relevant Are Host-economy and Industry Characteristics", *Transnational Corporations*, 13(3): 53–86.

OTC (2000). *Compendium of Textile Statistics*, Bombay: Office of the Textile Commissioner.

Ocampo, José Antonio (2017). "Dynamic Efficiency: Structural Dynamics and Economic Growth in Developing Countries", in Akbar Noman and Joseph E. Stiglitz (Eds.), *Efficiency, Finance and Varieties of Industrial Policy: Guiding Resources, Learning, and Technology for Sustained Growth*, New York: Columbia University Press, 65–102.

Ocampo, J. A., C. Rada, and L. Taylor (2009). *Economic Structure, Policy and Growth in Developing Countries*, New York: Columbia University Press.

OECD (2000). "Main Determinants and Impacts of Foreign Direct Investment on China's Economy", *OECD Working Papers on International Investment*, 2000/04, Paris: OECD Publishing.

182 *References*

OECD (2004). *Innovation in the Knowledge Economy: Implications for Education and Learning*, Paris: OECD.

OECD (2015). "The Participation of Developing Countries in Global Value Chains: Implications for Trade and Trade-Related Policies", *Trade Policy Paper No. 179*, Paris: OECD.

Pack, H., and L. E. Westphal (1986). "Industrial Strategy and Technological Change: Theory versus Reality", *Journal of Development Economics*, 22(1): 87–128.

Panagariya, Arvind (2004). "Growth and Reforms during 1980s and 1990s", *Economic and Political Weekly*, 39(25): 2581–2594.

Panchamukhi, V. R. (1974). "A Quantitative Analysis of Trade Policies in India", in J. C. Sandesara (Eds.), *The Indian Economy: Performance and Prospects*, Bombay: University of Bombay.

Pant, Manoj, and Manoranjan Pattanayak (2005). "Does Openness Promote Competition? A Case Study of Indian Manufacturing", *Economic and Political Weekly*, 40(39): 4226–4231.

Parida, Purna Chandra, and Kailash Chandra Pradhan (2016). "Productivity and Efficiency of Labour Intensive Manufacturing Industries in India: An Empirical Analysis", *International Journal of Development Issues*, 15(2): 130–152.

Patnaik, Utsa (2019). "Dispossession, Deprivation, and Development", in A. Banerjee and C. P. Chandrasekhar (Eds.), *Dispossession, Deprivation, and Development: Essays for Utsa Patnaik*, New York: Columbia University Press.

Pérez, Carlota (2001). "Technological Change and Opportunities for Development as a Moving Target", *CEPAL Review No. 75*, Santiago: UN-ECLAC, 109–130.

Pierson, Paul (2004). *Politics in Time: History, Institutions, and Social Analysis*, Princeton, NJ: Princeton University Press.

Pint, E. (1991). "Nationalization vs. Regulation of Monopolies: The Effect of Ownership on Efficiency", *Journal of Public Economics*, 44(2): 131–164.

Planning Commission (2011). *High Level Expert Group Report on Universal Health Coverage for India*, New Delhi: Planning Commission, Government of India.

Prebisch, Raul (1959). "Commercial Policy in the Underdeveloped Countries", *American Economic Review*, 49(2): 251–273.

Pushpangadan, K., and N. Shanta (2008). "Competition and Profitability in Indian Manufacturing Industries", *Indian Economic Review*, 43(1): 103–123.

Raihan, Selim (2020). "Avoiding Premature Deindustrialization in India: Achieving SDG9", in S. Hazra, and A. Bhukta. (Eds), *Sustainable Development Goals: An Indian Perspective*, Cham: Springer: 139–151.

Rajaraman, V. (2012). *History of Computing in India (1955–2010)*, Bangalore: Supercomputer Education and Research Centre, Indian Institute of Science.

Ramaswamy, K. V. (2006). "State of Competition in the Indian Manufacturing Industry", in Pradeep S. Mehta (Ed.), *Towards a Functional Competition Policy for India*, New Delhi: Academic Foundation, 155–164.

Rao, K. S. Chalapati, and Biswajit Dhar (2018). *India's Recent Inward Foreign Direct Investments: An Assessment*, New Delhi: Institute for Studies in Industrial Development.

Ray, P. K., and S. Rahman (2006). "The Propensity for Local Innovation and Inter-Firm Linkages in Transnational Corporations versus Local Enterprises in India", *Transnational Corporations*, 15(2): 71–98.

RBI (2020). *Report on Trend and Progress of Banking in India*, Mumbai: Reserve Bank of India.

References   183

Reinert, E. S. (2007). *How Rich Countries Got Rich . . . and Why Poor Countries Stay Poor*, London: Constable.

Rin, Marco Da, and Thomas Hellmann (2001). "Banks as Catalysts for Industrialization", *William Davidson Institute Working Paper Number 443*, Ann Arbor, MI: University of Michigan.

Rodrik, Dani (2004). "Industrial Policy for the Twenty-First Century", *CEPR Discussion Paper No. 4767*, London: CEPR.

Rodrik, Dani (2009). *One Economics, Many Recipes: Globalization, Institutions, and Economic Growth*, Princeton, NJ: Princeton University Press.

Rodrik, Dani, and Arvind Subramanian (2004). "From Hindu Rate of Growth to Productivity Surge: The Mystery of Indian Growth Transition", *IMF Working Paper WP/04/77*, Washington, DC: International Monetary Fund.

Rose, Mary B. (2006). "International Competition and Strategic Response in the Textile Industries Since 1870", in Mary B. Rose (Ed.), *International Competition and Strategic Response in the Textile Industries Since 1870*, London: Routledge, 1–8.

Roy Choudhury, P., and B. Chatterjee (2017). "Growth in India's Service Sector: Implications of Structural Breaks", *Journal of Quantitative Economics*, 15(1): 75–99.

Saluja, M. R. (1968). "Structure of Indian Economy: Inter-Industry Flows and Pattern of Final Demands 1964–65", *Sankhyā, Series B*, 30(1&2): 97–122.

Sandesara, J. C. (1979). "Size of the Factory and Concentration in the Factory Sector in India, 1951 to 1970", *Indian Economic Journal*, 27(2): 1–34.

Sanyal, Amal (2018). "The Making of a Mythical Forerunner", in Sanjaya Baru and Meghnad Desai (Eds.), *The Bombay Plan: Blueprint for Economic Resurgence*, New Delhi: Rupa, 19–63.

Saqib, N., M. Masnoon, and N. Rafique (2013). "Impact of Foreign Direct Investment on Economic Growth of Pakistan", *Advances in Management & Applied Economics*, 3(1): 35–45.

Saraswathy, Beena (2016). "An Analysis of Foreign Acquisitions in India's Manufacturing Sector", *ISID Working Paper No. 193*, New Delhi: ISID.

Sawhney, P. K., and B. L. Swahney (1973). "Capacity Utilization, Concentration and Price-Cost Margins: Results for Indian Industries", *Journal of Industrial Economies*, 21(2): 145–153.

Scherer, F. M. (1980). *Industrial Market Structure and Economic Performance*, Chicago: Rand McNally.

Schmalensee, R. (1989). "Inter-Industry Studies of Structure and Performance", in R. Schmalensee and R. Willig (Eds.), *Handbook of Industrial Organisation*, Amsterdam: North Holland.

Schumpeter, J. A. (1934). *The Theory of Economic Development*, Cambridge, MA: Harvard University Press (first published in German in 1911).

Schumpeter, J. A. (1950). *Capitalism, Socialism and Democracy*, New York: Harper and Row.

Schwalbach, J., U. Grasshoff, and T. Mahmood (1989). "The Dynamics of Corporate Profits", *European Economic Review*, 33(8): 1625–1639.

Sen, Abhijit (2015). "Demographic Drivers of Economic Growth – Role of Human Capital", *Durgabai Deshmukh Memorial Lecture*, New Delhi: Council for Social Development.

Sen, Kunal (2010). "Trade, Foreign Direct Investment and Industrial Transformation in India", in Premachandra Athukorala (Ed.), *The Rise of Asia: Trade and Investment in Global Perspective*, London: Routledge, 182–206.

184 References

Sengupta, Jayashree (2007). *A Nation in Transition: Understanding the Indian Economy*, New Delhi: Academic Foundation.

Sharma, Dinesh C. (2009). *The Long Revolution: The Birth and Growth of India's IT Industry*, New Delhi: Harper Collins.

Sharma, Dinesh C. (2013). "Nehru: The Unlikely Hero of India's Information Technology Revolution", *NMML Occasional Paper, Perspectives in Indian Development, New Series 8*, New Delhi: Nehru Memorial Museum and Library.

Sharmila, R., and Manjappa D. Hosamane (2014). "An Empirical Analysis of Total Factor Productivity Growth of Manufacturing Sector in Karnataka", *Journal of Management and Commerce*, 1(1): 5–8.

Siddharthan, N. S., and A. K. Dasgupta (1983). "Entry Barriers, Exports, and Inter-Industry Differences in Profitability", *Developing Economies*, 21(1): 14–23.

Silva, Thiago Christiano, Benjamin Miranda Tabak, and Marcela Tetzner Laiz (2019). "The Finance-Growth Nexus: The Role of Banks" *Working Paper Series No 506*. Brasília: Banco Central do Brasil.

Singer, H. W. (1950). "The Distribution of Gains Between Investing and Borrowing Countries", *American Economic Review*, 40(2): 473–485.

Singh, Ajit (2008). "The Past, Present and Future of Industrial Policy in India: Adapting to the Changing Domestic and International Environment", *Working Paper No. 376*, Cambridge: Centre for Business Research, University of Cambridge.

Singh, Ajit, and Bruce A. Weisse (1998). "Emerging Stock Markets, Portfolio Capital Flows and Long-term Economic Growth: Micro and Macroeconomic Perspectives", *World Development*, 26(4): 607–622.

Singh, Fulwinder Pal (2012). "Economic Reforms and Productivity Growth in Indian Manufacturing Sector – An Inter-State Analysis, International Journal of Marketing", *Financial Services & Management Research*, 1(12): 1–22.

Sivasubramonian, S. (2000). *The National Income of India during the Twentieth Century*, New Delhi: Oxford University Press.

Solow, R. M. (1957). "Technical Change and the Aggregate Production", *Review of Economics and Statistics*, 39(3): 312–320.

Srinivasan, T. N. (2006). "China, India and the World Economy", *Economic and Political Weekly*, 41(34): 3716–3727.

Srinivasan, T. N., and Suresh Tendulkar (2003). *Reintegrating India with the World Economy*, Washington, DC: Peterson Institute for International Economics.

Stigler, George J., and James K. Kindahl (1970). *The Behavior of Industrial Prices*, New York: National Bureau of Economic Research, Inc.

Stiglitz, Joseph, and Bruce Greenwald (2014). *Creating a Learning Society: A New Approach to Growth, Development, and Social Progress*, New York: Columbia University Press.

Street, J. H. and D. D. James (1982). "Institutionalism, Structuralism, and Dependency in Latin America", *Journal of Economic Issues*, 16(3): 673–689.

Taglioni, Daria, and Deborah Winkler (2014). "Making Global Value Chains Work for Development", *Economic Premise 143*, Washington, DC: Poverty Reduction and Economic Management (PREM) Network, World Bank.

Taylor, Lance (1983). *Structuralist Macroeconomics*, New York: Basic Books.

Tewari, Meenu (2006). "Adjustment in India's Textile and Apparel Industry: Reworking Historical Legacies in a Post-MFA World", *Environment and Planning A: Economy and Space*, 38(12): 2325–2344.

References   185

Thelen, Kathleen (2004). *How Institutions Evolve: The Political Economy of Skills in Germany, Britain, the United States and Japan*, New York: Cambridge University Press.

Tintin, C. (2012). *Does Foreign Direct Investment spur Economic Growth and Development? – A Comparative Study*. Brussels: Institute of Foreign Studies, Vrije Universtiet Brussels.

Tregenna, Fiona (2009). "Characterising Deindustrialisation: An Analysis of Changes in Manufacturing Employment and Output Internationally", *Cambridge Journal of Economics*, 33(3): 433–466.

Tybout, James, Jamie de Melo, and Vittorio Corbo (1991). "The Effects of Trade Reforms on Scale and Technical Efficiency: New Evidence from Chile", *Journal of International Economics*, 31(3–4): 231–250.

UNDP (2015). *Is the Private Sector More Efficient? – A Cautionary Tale*, Singapore: United Nations Development Programme, Global Centre for Public Service Excellence.

Upender, M. (1996). "Elasticity of Labour Productivity in Indian Manufacturing", *Economic and Political Weekly*, 31(21): M-7–M-10.

Uwubanmwen, A. E., and M. G. Ajao (2012). "The Determinants and Impacts of Foreign Direct Investment in Nigeria", *International Journal of Business and Management*, 7(24): 67–77.

Verma, S. (2002). "Export Competitiveness of the Indian Textile and Garment Industry", *Working Paper 94*, New Delhi: Indian Council for Research on International Economic Relations.

Vernon, Raymond (1966). "International Investment and International Trade in the Product Cycle", *Quarterly Journal of Economics*, 80(2): 190–207.

Vickers, John, and George Yarrow (1988). *Privatization: An Economic Analysis*, Cambridge, MA: The MIT Press.

Wallack, Jessica S. (2003). "Structural Breaks in Indian Macroeconomic Data", *Economic and Political Weekly*, 38(41): 4312–4315.

Wang, Chengqi, and Zhongxiu Zhao (2008). "Horizontal and Vertical Spillover Effects of Foreign Direct Investment in Chinese Manufacturing", *Journal of Chinese Economic and Foreign Trade Studies*, 1(1): 8–20.

Waring, G. F. (1996). "Industry Differences in the Persistence of Firm-Specific Returns", *American Economic Review*, 86(5): 1253–1265.

Waterson, M. (1984). *Economic Theory of the Industry*, Cambridge: Cambridge University Press.

Weiss, John (1992). "Export Response to Trade Reform: Recent Mexican Experience", *Development Policy Review*, 10(1): 43–60.

Wen, Yi (2016). *The Making of an Economic Superpower: Unlocking China's Secret of Rapid Industrialization*, Singapore: World Scientific.

Westphal, L. (1982). "Fostering Technological Mastery by Means of Selective Infant-industry Protection", in M. Syrquin and S. Teitel (Eds.), *Trade, Stability, Technology, and Equity in Latin America*, New York: Academic Press.

Westphal, L. (1990). "Industrial Policy in an Export Propelled Economy: Lessons from South Korea's Experience", *Journal of Economic Perspectives*, 4(3): 41–59.

Westphal, L., and K. S. Kim (1977). "Industrial Policy and Development in Korea", *World Bank Staff Working Paper 263*, Washington, DC: World Bank.

186   *References*

Williamson, John (1998). "On Markets and Regulation", *Paper Presented to a Conference Held at the University of California, Santa Cruz, November 20–21*, New York: Peterson Institute of International Affairs.

Wolfgang, Streeck, and Kozo Yamamura (Eds.) (2001). *The Origins of Nonliberal Capitalism: Germany and Japan in Comparison*, Ithaca: Cornell University Press.

Wruuck, Patricia (2015). "Promoting Investment and Growth: The role of Development Banks in Europe", *EU Monitor – Global financial markets*, Frankfurt: Deutsche Bank Research.

Yeyati, E. L., A. Micco, and U. Panizza (2004). "Should the Government Be in the Banking Business? The Role of State-Owned and Development Banks", *Working Paper #517*, Washington, DC: Inter-American Development Bank.

Index

absolute competitive advantage (ACA) 83–85, 100–102, 130, 158, **160**
access to technology 7, 23, 28, 103, 127, 132; *see also* intellectual property rights (IPR)
acquisition by foreign firms 37, 132, 154
acquisition-type FDI 28, 37, 123, 154
aggregate demand 62
agricultural growth 52, 63
agricultural sector 6, 52, 60, 63, 73, 157
allocative efficiency 10n1, 13, 18, 77; *see also* technical efficiency
alternative measures of performance 83; *see also* industrial performance, measurement of
anti-dumping actions 161
Argentina 85, 142–143
Atomic Research Centre 125
Australia 1, 2, 113
automobile industry: competition in 140, 142, 145, 148–151, 159–160; efficiency/performance of 86–88, 90–93, 102, 130, 158–160; exports and imports 30, 72, 100; FDI in 3, 105, 123, 131, 163, 166–167; global development in 95, 102, 105, 131; growth and development of 102, 107, 131–132, 146, 148, 156; history of 103–104; importance of 103; policy issues 3, 40, 48, 105, 108, 131–133, 163; technology 105, 131–132, 166

backward and forward linkages 27, 103; *see also* technology spillover
Bagchi, A. K. 26, 65
Bain, J. S. 39, 135, 138
Balakrishnan, P. 80
Balassa, B. 8, 78
Bardhan, P. K. 15

basic metals industry: competition in 146, 148–150, 152, 159–160; efficiency/performance of 80, 82, 86–87, 89, 95, 99–102, 158–160; exports and imports 86, 100; growth and development of 93–94, 107, 131, 145; history of 106, 116; importance of 105–106; policy issues 40, 43, 106–107, 123, 130, 132–133, 163; technology 132; *see also* iron and steel industry
Bata 169n1
Bhabha, H. J. 124, 125, 130, 134n6
Bhabha Committee 125
Bhagwati, J. N. 30
Bharat Heavy Electricals Limited (BHEL) 114
Birla, G. D. 65
Bombay Plan 65
bounded rationality 8
Brazil 21, 24–35, 85, 108, 110, 113
Britannia 169n1

Canada 29, 31, 90, 91, 113
capacity utilization 3, 80, 82
capital flows 33, 123
capital formation 37, 55, 57, 154; acceleration in 57; savings and 55
capital market 22, 166; deregulation of 166
cartel 32
cartelization 152
Caves, R. E. 15
Centre for Development of Advanced Computing (C-DAC) 127
Centre for Development of Telematics (C-DoT) 127
Chadwick, Andrew 26
Chaudhuri, S. 112, 165

188 *Index*

Chang, Ha-Joon 1, 17, 21, 30, 168
chemicals industry: efficiency/
  performance of 81–82, 86–89, 95, 97,
  100–102; exports and imports 82,
  100–101, 115; global development in
  92–95; growth and development of
  113; history of 111; policy issues 70,
  113; *see also* pharmaceutical industry
Chenery, H. B. 14
China 7, 12, 16, 21–22, 24, 28, 33–35,
  37, 59, 67–68, 72, 82, 90–92, 94–99,
  102, 106–108, 113–117, 123, 128,
  154, 156, 160–163, 165–166
Colgate 169n1
comparative advantage 9, 78–79,
  81–85, 130
comparative advantage-defying 7
comparative advantage-losing 7
comparative advantage theory 8–9, 13,
  78–79; *see also* revealed comparative
  advantage (RCA)
competition: degree of 10, 132,
  140, 149; foreign/import 14, 110,
  117, 140, 142, 169; impact on
  performance 8, 13–15, 20, 30,
  159–160; in an industry 7; and
  innovation 13, 138; intensity of 9,
  10, 135–138, 140–142, 150–152,
  159–160; market structure and
  135; nature of 137–138, 140, 143,
  145, 149, 151; perfect 12; policy
  13, 28, 30–31, 112–113, 132, 137,
  139, 153, 159 (*see also* MRTP Act);
  profitability and 10, 147, 152n2;
  short-term 159; stage of 12
competitiveness: assessment of 81–82,
  102, 140; impact of economic
  reforms on 141; management of 8,
  123; measure of 84–85, 130, 158;
  policy initiative 2
competitive performance index (CPI)
  84–86, 88–90, 100, 102, 158, **160**
compound annual growth rate (CAGR)
  120, 128
Computer Management Corporation
  (CMC) 126
Connolly, R. A. 141–142
coordinated market economy 4–5, 10,
  26, 31, 34, 69, 72, 156, 167
core-periphery 6, 160; *see also*
  structural/structuralist economics
Cournot, A. A 136, 138
creative destruction 11–12, 75; *see also*
  innovation, Schumpeterian

Cubbin, J. S. 136, 138
CUTS 111, 114

Dasgupta, A. K. 64, 65
Dasgupta, K. C. 138
Dalda 169n1
deindustrialization 5, 7, 26, 160, 165;
  premature 5, 7, 160, 165
De Long, J. B. 49
Department of Atomic Energy (DAE) 125
development finance (DF) 35, 57, 105,
  108, 110, 113, 119, 131, **133**, 163
development finance institutions (DFI)
  34–35, 57, 69
development planning 64, 69, 72–73,
  155–157
Dhar, Biswajit 66, 127, 165
district industries centres (DIC) 3, 42
Dollar, D., and A. Kraay 16
dynamic competition 10, 76, 138,
  143, 149–151, 159; Schumpterian
  notion of 10, 138; *see also* profit,
  persistence of
dynamic efficiency 75
dynamic performance 7, 13

East Asian countries/economies 1, 4, 28,
  30, 38, 50, 56–57, 155
East Asian growth experience 38, 154
East India Company (EIC) 29
economic growth: foreign investment
  and 27–29; financial development
  and 62; global economic environment
  and 35–37, 167; in India 50, 57,
  73, 157; and productivity 14; trade
  liberalization and 16, 36, 39, 49,
  72, 157
economic reforms: adjustment costs of
  66–67; advocates of 48–49, 73n1; in
  developing countries 31; economic
  crisis and 62; and economic growth
  48–49; in India 1, 48, 70–71, 140,
  164, 168; and industrial performance
  39, 141, 164, 168; World Bank and
  IMF and 31
economic structure 54–56, 69, 72
education 13, 20, 40, 167–168
effective demand 6
effective rate of protection (ERP) 17, 82
Egypt 113
Eichengreen, B. J. 32
electrical machinery: competition
  in 142–148, 159; efficiency/
  performance of 86–88, 90, 100–102,

Index 189

130, 142–148, 158–159; exports and imports 100–101; global development in 93–94, 131; growth and development of 113–114, 145; history of 113–114; importance of 113; policy issues 107, 113–114, 132–133
Electronics Commission 125–126
Electronics Committee 125–126
electronics industry: competition in 148–152, 159–160; efficiency/performance of 82, 95, 97, 100–102, 159–160; exports and imports 100–101; FDI in 127–128; global development in 128–129, 168; growth and development of 124–130; history of 124–128; importance of 103, 124; policy issues 48, 124–129; technology 128–131
environment: business 2, 45; competitive 23, 137–138, 144, 151; economic 35, 143; enabling 168; global 5; industrial 20; institutional 20; *laissez-faire* 1; liberalized 3; operational 20; patent 113; policy 20, 118; political, economic and social 58; regulatory 162–163
equality of long-term profit 148–149
Estrin, S. 20, 22
European Union (EU) 32, 59, 104
EXIM Bank 47
export-import policy 9, 46–48
export-led growth/industrialization 5, 9–10, 30, 46, 62, 72, 131, 156, 161
export processing zone (EPZ) 46–47, 72, 156
export promotion 30, 46–48, 68, 70, 117, 121–122, 156

favourable policy for consuming sectors 108, **133**
five year plan: eleventh 73n4; first 2, 46; second 47, 65, 106, 118, 124; seventh 48, 120; sixth 120; third 70, 118, 156
flying geese pattern of development 36–37, 154
foreign direct investment (FDI): acquisition-type 28, 37, 123, 154; automatic route 44–45, 123; and competition 67, 123, 140, 143; and economic growth 27–29, 46, 154; efficiency-seeking 29; greenfield 28, 37, 154, 167; liberalization of 44–45, 67, 70–71, 104, 127–128,

156; market-seeking 29; regulation of 28–29, 44, 104, 127, 154, 166–167; resource-seeking 29; as source of financing 12, 27, 37, 123, 131, 154, 166; and technology 12, 26–29, 105, 154
foreign exchange: constraint/crisis/shortage 46, 118–119
Foreign Exchange Regulation Act (FERA) 42, 44, 126–127
foreign investment 127, 131, **133**, 154, 167; along with performance requirements **133**; *see also* foreign direct investment (FDI)
Foreign Investment Promotion Board (FIPB) 44
foreign remittances 57
Foucault, M. 85
France 6, 18, 20, 31, 90–91, 94, 113, 141
free trade agreement (FTA) 45, 132, 165

Galbraith, J. K. 63, 163–164
Gandhi, Indira 60, 64
Gandhi, Rajiv 43
GDP growth 48–52, 54–57, 69, 72–73, 73n1, 157
General Agreement on Tariffs and Trade (GATT) 67
Georgescu-Roegen, N. 78
Germany 2, 4–5, 31–32, 34–35, 38, 62–64, 67–69, 85–86, 92, 94, 108, 113, 141, 155–156, 163, 167
Geroski, P. 38n1, 141, 143, 149
Glenn, J. 142–143, 146
global competitiveness ratio (GCR) 84–89, 95–99, 100–102, 130, 158, **160**
global economic environment 35–37
global market 12, 36, 67–68, 76, 78, 81, 95, 100, 113, 124, 154, 158, 160–161
Goldar, B. N. 79, 80–81, 140
governance 13, 22, 28, 167
government procurement 111, 114; *see also* public procurement
greenfield FDI 28, 37, 154, 167
gross domestic product (GDP) 4–5, 16, 26, 40, 44, 48–57, 59, 63, 66, 69, 72–73, 73n1, 92, 103, 106, 110, 113, 116, 157, 161, 168
Growth Centre Scheme 43

half-life (for short-run profit) 143, 149–**150**, 152n6

190 *Index*

healthcare 13, 20, 113, 167, 169
hindu rate of growth 49, 73
Hindustan Copper Limited (HCL) 107
Hindustan Lever 169n1
Hindustan Motors 103
Hirschman-Herfindahl Index (HHI)
 136, 140, 141
Hodrick-Prescott trends 51, *54*, 73n3
Hong Kong 31
Hussain, Abid 120

import-substituting industrialization
 1, 3, 5, 9–10, 15, 30, 40, 46, 70, 72,
 131, 156; *see also* industrialization,
 strategy
Indian growth experience 54
Indian growth performance 35, 52
Indian Oil Corporation 109
Indian Petrochemical Corporation
 Limited (IPCL) 110
Indonesia 18, 90–*91*, 102
Industrial Credit and Investment
 Corporation of India (ICICI) 119
Industrial Development Bank of India
 (IDBI) 119
Industrial Finance Corporation of India
 (IFCI) 119
industrial growth 4, 9, 13, 26, 39, 45,
 47, 49–52, 56–57, 60, 153, 166
industrialization: capital for 33–35, 66,
 154; foreign investment and 26–27;
 global experience in 1–2, 4, 31–35,
 37, 48, 67, 70, 72, 114, 131–132,
 154, 162–163; performance 21,
 153; policy issues 1–5, 9–11, 13,
 16, 29–31, 35–37, 40, 46, 48–49,
 70, 72, 75, 124, 153, 164, 168–169;
 strategy 3–4, 30, 33, 67, 70, 72, 131,
 155–156, 168; technology for 2, 12,
 22, 24, 131
industrial licensing 41, 49, 67, 135, 139
Industrial Licensing Inquiry
 Committee 41
industrial performance: assessment of
 9, 79–83, 85–102; definitional issues
 in 75, 153; effect of productivity
 growth on 14; factors affecting
 13–37, 39–40, **133**, 157, 168; FDI
 policy and 26–29, 166–177; global
 economic environment and 35–37,
 40; impact of industrial policy on 7,
 39, 145, 153, 159, 160, 167; impact
 of sectoral policy on 2; in India 5, 7,

9, 72, 157–159; industrialization and
 4; measurement of 7, 76–79, 83–85,
 130, 157–158; price-cost margin as
 76, 135–136; productivity growth as
 76–82; role of state and 13, 18–22,
 29–33, 163–164; in structure-
 conduct-performance 10–11, 36,
 135–136, 153; trade performance as
 proxy for 8, 76, 78–79, 81–82; trade
 policy and 13–18, 164–166
industrial policy: and access to finance
 33–35; aspects of/elements of 9–10,
 12–37, 132, 158, 168–169; in China
 160–163; definition of 1, 12–13; in
 East Asian countries 30; and foreign
 investment 26–29; in Germany 2;
 and global economic scenario 35–37;
 impacts on industrial performance
 7, 39, 145, 153, 159–160, 167; in
 India 2–5, 39–46, 48–49, 64–66,
 68, 70, 72, 117, 156, 160–169;
 instruments of 35; interventionist 7;
 in maintaining industrial dynamism
 1; "no policy" as the default 1;
 as a process 7; and public sector
 participation 18–22; and regulation
 and public support 29–33; strategic
 4, 7, 12, 153; and technology and
 IPR policy 22–26; and trade policy 8,
 13–18; in the US 2
Industrial Policy Resolution 1, 2, 40–41
Industrial Policy Statement 1, 12, 42, 68
industrial production 12, 27, 84, 106,
 113; global 84, 86, 90–*91*, 94, 130;
 growth of 92
industrial structure 2, 8, 36, 116, 143;
 global 36
Industries (Development & Regulation)
 Act 40
Information Technology Agreement
 (ITA) 127, 165
infrastructure: investment in 68–69,
 108, 161–162; public support in 1,
 32–33, 68–69; regulatory 22; services
 41, 43, 45, 59, 67–68, 122, 125, 131
innovation: cycle 7; and
 industrialization 22, 24, 36, 131,
 157, 167–168; IPR, technology
 and 12, 22–23, 26, 167; monopoly/
 profits through 12–13, 23, 76,
 137–138; policy/programme 2, 26,
 46, 128, 167; and productivity 14;
 Schumpterian 8

Index 191

institutional development 28
intellectual property rights (IPR): and
access to technology 12, 22–24, 26,
37, 112, 132, 154, 163, 167; and
innovation 23–24, 26, 167; and
market power 95, 167; payments
for use of 24–25; and product
patent regime 70–71, 111; relaxed
protection/regime 8, 24, **131–133**
(*see also* environment, patent);
royalty on 24, 26; and technology
transfer 12, 24, 26
intensity of competition 9–10, 135–138,
140–142, 150–152, 159–160;
see also competition, degree of
International Business Machines (IBM)
106–107
iron and steel industry: efficiency/
performance of 82, 148–50, 152,
159–160; exports and imports 82;
history of 106; importance of 21, 40,
42, 105, 116, 145–146; policy issues
40, 42–43, 123; *see also* basic metals
industry
Italy *91*

Jacobsen, R. 141, 142
Japan 2, 12, 15, 21, 26, 31, 35, 37,
90–95, 97–99, 104, 106, 112, 114,
116–117, 123, 128, 154

Khadi and Village Industries
Commission 117
Kohli, Atul 49
Krugman, Paul 30, 84

Lall, Sanjaya 85, 108
Lin, J. Y. 7, 22, 33
linking policy and performance
102–130, 160–163

Maddison, A. 13, **53**
Magdoff, H., and P. Sweezy 78
Mahalanobis, P. C. 124, 130
Make in India 45, 82, 122, 128, 168
Malaysia 37, 90–*91*, 102, 113, 143, 154
manufacturing sector/industries:
competition in 140–143, 145–147,
149–151, 158–159; efficiency/
performance of 4, 9–10, 15, 20,
79–82, 85–89, 100–101, 158–159;
exports and imports 81, 100–101;
FDI in 28, 127–128, 167; global

development in 92–94; growth and
development of 1, 4, 103, 100, 110,
112–113, 117, 131–132; policy issues
15–17, 30, 33–34, 44–45, 62–63,
104–105, 128, 133n1, 168–169;
share in employment 5, 140; share
in GDP 4, 26, 44, 49; technology
44, 128
market concentration 11, 135–136,
139–142; *see also* market structure
market structure: effect on dynamic
efficiency/technological progress
75; global 160; index of 136; and
industrial performance 11–12, 36, 39,
76, 135, 159; and innovation 14
measuring competitive performance
85; *see also* absolute competitive
advantage (ACA)
measuring performance 75–76, 137
Minerals and Metals Trading
Corporation (MMTC) 46, 107
Ministry of Electronics and Information
Technology (MEITY) 124, 128, **129**
mixed economy 1, 33, 64–65, 69, 155
monopolies and restrictive trade
practices 3, 41, 60, 139; *see also*
competition policy
Monopolies Inquiry Commission
41, 138
monopolization 14
monopoly power/position 11–13,
77, 138
motor vehicles 86–88, 90, 93–95, 102
MRTP Act 3, 41, 43, 60, 61, 67–68,
127, 139
Mueller, D. C., 141, 143, 147
Mukherjee, S. P., 65, 70, 156
Multi-fibre Arrangements (MFA) **71**,
82, 119, 121, 123, 152, 165
multi-national corporation/companies
126–128

Nagaraj, R., 49, 74n10, 162
Nanda, N., 16, 18, 24, 28, 31, 50,
57, 61, 63, 68, 73n6, 111, 152n2,
161–162, 169
National Development and Reforms
Commission (NDRC) (of China)
33, 163
national investment and manufacturing
zone (NIMZ) 45
National Manufacturing Policy (NMP)
44–45

192 Index

National Small Industries Corporation (NSIC) 44
National Textile Corporation (NTC) 118–120, 122
National Textile Policy 117, 119–120, 122
Nayyar, Deepak 4, 13, 35, 39, 49, 50, 57, 67, 69, 105, 108, 110, 113, 131, 157, 161
Nehru, J. L. 4, 49–50, 60, 65–67, 70, 126, 156
New Economic Policy (of 1991) 43, 67, 127–128
New Electronics Policy 127
Newly Industrialized Countries (NICs) 31
Nigeria 29, 110, 113
non-metallic mineral products 86–87, 89, 102, 133n2
non-tariff barriers 16, 36, 84, 104
normal competitive return 144–148, 151

Ocampo, J. A. 22, 132
Oil and Natural Gas Corporation (ONGC) 109
Organization for Economic Cooperation and Development (OECD) 22, **24–25**, 28, 132

Panchamukhi, V. R. 139
Peru 142–143
petroleum products/refining industry: efficiency/performance of 81, 86–89, 95, 99, 100–102, 130, 158; exports and imports 100–101, 109–110; FDI in 109, 166; global development in 95, 109; growth and development of 108–110; history of 109–110; importance of 108; policy issues 109–110, 115, 131, **133**, 145; technology 109, 132
pharmaceutical industry: competition in 148–152, 159–160; efficiency/ performance of 102, 130, 159–160, 167; exports and imports 72, 131; FDI in 113, 132, 166–167; global development in 23, 95, 112–113, 152; growth and development of 72, 110–113, 169; history of 111–112; importance of 110; market structure of 136, 141; policy issues 70, 95, 111–113, 130–133, 136, 163, 165;

technology 23, 111, 131–132; *see also* chemicals industry
planned economy 3, 5, 10, 64, 69–70, 155–156
Planning Commission 64–65, 113, 122
Pohang Iron and Steel Company (POSCO) 21, 164
policies influencing performance 153
Prebisch, Raul 7
preferential access to raw materials **133**
preferential public procurement **133**
premature deindustrialization 5, 7, 160, 165
price-cost margin (PCM) 7, 11, 19, 75–77, 83, 137, 139–141, 143, 151
price regulation 111–112, **133**
private sector 19, 21, 40–41, 43, 64, 68, 71, 73n5, 110, 117, 126, 155, 160, 162–164
privatization 18–22, 31, 33, 74n9, 162, 164, 168
product cycle hypothesis 36
productivity: competition and 8, 14; and economic growth 3, 14, 32, 45; effects of protection on 13, 15, 80–81; and efficiency 8, 15, 37, 76–79, 85, 153; FDI and 27–28; innovations and 14; measurement of 76–78, 83; and state ownership 20; trade policy and 13, 15–16
profit: abnormal 76, 137–138, 141–143, 145; above-normal 137–138, 144, 151; determinants of persistence of 142; estimates of persistence of 146–152; long-term 146–152; measurement of persistence of 143–145; persistence of 138, 141–144, 146, 149, 151–152, 159; short-term 146, 148–149, 151
profitability: and competition 10, 138, 152, 159; and efficiency 11, 14, 34, 76; market share and 136, 139, 142; measurement of 76–77; as measure of performance 135, 137; or price-cost margin 11, 75, 83; protection and 14; in public *vs.* private firms 18, 34; as rate of return 76–77, 135
protectionism 29–30
public procurement 190–191, 232; *see also* government procurement
public sector 28, 158, 232
public sector enterprise (PSE) 22, 33, 49, 107, 108, 130, **132–133**, 163

Index 193

public sector participation 12, 18–22, 163

quantitative restrictions 44, 48, **70–71**, 122, 136, 140, 143, 165

rent: firm specific permanent 144, 147, 151–152; transitory 144, 146, 151
research and development (R&D) 1, 12, 23, 46, 112, 125, 128, 137–139, 141–142, 145, 163
Reserve Bank of India (RBI) 63, 73n5, 73nn7–8
return: on capital 137; guaranteed 68; normal competitive 144–148, 151; private 34; rate of 73n5, 76–77, 135, 137–138, 141; social 34
revealed comparative advantage (RCA) 78–79, 81–85, 130; *see also* comparative advantage theory
Rodrik, Dani 1, 2, 49
role of state 31, 163

Sandesara, J. C. 139
Sarabhai, Vikram 125
Scherer, F. M. 38n1, 76
Schmalensee, R. 76
Schumpeter, J. A. 11, 13, 33, 75, 138
Schumpeterian innovations 8
services sector 50–52, 157, 169
Shastri, L. B. 60
Siddharthan N. S., and A. K. Dasgupta 139
simulated free markets 30
Singapore 18, 31, 168
Singh, Ajit 33, 67
small scale industries (SSI)/Sector 3, 42–43, 66, 108, 122
socialistic pattern of society 64–65
South Korea 3, 5, 21, 31, 32, 34–35, 37, 48, 62, 64, 67, 69, 70, 72, 90, 92, 95, 102, 114, 128, 142, 154–155, 156, 161, 163, 164, 167
State Bank of India 42, 64, 155
state involvement 3, **132–133**; in consuming sectors **133**; *see also* public sector participation
state support 33–34, 113
State Trading Corporation (STC) 46, 107
Steel Authority of India Limited (SAIL) 106
Stigler, G. J. 11
Stiglitz, J. 22

structural break 50, 52, 73, 157
structural change 6, 7, 35, 89, 94, 121
structural/structuralist economics 5–9, 160
structure-conduct-performance (SCP) 7, 8, 10, 11, 38n1, 135–136, 140–141
subsidies 30–32, 68, 110
supply rigidities 6
supply surge 136
Surf 169n1

Taiwan 3, 12, 15, 30–32, 37, 48, 69, 79, 128, 154, 156, 161, 163–164, 167
tariff: applied 67; average 15, 17, 105, **115**; barriers 16, 36, 39, 58, 84, 140; barriers, non- 16, 36, 84, 104; cut/ reduction 16, 43, 58, 122–123, 127, 140, 143, 165; peak 105, **115**; policy 105; profile/structure 17, 30, 72, 104, **115**, 168; protection 17, 30, 45, 48–49, 67, 105, **133**; rates 43, 131; revenue 18, 68
Tata, J. R. D. 65
Tata Institute of Fundamental Research (TIFR) 124
Tata Iron and Steel Company (TISCO) 106
Tata Motors 132
Taylor, Lance 6
technical change 77, 129, 141; *see also* technical/technological progress
technical efficiency 10n1, 14, 15, 77, 78, 80–82, 130, 133n2, 158
technical/technological progress 11, 75, 77, 80
technology acquisition 44, 127, 168
Technology Acquisition and Development Fund (TADF) 44, 45
technology spillover 105
Technology Upgradation Fund Scheme (TUFS) 122
textiles/apparel industry: competition in 148–152, 159–160; efficiency/ performance of 81–82, 86–87, 95–96, 100, 102–103, 131, 158–160, 165; exports and imports 82, 100, 116–118, 123; FDI in 116, 123, 131; global development in 17, **71**, 82, 95, 119, 123; growth and development of 118–121, 123, 134n5; history of 17, 114–121; importance of 114–116; policy issues 40, 44, 115–123, 131; technology 114, 118, 121–122

194 *Index*

TFP growth 29, 80–82
Thailand 37, *91*, *102*, *128*, 142–143, 154
total factor productivity (TFP) 14–16, 29, 77–82, 85, 130
trade performance 8, 78, 84, 100
trade policy(ies) 3, 8, 12, 13–18, 30, 31, 35–37, 48, **115**, 153–154, 164; and industrialization 37, 154; and industrial performance 13–18, 164; *see also* tariff, policy; tariff, profile/structure
trade related aspects of intellectual property rights (TRIPS) 23, 28, 37, 152, 154
transnational corporation (TNC) 21, 112–113, 154

United Arab Emirates (UAE) 113
United Kingdom (UK) 20, 31, 33, 58, 90–*91*, 108, 113–114, 117, 124, 141–142
United Nations Development Programme (UNDP) 20

United Nations Industrial Development Organization (UNIDO) 85–99, 100, 158
United States (US) 1, 2, 4, 15, 17, 18, 20, 31, 34, 48, 58–59, 63, 90–99, 104, 108, 111–114, 128, 142, 155, 163

value added 85, 92–94, 110, 113, 130, 137, 140
value addition 16, 37, 46, 128, 134n8, 158
value chain 16–17, 27, 116, 128, 132; global 16–17, 132
Vietnam 28

World Trade Organization (WTO) 23, 28, 67, 70, 92, 104–105, 112, **115**, 130, 143, 161–162, 164–167; Agreement on Trade Related Aspects of Intellectual Property Rights (TRIPS) 23; Uruguay Round 67, 70, 143, 164

X-efficiency/X-inefficiency 14–15, 152n1